THE SCHOOL OF HARD KNOX

THE AUTOBIOGRAPHY OF ARCHIE KNOX

ARCHIE KNOX

WITH

ROGER HANNAH

First published in 2017 by

ARENA SPORT
An imprint of Birlinn Limited
West Newington House
10 Newington Road
Edinburgh
EH9 1QS

www.arenasportbooks.co.uk

ISBN: 978-1-909715-55-4
eBook ISBN: 978-0-85790-946-6

British Library Cataloguing-in-Publication Data
A catalogue record for this book is available on request from the British Library.

Designed and typeset by Polaris Publishing, Edinburgh

Printed and bound by CPI Group (UK) Ltd, Croydon, CR0 4YY

CONTENTS

ACKNOWLEDGEMENTS

Over the years, working in football, I've been lucky to have met and made many great friends some of whom are mentioned in the book.

Although football consumed my life, any success wouldn't have been possible without the support of my family.

To my wife Janis who moved house on a regular basis whilst trying to pursue her own career in teaching and who sadly passed away in 2006, to Susan and Lesley who also had to contend with moving schools during the early years but never complained and who both now have families of their own. Having three granddaughters and one grandson has brought a different perspective on life and filled the gap left by retiring from the football.

Anna and Olivia live locally and being able to see them grow up is special and probably something I missed with my own girls.

April and Archie are a bit further away in Spain and, although we keep in regular contact, going to visit is always something special.

To my brothers Jimmy, Arthur, Jack and sisters Margaret and Evelyn for keeping my feet firmly on the ground.

Lastly I would like to thank Roger for his considerable effort in making the book possible.

Archie Knox

This book wouldn't have been possible without the advice, assistance and, most importantly, patience of Pete Burns at Arena Sport.

Martin Greig of BackPage Press offered much-appreciated encouragement from the first moment and helped enormously.

Thanks to all on the sports desk at the *Scottish Sun* and to picture desk colleagues Darren O'Neill, Keith Campbell, Mike Schofield and David Henderson.

Sam Wallace and Ken Lawrence opened their enviable contacts books to bring some of England's finest players to the table.

Thanks, too, to Satty Singh for his support in the project and helping us launch this book.

The staff of Nonna Gina's in Newton Mearns must be mentioned for keeping us fed and watered during our numerous breakfast summits.

And thanks go to everyone from Sir Alex Ferguson at the start of this story to Jim McSherry in the final paragraphs. Without each and every one of you, *The School of Hard Knox* would never have developed past kindergarten.

Thanks to Susan and Andy Baird for digging into their loft, garage and cupboards for family photos and mementoes.

Thanks to Derek and Amanda Templeton for keeping our glasses charged as we passed round those photos and mementoes. It's been dyno . . .

And, of course, huge love and thanks to Fiona, Mark and Katie for putting up with me and the clatter of the laptop keys at the kitchen table. I promise there will be no more late-night cursing when the internet router goes down and I can't Google the Forfar Athletic squad from 1978.

Finally, a big thanks to Archie. It's been wonderful to hear all your stories and gain a glimpse into a life less ordinary.

I told you folk would buy it!

Roger Hannah

FOREWORD
SIR ALEX FERGUSON

In the summer of 1980, Aberdeen celebrated a first league title in a quarter of a century – but one major change was on the horizon at Pittodrie. I had lost Pat Stanton as my assistant. I think his family wanted to move back closer to Edinburgh and he decided to take the manager's job at Cowdenbeath. Despite our New Firm rivalry, I was close to Jim McLean – the manager of Dundee United – and I sought his counsel on a replacement. Jim instantly recommended Archie Knox, who was manager of Forfar Athletic at the time but had played and coached under him at Tannadice.

Jim told me 'He works like a beast, is dedicated, is as straight as a die and you can trust him.' Those are all the qualities you need in an assistant.

Archie was prepared to work all right. He was also honest and I quickly found out that I could trust him to watch my back all the time. Choosing someone you can trust is the most important thing. But Archie also had energy, dedication and a terrific work ethic. What you see is what you get with Archie and we had a fantastic relationship. Mind you, he could be like a bull in a china shop at times. We had a million arguments – it was never a honeymoon. But I trusted him 100 per cent and he always gave me the right advice.

We used to travel all over the place to games. We would leave our wives, Janis and Cathy, in Aberdeen and drive everywhere. I would drive down the road from Aberdeen and Archie would sleep in the car, then Archie would drive back up and I'd get some sleep. That was the arrangement. Goodness knows how many trips we made down that road. We put in an unbelievable amount of work.

But we had an unbelievable amount of fun, too. We used to play a game called 'Tips' in the gymnasium at Pittodrie after training on a Friday and it could go on for hours. There were lots of little goals all over the gym – which was built underneath one of the stands – and you'd have to outscore your opponent. Sometimes the players were involved but most of the time it was just the two of us and we'd haul in a young player to referee. We grabbed Brian Mitchell one day and he was sh***ing himself. He gave a bad decision against me and I warned him that one more wrong call and he'd be running round the track. He then gave a bad one against Archie and got the same warning from him. I can't remember what happened next but, needless to say, it ended with Brian running round the track.

We played for another couple of hours before finishing. Teddy Scott, our coach at Aberdeen, would have a cup of tea ready for us. At that point, Teddy asked us what we should do with Brian because he was still out running round the track. We'd forgotten all about him!

I lost Archie twice, once to Dundee as manager in 1983 and then again to Rangers as assistant manager in 1991. I always remember in Gothenburg after the European Cup Winners' Cup final win over Real Madrid, I was at the bar with Teddy at four in the morning. He said 'Someone will be coming in for Archie. I've heard rumours.' Of course, Dundee came in and he did very well for them as manager for three years.

I attracted him back to Aberdeen in 1986. I didn't want him going from being a manager to an assistant manager, so we became joint-managers. I was perfectly comfortable with it and so were the board. But then, just a few months later, Manchester United came in and we were both off. I'm pretty sure Dick Donald offered Archie the job at Aberdeen on his own at that stage but he chose to come down to United.

Being manager of United at the start was fraught with all sorts of problems. The only thing we could do was work hard to correct it.

Together, we sorted the coaching, we sorted the scouting, we sorted everything. We had a tremendous work ethic and the energy to get it right. When we went down at first, the kitchen staff at The Cliff didn't start until 9 a.m., so we used to go to the laundry at 6.45 a.m. for tea and toast with the girls.

It was unfortunate for United that Walter Smith got the Rangers job, but I could understand why Archie went there. Walter was his friend and United wouldn't match the financial offer from Rangers. That said, Archie definitely would have made a great manager in his own right. I wasn't going to retire any time soon but Archie could easily have followed me at United if he had stayed that long. Mind you, neither of us might have been around too long after I tried to cook us breakfast one Sunday morning. We were in digs when we first moved to United then stayed in the Four Seasons Hotel for a while but we eventually moved into a flat in Timperley, a village near Altrincham. We'd take turns at cooking and I was making the eggs, bacon and sausages for breakfast one Sunday morning. Archie was sitting at the kitchen table with the Sunday papers and I'd stuck the plates in the top oven to warm. Suddenly, the oven exploded and the plates and everything else just flew across the kitchen. Archie was screaming and I thought I was going to kill the two of us!

Archie has been such a good friend and we have always remained close. I have always appreciated his honesty, his support for me and his wonderful friendship.

CHAPTER ONE

PICKING UP TIPS FROM FERGIE

YEARS BEFORE escaping the exploding oven in Timperley, Archie Knox survived another major scare at the hands of Alex Ferguson.

Archie recalled: 'The first time Alex nearly killed me was when we were driving down from Aberdeen to Helenvale in Glasgow to coach some youngsters. There is a railway bridge over the road just after Stonehaven and there's a sharp turn in the road. Alex had the foot down, the road surface was wet and he suddenly put the brakes on. We went straight on, straight across the road, hit the kerb on the other side and bounced back into the road – the opposite side of the road. If there had been anything coming the other way, we'd have been dead.

'Amazingly, there didn't seem to be any notable damage to the car – we didn't even have a puncture – so we got ourselves together again and continued the journey. What we didn't realise until the next day, when we got the mechanic to look it over, was that we'd fractured an axle and we could have lost a wheel and crashed anywhere on the road that night.'

The road to glory for Knox and Ferguson was often littered with obstacles. That they overcame them all to lead Aberdeen to a golden era of success said everything of the relationship between the pair.

Dons legend Alex McLeish, who won every domestic honour under them as well as the 1983 European Cup Winners' Cup final against the mighty Real Madrid, remembers it well.

Big Eck said: 'You could see an instant bond between the two of them. They had a great camaraderie from the start. They used to walk round the corridors inside Pittodrie and they'd be shouting and singing. They were just like a couple of best pals.'

The closeness of the bond between them was all the more surprising given they hardly knew each other before Archie's appointment as No.2 in 1980. He'd spent his playing and coaching career at Forfar Athletic, St Mirren, Dundee United and Montrose. Ferguson, five years his senior, had moved into management aged just 32 and their paths had rarely crossed. Indeed, they were only drawn together after a feud over frozen pies and a deal to earn a bumper £20-a-week pay rise.

Archie remembers: 'I didn't really know Alex at the time, although I'd met him on a couple of coaching courses.

'I'd started a Tayside Reserve League to allow the likes of United, Dundee, St Johnstone and the Angus clubs to give their fringe players more game-time. It was cleared by the SFA and was proving quite popular as the arrangements were quite loose and could be changed to suit the teams.

'The only outspoken critic of the idea was Albert Henderson, the Arbroath manager, who was worried about what would happen if clubs ordered too many pies and they weren't all eaten. Once Albert was assured the pies could be frozen and used at the next home game, everyone was happy.

'Alex quickly got involved and brought Aberdeen's reserves down to Station Park to play Forfar in the new league. He asked me for a quick word before kick-off. I took him into my pokey wee office under the main stand at Station Park and he didn't waste time with any preliminaries. He just said, "How would you like to be my assistant manager at Aberdeen?" I said that would be great. He asked when could I start and I said the next day. Less than 24 hours later, I was at Pittodrie for a friendly against Twente Enschede.

'I spoke to the Aberdeen chairman, Dick Donald, and agreed a package that meant I was getting £1,000-a-year more than I was currently on. With my job at Bett Brothers, the builders in Dundee, and my part-time work at Forfar, I was on £8,000-a-year. Aberdeen offered to put it up to £9,000. Then I realised I had a car at Forfar and wasn't getting a car at Aberdeen so my new pay rise instantly went on a new motor!'

Never mind a new car, Archie soon realised he had stepped aboard a juggernaut which was hastily moving through the gears. Ferguson had led the Dons to a first league championship in 25 years – clinched with a 5-0 win over Hibs at Easter Road on the penultimate weekend of the season – just weeks before Archie arrived in the Granite City. The vast bulk of the side which would go on to win the Cup Winners' Cup in Gothenburg three years later was already in place.

McLeish and club captain Willie Miller were together at the heart of the defence, with Jim Leighton behind them in goal. Scotland international Gordon Strachan contributed 15 goals from midfield, Mark McGhee ten from attack. Steve Archibald, soon to be sold to Tottenham Hotspur for a club record fee of £800,000, was leading goalscorer with 22.

Now Ferguson had chosen to add Knox's training ground nous to oil the wheels of the Dons' machine, even if the boss needed the odd reminder.

Archie said: 'I'd only been at Aberdeen for a couple of weeks when I had to speak to Alex. All I'd done was watch training and work with the young lads in the afternoons. I said to him, "What am I doing here?" Alex didn't understand what I meant but I told him I hadn't just come to the club to stand and do nothing.

'He came back to me later that same day and said, "You're right. From now on, you take the training and I'll watch."

'There was no drama but I think he wrote in one of his books many years later that it was one of the best decisions he'd ever made. It allowed him to do the things he was good at, and it allowed me to concentrate on the things I was good at, too.'

It was an arrangement which proved popular with the players as well. Centre-back McLeish – who had 16 years and 500 appearances at Aberdeen – believes Knox was an inspired appointment. He said: 'Fergie and Archie created a great atmosphere at the club. When it was serious, it was serious and they prepared us to win. But they were great advocates of down time, too, and we'd have golf or cricket or get away to the sunshine for a bit of Vitamin D in the body. We'd go to Mallorca or Marbella. We even went to Egypt once and I remember us visiting the Pyramids.

'The cricket could be great. There was one time when Fergie fell out with Steve Cowan, one of our strikers, when he caught and bowled him. We were playing at Gordonstoun and Steve had actually got Fergie out in the first over but the gaffer said he wasn't allowed to be out in the first over! Steve caught and bowled him a second time and shouted something like, "Right, you're out this time." Fergie threw his bat at him and ordered him away to run round the pitch until he was told otherwise.

'We were back inside having some dinner when Archie pointed out that Steve was still outside running. Fergie had forgotten about him. He immediately went to apologise and said, "Sorry about that Steve." Cowan replied, "Don't worry – it was worth every lap!"'

Archie, born in the Angus village of Tealing, was just 33 when he succeeded Pat Stanton as assistant to Ferguson. The manager himself was well shy of 40 and the energy and enthusiasm they shared for their task drove on the Dons. The squad was relatively young, too, with home-grown players such as Neil Simpson and Gothenburg goal hero Eric Black slowly bled into the first team.

Black, who has gone on to coach at Celtic and several clubs in England's Premier League including Southampton, recalled: 'At the time, I didn't know any different than Archie and Fergie told me. I was 16 when I signed, 17 when I broke into the first team and everything seemed normal as I had nothing to compare it to. I thought you just turned up, they shouted, you ran, you won a couple of trophies, went on holiday for a week or two then came back and did it all again.

'How lucky was I to have landed with that group of players and that management team at such a young age? Mind you, I didn't always think that at the time.

'They definitely formed me. You have your own character but they tested you and through my whole career I have kept that discipline, work ethic and humility with me. Archie was the one who put that into me. He used to stay behind in the afternoons and work with us as kids. Even when we were in the first team, he constantly tried to make me better. I owe an enormous debt to Archie Knox.

'They did put you under pressure but it was a pressure to make you better. It was top-class management. They were the kind that, once they'd climbed Everest, they'd be looking around asking where the bigger mountain was.

'I've worked with people who could do it five or six days a week. They were the only ones who could do it seven days a week. They were constantly at you – questioning, encouraging, criticising and helping. Archie was always at us on the training ground, but it helped us grow.'

As Knox and Ferguson got to know each other better, the working relationship strengthened and so too did the off-field bond. They'd share nights out with wives and friends, they'd chew over the latest win or a forthcoming contest over a pint or two. A friendship which endures to this day would intensify as the pair realised they shared the common goal of bringing glory to Aberdeen.

And they didn't suffer fools gladly.

Archie said: 'We used to socialise a lot in Aberdeen in those days. We'd go for a few pints after games or out with the wives. I can remember one night we were in the Palm Court, a place in Aberdeen owned by Ricky Simpson, a hairdresser and businessman who was a close friend of Rod Stewart. We'd lost to Rangers at Ibrox and a fan, a lad called Callum Shand who was often seen around the club in those days, approached Alex to discuss the game. He said, "Alex, what the players lacked today was PMA." Alex asked him what he was talking about and what he meant by PMA. Callum explained it was "Positive Mental Attitude" that they were lacking. Alex explained that he could take his PMA and GTF.'

The fire which burned deep inside Knox and Ferguson often came to the surface on the 'Tips' court deep in the bowels of the stadium. As Ferguson says in his foreword, Brian Mitchell once spent two hours running round the Pittodrie track after making a poor decision when press-ganged into refereeing one of the notorious contests. But Knox remembers the one-on-one clashes often lasted even longer as they let off steam at the end of another tough week. He said: 'We had some incredible rammies when playing Tips. There were six goals and all the boys could be involved. There could be anything up to 12 players involved at one time, dodging round the pillars which held up the stand and shooting for goal. It was one touch and if you lost three goals, you were out.

'Alex and I used to play ourselves with diagonal goals and two touches. We could be in there for two or three hours playing non-stop. We loved it but, unfortunately, Stuart Kennedy got smashed in the eye by the ball one day and suffered a detached retina. He was a crucial player – a Scotland international who'd been to the 1978 World Cup finals in Argentina with Ally MacLeod – and had now suffered this bad injury because of a game of Tips. That was the end of that.'

But memories of the way Tips shaped the Fergie/Knox era – and drew management and players closer – endure to this day. Even if outsiders couldn't quite understand what was happening. Strachan, later to manage Celtic and Scotland, recalled: 'I remember a lad, I think he was from Hungary, came over to watch us. Lots of people wanted to come and study this little team from Scotland which was doing so well, but the weather was so bad all we could do was play games of Tips in the gym.

'Within five minutes, he'd cleared out fearing he was in danger of being badly hurt. I think the only word he wrote in his notebook was the Hungarian word for "mayhem". Archie and the gaffer would literally smash the ball off people's faces when they were playing Tips.

'I went in one day when they were playing. I needed to speak to the gaffer about something or other. Archie said, "You saw that – was it a goal?" I said I wasn't sure if it was a goal or not and Fergie shouted, "F*** off, what do you know?" The next thing they were shoving and pushing each other. I left the gym but they came out raging with each other – and I mean raging.'

Legendary Dons skipper Miller, who would later manage the club and serve on the board, also recalls the feuds over Tips. He said: 'The two of them draped a net between two pillars and just battered a ball at each other – and at the younger lads. It let them vent their frustrations and get out any tension. But I'm not sure it's something you'd get away with nowadays.'

One of those younger lads was goalkeeper Bryan 'Big Ben' Gunn, who would serve as understudy to first-choice shot-stopper Leighton. Gunn, who would later win caps for Scotland, signed his first professional forms in the summer of 1980 – just as Knox also penned his deal to join the club. Ousting Leighton from between the sticks was, of course, a sizeable task. But even that couldn't faze him quite like Tips. Gunn said: 'You each had three lives and it was a battle royal at the end. A life was a shot which went inside your white lines. Of course, there was no electronic goal-line technology in those days and it always ended in arguments. The floor was also painted in a horrible black paint which would peel off and leave you filthy, sweaty and dirty.

'The highlight was a Friday afternoon when Archie and Fergie would have their own play-off. It was not to be missed. The younger ones had to stay behind and watch it – and an unlucky one had to referee it – and it was blood-curdling, ferocious, one-on-one stuff. Archie favoured what he called the "blooter". Fergie went for a more dainty approach and would often chip a ball over Archie's head into his goal.

'Archie was there to take bodies and inflict pain. He didn't care that it was the boss on the other end of it – it was last man standing for sure.

'If you were caught cheering for one of them, you knew that the other one would keep it in the memory bank.

'Archie often had a "blooter" which would hit the boss on the head and send him spinning. The key was to make sure we had stopped laughing before he sorted himself out.

'We all wanted Archie to win but we knew the punishment meted out would be worse if Fergie lost so we had to be as diplomatic as possible.

'There was more than one occasion when one of the boys had to run to get Teddy Scott to do his Henry Kissinger bit. I remember Fergie winning one game and one of the boys cheering. Archie sent us out into the snow in our T-shirts to do ten laps of the pitch.

'It could be a fight to the death but it was also a fun way to end a tough week of training ahead of the game on a Saturday.'

And there were plenty of 'tough' weeks at Pittodrie as Knox and Ferguson placed the Old Firm and north-east rivals Dundee United firmly in their sights.

As the title of this book suggests, they took a no-nonsense approach to their jobs – with the players either embracing their methods or being left in their slipstream. When Black was invited to contribute to this book, he joked by text: 'Roger, got your message – will have a think and get back to you. Psychologically, only just recovering from Archie and Fergie and now you're bringing it all back up!!'

Lesser men couldn't cope with the demands placed on them by the management. But Strachan, like Black, is a devotee of the 'what doesn't kill you, makes you stronger' maxim. He looks back on the Ferguson/Knox dugout axis as pivotal to the development of that Dons squad, shaping them as players and people. He said: 'It was character-testing. As a football player, you get tested on the field and you are on your own to deal with mental and physical crises. These two tested you every day so that when these tests came round on the pitch, you were ready for them.

'I look back on those Ferguson and Knox barrages and think, "They didn't kill me, they didn't turn me into a psychotic killer, they didn't make me a depressive." I look back and laugh and say, "I'm all right." They made it easier for me to deal with things as a manager in later years because I'd been tested.

'Archie always had a sense of humour which endeared you to him. I don't think he could have done it without that sense of humour, and he genuinely wanted to make people better. You could feel that as a player, the fact that he was trying to make you better.'

McLeish, who would later manage Rangers to a domestic Treble and lead Birmingham City to the English League Cup after bossing Scotland, agrees with Strachan's assessment. 'There was always a great bond between Fergie and Archie and the players. It just seemed to work. Archie knew how to calm down Fergie when he was having a go. But he could also take the bull by the horns at times. He wasn't a man to be messed with. I tried to improve my game as much as I could and Archie would work with me to improve my range of passing. He'd try to get me to mix up my game and my use of the ball, to hit different diagonals to team-mates. We'd work on the Pittodrie pitch after training to perfect the accuracy of my distribution from the back.

'I made a pass during the 1990 World Cup finals in Italy, a big diagonal out to Robert Fleck on the touchline in Scotland's game against Sweden. Ronald Koeman and company would have been proud of it. Wee Flecky controlled it and put it into that corridor of uncertainty in the penalty box. Big Roy Aitken went down, we got a penalty and won the game 2-1. That pass was a result of all the work I'd done years earlier with Archie. It was about shifting the ball from one foot to the other and changing the direction of play.

'Archie took a coaching course I was on at Largs years after leaving Aberdeen. He was so enthusiastic and skilled. I saw a different side of him. For years, he'd been the boss and you didn't want to get on the wrong side of him – but now we have ended up great pals.'

Bonds forged at Pittodrie have remained strong over almost four decades. Miller, Strachan and McGhee – as well as Ferguson and countless others – were guests at Archie's 70th birthday party in May 2017. At such social occasions, it's only human nature that old tales are stretched a bit. But the Dons legends speak as one when recalling the strict regime which developed them into kings of Europe.

Gunn said: 'People tell stories about Archie swinging a baseball bat in a darkened room at Pittodrie. The stories are as true as can legally be written without anyone getting into trouble. But it was a fun time to be around Aberdeen and it helped all the young lads grow up very quickly and focus on what we needed to do to make it in the game.

'Archie was a massive part of my development. I think Eric and I went full-time in the summer of 1980, just as Archie arrived from Forfar. You only need to look at the number of boys from that team who went on to have careers in coaching or management to realise his influence.

'It was great to work under Fergie, but it was Archie who would stay behind and do extra sessions with us. The coaching techniques and methods were way ahead of their time. Little wonder that team won so much.'

Archie admits it was not an atmosphere in which a player could ever find a 'shoulder to cry on'. All of them were expected to pick themselves up after a verbal battering and carry on. He added: 'I did have a baseball bat and I would sometimes go into the bootroom and let fly at a few of them. It was never too serious and you have to remember these were very different times in all sorts of ways. Aberdeen were just emerging as a force worthy of challenging the Old Firm clubs and taking on Jim McLean's Dundee United. We had to do it the hard way. But we were determined to do it, no matter what stood in our way.

'It's amazing to look back and remember that so much of our training in those early days at Aberdeen was on Seaton Park, a council-owned area of land. If it snowed – and that was not unusual in Aberdeen in the winter – we'd have to go down to the beach. I'd go down early and mark out a full-size pitch on the sand when the tide was out. The sand was hard and made for a decent surface. We'd play games and practise our shooting, crossing and finishing. The problem was that, as the tide came in, we'd have to move the goalposts every ten minutes. The pitch would get narrower and narrower as the session went on, but none of the players ever batted an eyelid. They wanted to play on, they wanted to work, they wanted the same success that Alex and I wanted for them.'

Miller had tasted success in the form of that first title and also the 1976 League Cup under former boss Ally MacLeod. But he knew something special was brewing in Aberdeen as Ferguson and Knox got together. Even if the pair could annoy, offend and infuriate their squad on an almost daily basis. Miller said: 'Archie made a huge impact when he arrived at the club through his talent as a coach and through his big personality. You always knew Archie was going about the place. He was so big and loud that he'd give you a sore head. He was very outgoing and a big character. He has a quiet side but I think it was part of his role with Fergie to keep the place at a high tempo and lively. It didn't always sit well with me in the morning because I was a slow starter.

'He worked well with Fergie but he could also pour oil on the fire. They were a great combination. From time to time, they were bad cop, bad cop!

'Archie came in when Pat Stanton left but they were like North Pole and South Pole. I can remember one day when Fergie was hammering Stuart Kennedy because of the quality of his crosses. Fergie went on and on but Stuart just couldn't see his point. Stuart thought everything he did was perfect – not just his crossing. It got to the point where Fergie looked to Archie for assistance. He said, "Archie, will you tell him his crossing is pathetic." Archie tried to be diplomatic and said, "Well boss, it has improved." But Stuart took it the wrong way and moaned, "So, it's improved to pathetic!" That was the end of the drill because the rest of us could do nothing for laughing.'

CHAPTER TWO

THE DONS' DEEP POOL OF TALENT

THE FOREWORD to this book features the tale of Archie Knox cheating death at the hands of an exploding oven. The first chapter reveals another close encounter as Alex Ferguson lost control of the wheel of a car. It might be considered dangerous to suggest Archie is a cat with nine lives. Then you discover he almost drowned when Gordon Strachan pushed him into a Balearic swimming pool during a champagne-soaked end-of-season trip to the sunshine. If ever one incident summed up the camaraderie and spirit which Knox and Ferguson instilled in Aberdeen's all-conquering squad, this was it.

They would often leave opponents breathless. But this time it was the assistant manager – a non-swimmer to this day – who was left gasping for air. Archie recalled: 'Wee Gordon pushed me into the pool. I couldn't swim and I thought I was going to drown.

'It had been a chaotic trip from the moment we left Scotland. For some reason, the squad travelled in two separate planes. We used a well-known travel agent called Harry Hynds and he couldn't get us all on the one plane for the trip. Alex went direct with some of the team and I had to take the other half to Menorca overnight then catch a flight across to Mallorca the next morning. It was quite a memorable trip because there always seemed to be something happening – even before I was thrown in the pool!

'The Menorca boys had had a few drinks on our one night on the island when Jim Leighton confided in Mark McGhee that his brother was a spy in Russia. I've no idea whether it was true or not but Jim said it was a secret and McGhee must not tell anyone. Unfortunately for him, he told the wrong man and everyone knew within minutes!

'When we eventually made it to Mallorca, the rest of the boys were all stretched out by the pool relaxing. They were enjoying the rather odd combination of Dom Perignon champagne and hamburgers. What a mix!

'All of a sudden, Wee Gordon appeared from nowhere and shoved me into the pool. I came back up to the surface and shouted that I couldn't swim. They were all laughing and didn't believe me. I went down two or three times before McGhee and some of the others jumped in to get me out.

'I chased Wee Gordon for the rest of the trip and told him I'd kill him if I got my hands on him. Of course, I never did!'

Even the perpetrator of this heinous crime admits he got a scare when he realised Archie had never learned to swim. 'I got a fright,' said Strachan. 'I didn't know he couldn't swim. He had a hat on when I shoved him in the pool. The hat came back up and floated on the surface, but Archie didn't. At first, I thought he was taking the mickey. When they got to him, he came out of the water like the evolution of man. Mind you, he's a funny shape to swim – shall we say "heavy-boned". I should have thought of that before I pushed him in.

'I was cruel on him but, then again, he'd been cruel on me.'

Defensive lynchpins Miller and McLeish looked on in amazement as Archie quickly went in and slowly came out of the pool. They'd seen it all before in the 'work hard, play hard' environment which Knox and Ferguson presided over at Pittodrie. Captain Miller recalled: 'I think the trip was at the end of the 1980/81 season, Archie's first at the club. Mark McGhee had just won the PFA Scotland Players' Player of the Year award after a fine season and he and Wee Gordon were the ringleaders. They got hold of Archie and he was shouting loudly that he couldn't swim. Of course, none of the boys believed him.'

McLeish added: 'Somebody shouted that Archie was a "standing target" so they pushed him. He went to the bottom of the pool in the deep end. We didn't believe him and thought he was holding his breath. Then we thought, "Wait a minute, he's not coming back up". We gave it a few more seconds then about ten of us dived in to pull him out.'

Knox was renowned for dishing it out as he ruled with an iron fist at Pittodrie. But he'd also have to take it, with even kids like Eric Black and Bryan Gunn ready to turn on him from time to time. Black recalled: 'Archie used to make us sing songs as a forfeit if we'd done something wrong. I remember getting into trouble with Big Ben for playing hide and seek at our digs. The landlady had complained to Archie that we were wearing out her carpet with all the running around. Singing was the punishment and we had to stand up in front of all the other "S" Forms and belt out a song. I can't remember what I sang, but I do remember that kind of thing was brilliant in keeping up a positive atmosphere around the place.

'He would also get us in this strange kind of lock. He would put his arms up against us and pin us to the wall inside the corridors at Pittodrie. We'd be inside his two forearms and he was a big, powerful man. It was his way of keeping us going, keeping us focused.

'One day Big Ben and I caught him. He was singing in the shower – as he did – and was washing his hair. He didn't hear us or see us and we managed to sneak up with some wet towels and whack him as hard as we could. We took off but he raced after us. I'd like to say he'd picked up one of the towels to cover himself, but I'm not too sure that was the case. It was November and it was snowing outside but he was chasing us around the Pittodrie pitch, trying to catch us, until he ran out of steam.'

The team spirit was legendary and, while Aberdeen ended Archie's first season without any significant silverware, the seeds were being sown for future successes. And if that meant being the butt of the occasional prank or practical joke then Archie felt it was a price worth paying in the name of morale. He added: 'A few of the young lads also got their own back on me one Christmas when a gang of them grabbed me, stripped me naked and dragged me out into the centre circle at Pittodrie before pelting me with snowballs. I think it was after I'd given them trouble for causing chaos in their digs.

'One of my jobs was to liaise with the landladies who looked after the young boys in digs through the week. I remember regular complaints that the boys were using the telephone too often. Of course, it was long before all the players had mobile phones.

'When I called one lady to discuss the complaint, she added, "Archie, they are also wearing out my carpet running up and down the stairs". I told her that fit, young lads tended to run everywhere. She said, "I don't mind that – but they're playing hide and seek!" Imagine having to haul in some of Scotland's brightest young footballers – some who would go on to play for Scotland – and politely ask them to stop playing hide and seek.

'We had some great young lads. Eric Black, Bryan Gunn and a young lad from Kilmarnock called Billy Muir spring to mind. Billy ended up being released and signing for Rangers but I remember one reserve-team game at Tynecastle on a Friday night. Another one of my jobs was taking the reserves – and even driving the minibus to and from the away games. We were 2-0 up against Hearts with ten minutes to go and I'd promised the boys the weekend off if they won. All the mums and dads were in the stand and were awaiting the final whistle to take their boys away back home.

'Of course, we blew it and only drew 2-2. I lost my rag with them and told them they were all coming back to Aberdeen to train in the morning and tidy the place before the first-team game on the Saturday afternoon.

'One by one, they glumly got back into the minibus. I was in the driver's seat and there was a knock on my window. This man said, "I'm Billy Muir's dad. He says you're not letting them home and they've got to go back to Aberdeen".

'I explained the realities of it and said that even the first-team – big-name stars like Willie Miller and Alex McLeish – had suffered the same punishments when we'd lost at Ibrox or places like that.

'Mr Muir said quite calmly, "Well, that just confirms what I've always thought of you – that you're a f**king idiot".

'I said, "That may be so – but he's still coming back up the road".'

Whereas Muir ultimately left the club without making a major first-team breakthrough, pals Black and Gunn emerged as Dons heroes. The former scored the opening goal against Real Madrid in the 1983 European Cup Winners' Cup final in Sweden. The latter challenged Jim Leighton for the gloves before a huge career at Norwich City and international recognition. As they chased their big breaks, however, they were tasked with babysitting duties for Knox and Ferguson on Saturday nights.

Black recalled: 'Archie had two girls, Susan and Lesley, and Fergie had three boys – Darren, Mark and Jason. It wasn't so much a request to babysit – it was more of a summons. I was 18 and I had more plans for a Saturday night than babysitting and watching a film, but I didn't really have an option.'

Gunn added: 'I was caught for the first time when I was sweeping the dressing room and was too slow to dive for cover with the rest of the lads. Archie and Fergie must have been celebrating a win and decided they wanted to take their wives out for a drink and dinner. After that, we quite often had to forgo our Saturday nights out and stay in with either Archie's girls or Fergie's boys. Little did they know that we'd go out on a Sunday night instead – armed with the £20 they'd given us for babysitting. There was method in our madness.'

There was also method in the madness of Knox and Ferguson when they chose to extend the Black and Gunn babysitting services to senior players. At first, Strachan was thrilled to be offered their services in order to allow him to take out wife Lesley for the evening in Aberdeen. But it didn't take him long to smell a rat. 'Lesley and I had our family quite young and Bryan or Eric used to babysit for us, too,' he recalled. 'Archie and the gaffer were tricky because it allowed them to spy on us and find out when we got home, what condition we were in, whether we brought in a curry, who was with us, whether or not McGhee was there too. You couldn't believe that three years later one of these babysitters was scoring a goal in a European final and the other was getting a winner's medal on the bench.'

Babysitting wasn't the limit of the extra-curricular duties for the Dons youngsters in those days. Archie, having moved north with wife Janis and his two daughters, required to find a new family home in Aberdeen. Busy with training and plotting the team's assault on honours, he enlisted the help of some local 'estate agents' to unearth a desirable property. To their eternal credit, the players found one – even if Archie thought they were pranking him again. He said: 'I'd told John Hewitt, Eric Black,

Bryan Gunn and Andy Dornan that they had to keep their eyes open for a house for me. I was in digs with Drew Jarvie and his wife, Janet, when I first went up to Aberdeen but we needed a family home. The four lads came up with all sorts of options – not all of them ideal. Then one of them told me about Burnieboozle Crescent.

'As you can imagine, I thought it was a wind-up. Do they seriously think I'm falling for this one? Are they taking the piss? But somehow they convinced me to take a look and it was perfect. The new Knox family home – Burnieboozle Crescent, Aberdeen.'

By way of reward for their efforts on and off the pitch, Knox and Ferguson always sought to look after the home-grown youngsters. Contract extensions, wage rises, extra bonuses were all pushed their way – assuming the recipient was a deserving one. In the days long before the Bosman agreement and freedom of contract, the Dons' squad often relied on the goodwill of the management to enhance their terms.

Goalkeeper Gunn recalls his own negotiations over one new deal were unorthodox to say the least. 'Archie had an affectionate nickname for me. At least, I think it was affectionate. He thought I had a large head and was never convinced when I told him it was just a big shock of blond hair. He called me "Heid". And it was a nickname which only got altered after I plucked up the courage to ask the manager for a pay rise.

'Most of the boys were heading off on holiday overseas at the end of the season but I feared that I'd be stuck back in Invergordon for the summer months. I went in to see Fergie to ask about a pay rise but he asked why I needed any extra money. I told him I was thinking of going to Torremolinos with the boys. Archie overheard it and started calling me "Heidimolinos". From then on, I was just "Heidimolinos" to him. Luckily, Fergie told me to go up and see Barbara in the office to get the money I needed to go on holiday.

'As I walked out of the office, he shouted, "And tell Ian Taggart – the club secretary – that you're signing for another year for that money!' Another year as "Heidimolinos".'

Archie's first season saw the Dons finish seven points behind champions Celtic and eliminated from the cup competitions by Dundee – whom he'd later manage – and Morton.

Drybrough Cup final victory over St Mirren, with goals from Jarvie and Steve Cowan, was scant consolation for the fiercely ambitious management team. Archie recalled: 'I liked Stevie Cowan but he would always cause a rumpus and was always fed up with something. I lost count of the number of times I sent him back early from training with instructions to tell the manager exactly why he was back ahead of the rest. Sometimes we'd drive past him while he walked back and the lads would chap on the windows of the minibus to annoy him. I'd look in the rear-view mirror and see him giving me a sign of his frustration – usually with one finger!'

The trials and tribulations of Black, Gunn and Cowan as they grew up at Pittodrie often brought smiles to the faces of the senior pros. Maybe the kids didn't recognise it at the time, but this was an important part of their development. McLeish, a stalwart for Knox and Ferguson, said: 'The young boys used to run a mile when they heard the two of them coming. They feared getting some verbals or being ordered to clean up the showers. But it gave the boys a great sense of discipline and respect. They listened to what was being preached about humility and what they needed to do to become good professionals. We did a lot of repetition in training. It was stuff which ultimately sinks in and you do it without thinking about it.

'Eric Black and others who came through the system would eventually make the right runs at the right times because of the work they'd done in training. The defenders would work tirelessly as a back four against six attackers, trying to stop the overload. It got to the stage that the attackers could never score. The repetition made us so solid.

'I actually thought of Archie recently when I was talking to someone about the influx of overseas coaching techniques into the British game nowadays. They complained it's all about "tactical transition" and "methodology" and it made me think about Archie when I heard those words. I texted him and asked why he never spoke to us about "tactical transition". He texted back that all I needed to know was heading the ball out the park and keeping it out of our net.

'When I texted again to ask about his "methodology", he replied that his preferred method was to score more goals than the other team. And he was quite right.'

After so much success in his own managerial career, McLeish is bound to look back and lay some praise at the feet of Knox and Ferguson. But it's Knox alone who earns the credit for one of the most famous nicknames in Scottish football history. McLeish revealed: 'Archie was the first person to ever call me "Eck". In fact, he'd started by calling me "Shuggie" which I could never understand. He then called me "Eck". I'd never been called "Eck" in my life before that and I asked him why he started it. He said he knew someone down the road who was called Alexander Alexander, so they'd called him "Double Ecky". He just took it from there.'

Archie confirmed: 'Alexander Alexander was a well-known fan at Dundee when I was younger. My brother-in-law knew him and he was indeed known as "Double Ecky". So Alex became Big Eck, after I'd spent a while calling him Shuggie. That started because one of the first games after I joined Aberdeen was an away league game at Airdrie. We won 4-0 at the old Broomfield with Cowan, McGhee, Jarvie and Ian Scanlon scoring the goals. The teams were listed on the back of the match programme at Broomfield and Alex was wrongly listed as "Hugh McLeish".

After that I just called him "Shuggie". Well, until he became Big Eck and that one stuck.'

The influence of Knox began to permeate the Dons' squad as he dominated the training ground and Ferguson spent more time upstairs at Pittodrie. Every training session was chronicled on files he still possesses to this day. If it worked, it was brought out again. If not, it was consigned to the bin. Strachan recalled: 'Archie was a very good coach and we enjoyed his training. I'd played for Dundee before going to Aberdeen and, of course, Archie was at Dundee United but I can't really remember playing against him too often. I must have played against him in reserve team football at some stage, though, because I certainly remember that running style of his. When Archie started running with the ball, he grew smaller. He adopted a crouching, charging bull position.'

He certainly possessed the strength of a bull and a hide just as tough. But the Dons' dressing room – like any other group of footballers – went in search of weaknesses, with the inability to swim proving just one. A fear of blood was another, one which came to the surface – quite literally – during one of several trips to play friendlies against Highland League opposition. Club captain Miller said: 'I remember the squad being split into two teams one pre-season for two friendly matches on the same day. Fergie must have taken Teddy Scott to his game because Archie was left to be kitman, physio and coach for the other game. He took us to Inverness to play one of the teams over there and I remember going up for a high ball and being caught in the eye by their centre-forward. I felt the blood straight away and Archie came running on with the medical bag and the magic sponge.

He looked at my face, realised the extent of the damage and yelped, "There's blood everywhere, I can't stand the sight of blood". And he ran away again! He must have been the first physio in world football who couldn't deal with the sight of blood. I had to take myself to Raigmore Hospital to get stitches.

'Archie is nothing like the way he portrays himself at times. He'd like you to think he's Desperate Dan, but he's really just a big pussycat.'

Stuart Kennedy was first-choice right-back under Ferguson and Knox but suffered injury problems. During one spell on the sidelines, he assisted Knox with the reserve team – albeit not sharing the natural enthusiasm of the Dons No.2 for coaching. Kennedy recalled: 'I remember being told I had to help Archie in a reserve game at East Fife in midweek. I was looking for a razor blade to slash my wrists at the prospect, but Archie couldn't have been more enthusiastic.

'Our old minibus was dubbed "The Tumble Dryer" because the lads got shaken about on the seats as if they were inside a tumble dryer. For some reason, Archie insisted on taking the coast road back from Fife after the game and we got caught in thick fog. He was driving at about five miles per hour through the fog and still moaning about the boys' performance. It was 2 a.m. when we got back to Pittodrie and he was still telling some of the young lads where they'd gone wrong. As we lifted the hampers out of the back of the minibus, he said to two of the defenders, "Right, these hampers are strikers – so where should you be right now?" It was pouring with rain by this time but Archie was acting as though it was 10 a.m. and he was doing a normal training drill. He had another two lads lifting these heavy, rain-soaked hampers around Pittodrie Street with the defenders following them. It was only when he saw me looking at my watch and looking at the rain that he decided to call it a night.

'You couldn't fault his enthusiasm for the game or for coaching. You could fill an encyclopaedia with his knowledge of the game.

'I do a little bit of after-dinner speaking these days and I've got a take on Archie as part of it. I tell folk that Gianni Infantino, the FIFA president, wants to bring in Archie to speak about the importance of sports science ahead of the 2018 World Cup finals. After all, there is no better motivation for a player than Archie's baseball bat and balaclava. And who needs these modern-day ice baths when Archie could make you stand in the North Sea for 15 minutes at a time? I can still remember standing in that freezing water, looking at Archie's Desperate Dan chin and wondering if he shaved with a blowtorch!

'He's great fun, though, and having met him again recently at Gordon and Lesley Strachan's wedding anniversary, I can tell you that he still dances like John Travolta.'

After a European Cup first round victory over Austria Memphis in the autumn of 1980 – in Travolta's big-screen heyday – the Dons were set for a Battle of Britain against English champions Liverpool. Bob Paisley, having succeeded Bill Shankly at Anfield, had built a world-class side which had captured Europe's blue riband competition in 1977 and 1978. No one knew at the time, but they'd win it again later this same season.

Alan Hansen, Graeme Souness and Kenny Dalglish provided a Scottish spine which would present the ultimate test for Miller, McLeish, Strachan and Co.

Fergie fancied Aberdeen's chances and enlisted his No.2 for two spying missions which he believed would lay the foundations for a shock success and a place in the quarter-finals. Archie recalled: 'We went down to watch Liverpool before the first leg of the European Cup tie. They were playing against Middlesbrough in the League Cup. Bob Paisley was the Liverpool manager at the time but his predecessor, the great Bill Shankly, was in the tearoom when we arrived before the game. Alex had met him before but I'd never had the pleasure. I was thrilled when Alex said he'd introduce me. Bill said, "Aye son, I've heard all about your team and you're doing well up in Scotland and in Europe, too". I thanked him for his kind words.

'Alex sent me back down on the Saturday afternoon – the

weekend before the first leg at Pittodrie – to make a final check on them. It was a 1-1 draw against Ipswich Town and John Wark, the Scotland midfielder who would later sign for Liverpool, scored with a penalty. I'd been frantically scribbling down everything about Liverpool in my notebook and trying to pinpoint any subtle changes from the Middlesbrough game.

'I met Mr Shankly again in the tearoom at half-time and he said, "Aye son, I see you're down here again". I explained my mission and why I thought it would be crucial to spot any weaknesses. I was nervous and just blurting things out. He looked me in the eye and said, "Aye son, they've all tried that before". I just put my notebook in my pocket and didn't even bother with the second half.'

Shankly's words would prove prophetic as the Dons struggled to shackle the experienced Euro force of Liverpool. With hindsight, the scale of the two-legged defeat – 5-0 on aggregate – would give Knox and Fergie vital lessons for future continental forays. And, looking back, Archie recalls it also provided one of the best laughs he enjoyed in all his time at Aberdeen. 'We lost the first leg 1-0 at Pittodrie to an early goal from Terry McDermott so we were up against it for the return at Anfield. We also had injury problems at the back and Andy Dornan made his debut at left-back at the age of 19. We started fine but Willie Miller scored an own goal just before the interval and Phil Neal netted another on the stroke of half-time.

'We were all a bit low in the away dressing room at 3-0 down on aggregate but Drew Jarvie tried to rally the players with one of the best lines I'd ever heard. He said, quite genuinely, "Right boys, three quick goals and we're right back in this". I don't think Liverpool had conceded three goals at home in 25 years. They still wind up Drew about it to this day.'

CHAPTER THREE

THE REAL TALE OF GOTHENBURG GLORY

THE JOURNEY from Aberdeen to Gothenburg would never be straightforward. From port to port, the fans who travelled to the 1983 European Cup Winners' Cup final aboard the legendary St Clair covered 524 miles each way. The hardy souls among the 12,000-strong Red Army who went by car via the Low Countries, West Germany and Denmark managed triple that number of miles. The team? Their route to the Ullevi Stadium took them to the cities of Sion, Tirana, Poznan, Munich and Genk.

Archie Knox's most arduous journey on the road to Gothenburg, however, involved heat, hostility and a brief encounter with the legendary Alfredo di Stefano in sun-kissed Valencia. He recalled: 'Alex Ferguson had been to the Bernabeu to watch Real Madrid before the final but he wanted me to go out and make a final check. They were playing Valencia in the Mestalla and everything was on the line. Real needed to win to pip Athletic Bilbao to the Spanish title and Valencia needed to win to have any chance of staying up.

'Aberdeen were still using Harry Hynds as the club travel agent at the time, and he sent me to Valencia via London and Alicante. I had to pick up a hire car at Alicante airport – and that was where the problems really began. It was the smallest car I'd ever seen, even smaller than the smart cars on the roads today.

'I was directed onto a new road, a special toll road, which was supposed to take me to Valencia in no time at all. But it quickly became apparent that I was the only car on the new road – in either direction. Then the little car overheated and chugged to a halt. There was steam pouring out of it and no one within miles to help. By the time the engine cooled, time was the enemy. I finally reached Valencia but had no idea where the hotel or stadium was. It was in the days long before sat navs.

'I flagged down a taxi and asked him to drive to my hotel and I'd follow him. Real were staying in the same hotel and, as relations between the clubs had been cordial, had agreed to let me travel to the game on their team coach. Of course, by the time I was showered and changed into my blazer and Aberdeen club tie, they were long gone.

'Now I needed taxi No.2. But the traffic was chaotic and I was dropped a mile from the Mestalla for a sharp jog to the game. It was the start of summer, the temperatures were sky-high and I was saturated in sweat by the time I reached the ground.

'There were more problems ahead, however, as Real hadn't left my complimentary ticket at the stadium. I had no way of getting in – and the game was about to kick off. The only thing to do was make a run for it. I got past security, over a turnstile and in. I'd even made it up the first flight of stairs before security swarmed on top of me and frogmarched me out.

'As it was such a high-profile game, there were lines of police motorcyclists on duty in the streets outside the Mestalla. In desperation, I asked if any of them spoke English and, fortunately, one policeman came forward to listen to my plight. He clearly felt sympathy for me – and for Aberdeen – because he agreed to distract the stewards while I made a second charge at the turnstiles. This time I got in and I was two flights up and deep into a sea of bodies before I even looked behind me.

'But more problems followed. It was quite literally standing room only with every aisle and alleyway jammed with fans. I got out my notebook and tried to work out Real's formation, their set-piece moves and who picked up who at corners. But I was having to bow down and catch glimpses of the action through the legs of a fan who was standing on a barrier. Not quite the detailed scouting dossier which Alex had craved.

'Valencia scored from a corner kick, won the game 1-0, stayed up on goal difference and denied Real the title as Bilbao snatched it by a single point. I waited until the celebrating home fans had dispersed and took myself off to the nearest pub to cool down and calm down.

'Later that night, I got another taxi back to the hotel and some of the Real party were still hanging around. Their coach, the great Alfredo di Stefano, was standing at the hotel bar alone with a very large whisky. I was going to pull him up for leaving the hotel without me and not leaving my ticket at the door, but he seemed miserable enough without me adding to his woes. Yet.

'The final insult was when I checked out of the hotel and the concierge had found an envelope behind his desk. It was left by Real Madrid and addressed to Mr Billy McNeill, manager of Aberdeen FC. They really knew nothing about us at all!'

The seeds of the Cup Winners' Cup success had effectively been sown two seasons earlier as the relationship between Knox and Ferguson developed. A year without major silverware and the sheer scale of the Battle of Britain defeat to Liverpool in 1980 had left them much to ponder. It sharpened their appetite to take Aberdeen the extra yard. Never again would they allow themselves to end a campaign empty-handed and pondering 'what ifs'.

They struck a blow for Scotland – and gained a mark of revenge for the Liverpool loss – when they eliminated holders Ipswich Town from the UEFA Cup in autumn 1981.

They'd go all the way to the quarter-finals of the competition before finally exiting to a Hamburg team which would end the following season as European champions.

Ferguson and Knox were plotting a path which, a season later, would result in Cup Winners' Cup final glory over Real.

But it wasn't all plain sailing for the management team – or the players – as big personalities clashed in the Pittodrie dressing room. Gordon Strachan recalled: 'I remember they had one disagreement which ended with Fergie saying to Archie, "When was the last time Forfar were in Europe . . . ?"

'They were both disciplined, driven men. Archie probably had a better sense of humour but this was an era when it was demand, demand, demand – and they both put plenty of demands on you. Usually, assistant managers were quieter, softer spoken or would reassure you that everything wasn't that bad. Archie would assure you that everything really was that bad – and that it could get a whole lot worse if we didn't shape up.

'Everyone about the place was of strong character. We'd have our own arguments at half-time, even before the manager and Archie came in. We used to see a lot of conflict but it summed up the whole club. There was nothing politically correct about the place, but everyone had an opinion. They stood their ground off the pitch and we'd stand our ground on it.

'With the success of the team, we'd attracted foreign coaches to Pittodrie to study the coaching methods and techniques.'

The Dons' reputation on the continent would grow with each commendable win or, in the case of the Hamburg tie, narrow loss.

The 1981/82 season would end with the Scottish Cup final victory which would provide a passport into the following season's Cup Winners' Cup. A 4-1 extra-time win over Rangers at Hampden – with goals from Strachan, Alex McLeish, Mark McGhee and Neale Cooper – brought the silverware Knox and Ferguson demanded.

They also looked the part at Hampden, even if Ferguson's dress sense wasn't in keeping with the conditions. Knox recalled: 'We won our first Scottish Cup-tie that season down at Motherwell when John Hewitt scored after just 9.6 seconds to set a record. Before the game, Alex had said a pal of his could get us new trench coats for just £12. I'd never had a trench coat so we agreed to buy them. When they arrived, they were a dark green colour – almost like camouflage. We wore them for the first time at Fir Park and we won the game. Of course, that was it for Alex. He reckoned the new trench coats were lucky omens and we had to wear them in every round.

'The semi-final against St Mirren and the final against Rangers at Hampden were played on boiling hot days and, if you watch footage of the games, you can see the sweat pouring off us as we're standing on the touchline in those big coats.'

Aberdeen again were runners-up to champions Celtic in the Premier Division, albeit closing the gap to only two points after an incredible run of 15 wins in their last 16 games. They'd finish behind the Hoops on goal difference alone a year later, although Dundee United would beat them both to the title by a single point.

For Aberdeen, though, the 1982/83 season would revolve around the historic pursuit of a first European trophy. They swept 11 goals past Swiss minnows Sion in the preliminary round before squeezing past Dinamo Tirana of Albania 1-0 on aggregate courtesy of another McGhee goal.

Another trip behind the Iron Curtain was next on the agenda, with the mystery men of Lech Poznan standing between the Dons and the quarter-finals. Ferguson dispatched his trusted

No.2 to Poland for a crucial spying mission. But, yet again, not everything went to plan. Knox said: 'I always seemed to get the troublesome journeys. I remember being sent to Poland to scout Lech Poznan. It was still a Communist country in those days and Lech were due to play Widzew Lodz in a league game. I flew into Warsaw and was picked up by a driver. I was told he'd played for Lech in his heyday, but he didn't speak a word of English. There were no motorways and we seemed to drive for hours along tree-lined A roads with neither of us saying a word.

'We arrived at the Lech hotel for dinner but the only person at the club who spoke any English was the club doctor. The driver showed me to my room – which was also HIS room. There were two single beds and we had to share. He fell asleep instantly and broke into the loudest snore in Poland. I knew I'd not get a wink of sleep.

'To make matters worse, there was a loud bang at the door at 2 a.m. and the driver got out of bed to have an extremely loud argument with the stranger in the corridor. He went straight back to bed and straight back to snoring. I'm not sure I got a wink of sleep but I was treated to a tour of the city of Lodz before the game the next day. It was the first time I'd seen people queuing to buy bread. In fact, they were queuing to buy everything. Everything had a number on it and if, for example, you wanted a new pair of shoes, you'd be handed that number and sent to pick them up at a distribution centre elsewhere in the city.

'The rain was coming down in torrents when we arrived at a stadium which featured huge, dull concrete stands. And I was alarmed to find that while the fans were crammed on one side of the ground, I was the ONLY person on the other side – in a stand which would have fitted 15,000 people.

'There was no cover, my notes got drenched and it was another classic scouting mission for me.

'I actually returned to Poland in 2006 to watch the Scotland

Under-19s side coached by Archie Gemmill and Tommy Wilson when they reached the final of the European Championships against Spain. The Scotland team included the likes of Robert Snodgrass, Steven Fletcher and Lee Wallace. They lost the final 4-0 to a Spain side which featured Gerard Pique and Juan Mata.

'The place had changed beyond all recognition, but it sent my mind racing back to that ridiculous scouting trip – and our win.'

Home and away victories over Lech, without a goal conceded, paved the way for a far more glamorous tie in the last eight.

The Euro aristocrats of Bayern Munich were held to a goalless draw on their own patch in the first leg. Mark McGhee recalled an unusual build-up to the first leg as Archie was pushed onto the sidelines and Fergie took charge. McGhee said: 'The night before the first leg in Germany seemed just like any other night when we arrived at the stadium. But when we got out onto the pitch at the Olympic Stadium, Fergie declared that he was going to take the session. I'm sure he did it because people like Uli Hoeness were looking on. He probably felt that, as manager, he should be seen to be taking the training session.

'Archie stood facing away from the session in an absolute huff. The boss had pulled rank and Archie's mood wouldn't have been helped by all the players shouting stuff at him.

'Fergie's session was supposed to be a drill with players in four corners and three balls between us. The idea was that the balls got played in to the spare man and everyone would move to receive their pass. But what ensued was chaos. You'd be looking in one direction for the pass and a ball would hit you on the head from the opposite direction. The drill was shambolic – which only exacerbated Archie's frustration at not being allowed to take the session. We didn't let him forget it.

'We played brilliantly the next night to get a 0-0 draw. And, of course, we totally credited the display to Fergie's pre-match training session.'

What followed in the return at Pittodrie two weeks later has become the stuff of legend – almost more so than the final itself. Bayern, including World Cup legends Paul Breitner and Karl-Heinz Rummenigge, twice took the lead in Aberdeen. But the Dons stormed to a 3-2 win, highlighted by one of the most bizarre and well-remembered goals in Scottish football history.

Strachan and John McMaster both ran to take a free-kick on the edge of the penalty area and then stopped as though it was a mistake. The German defence paused and the break in concentration saw Strachan turn and whip in the set-piece when they were off guard.

Alex McLeish, who got his head on the end of the cross to score, said: 'Bayern were caught cold – absolutely caught cold. We relaxed and for a minute they dropped their guard and one or two put their hands on their hips, including the goalkeeper. I'm sure the routine was plagiarised from somewhere – and our one has probably been plagiarised a thousand times since then. We managed to catch Bayern off guard with it, but we'd been laughing in training all week as we couldn't get it to work. Then, in the greatest game ever seen at Pittodrie, it worked against one of the top teams in the world.'

Big Eck's header was sandwiched by goals from Neil Simpson and John Hewitt as the roof almost came off Pittodrie. And he says the roots of the Euro upset lay in the way they'd been prepared by Ferguson and Knox. He said: 'Nowadays you can't sit down and watch a full game with the players. Their attention span isn't good enough. But in those days, we were like sponges. There was no European football on television back then so you couldn't see the opposition. The only European club games broadcast on TV were the big finals. By and large, we had very little knowledge of the teams we were playing against. I kept up to speed by buying *World Soccer* magazine. I'd save them up to get as much information as I could. When Fergie and Archie showed us footage of the teams we were going to play, we sat through the whole game and never get bored as this was new-tech stuff for us.

'I think we saw Bayern play Bayer Leverkusen before we played them in the quarter-final. We sat down and took everything in.'

After mighty Bayern had been vanquished, the Dons' fans believed they'd steamroller the little-known Belgians of Waterschei in the semi-final.

So it would prove, with a 5-1 first-leg romp at Pittodrie effectively ending the tie there and then.

And so to Gothenburg.

To say the Granite City was overwhelmed by cup fever would be the understatement of all understatements. The Aberdeen *Evening Express* front page on the eve of the game – May 10, 1983 – included a telegram sent by Prime Minister Margaret Thatcher to the team.

It read: 'Congratulations to the Dons on reaching the European Cup Winners' Cup final. You have my admiration for what you have already achieved and my very best wishes for the big match.

'I hope you capture the cup but, above all, win or lose, I hope you win friends. Yours, Margaret Thatcher.'

Other messages of good wishes were published from Denis Law, Rod Stewart, former manager Billy McNeill and Scotland boss Jock Stein, who'd accompany the team to Sweden. Beechgrove Gardeners Jim McColl and George Barron put down their trowels to wish the Dons all the best. And even Saturday night entertainers Cannon and Ball penned the message: 'All the best for the final and thanks to everyone in Aberdeen for a fabulous five shows we did there. Rock on Dons.'

At the foot of the front page, Dons' captain Willie Miller was advertising cut-price suits to mark this special occasion. Without Bobby Ball's braces . . .

Amid all the excitement and anticipation, however, the two

coolest heads en route to Gothenburg belonged to Ferguson and Knox. They knew Real had the history and a name synonymous with European glory. But they also knew that Aberdeen possessed the players to win the game. Archie recalled: 'Alex had invited Jock Stein over to Sweden for the final. Jock had a blether with one or two of the players before the game and just him being there gave everyone a boost. Of course, he had been there and done it and had beaten the best Europe had to offer with Celtic back in 1967.

'I can remember Alex going to watch Real after the semi-finals. He phoned me after the match and said, "We can't tell the players, but we have a right chance of winning this Cup".'

Play the game not the name, was the management's mantra as they convinced their squad that they would beat Real. McLeish said: 'I could see the Real players looking across at us in the tunnel and some of them were laughing as if to say "look at this bunch here". But it looked like a nervous laugh. I could not see the same spirit in the Madrid team that there was in that Aberdeen team.'

So it would prove, with Black's close-range finish handing Aberdeen a priceless early advantage.

A rare error by McLeish, when he left a back pass to Jim Leighton short on a sodden surface, allowed Real the chance to equalise. Leighton had tripped Carlos Santillana as he sought to profit from Big Eck's mistake, with Juanito netting from the penalty spot.

Real had superstars such as Uli Stielike, Johnny Metgod and Jose Antonio Camacho among their number. But the Dons took the final into extra time, albeit things might have gone a lot differently for matchwinner John Hewitt.

Archie recalled: 'When we sent on Hewitt, the plan was to get him playing around Stielike, the German international who was dictating the play for Real. He'd only been on for about five minutes and Alex was screaming at me to take him back off as he wasn't getting close enough to Stielike.

'He was getting what we used to call "the curly finger". But before we could do anything about it, he'd scored the winning goal.

'It was a great goal. Peter Weir chipped the ball down the line and Dingus (Mark McGhee) put it right on Hewitt's napper with his left foot. We couldn't even imagine Dingus kicking the ball with his left foot, far less placing a cross like that right onto his head.'

McGhee remembers: 'A left-foot cross? I didn't have many of them in my career. I remember it was deep into extra time on a horrendously wet night and the pitch was very heavy. Peter Weir played me a ball down the left-hand side and I thought, "I've got to chase this". I knew the bold fella was on the bench and would be expecting me to chase it. I remember just trying to put every ounce of energy that I had left into just getting the ball off the ground. That's all I was concentrating on – on that muddy, wet pitch – getting the ball up in the air.

'I launched my left foot, which wasn't great by any stretch of the imagination, at the ball and Hewitt did a great job of getting on the end of it and scoring the winning goal.

'The next day, when we returned to Aberdeen and saw the hordes lining the streets and the stadium, we realised the scale of the achievement. The acclaim showed us how special it was.

'The timing of the win was big for us because it was round about the end of the period when a provincial club like Aberdeen were able to go and do that. By 1990, with the advent of Sky TV and all the money, all the big clubs like Real suddenly became big again and it became difficult for clubs like Aberdeen.

'Dundee United and ourselves both made a good fist of European football at that time but it was kind of the end coming up. To achieve what we achieved and win the European trophy that the manager had spoken to me about when he signed me years earlier was incredible.

'One of the masterstrokes Alex pulled in the days leading up to the final was that he made no case for Real at all. I'm not even sure I knew we were playing Real Madrid. He downplayed it so much that we didn't even know their names. We didn't know they were greats. He kept such a lid on it that everything was about us, about our performance and about us winning that cup at all costs. It took away nerves or any fear that we were playing the mighty Real Madrid.'

The celebrations commenced as soon as the ball hit the back of the Real net, with even TV reporters getting in on the act. Knox explained: 'On the day of the final, it emerged that Bob Patience – who was working for Grampian TV – hadn't received his accreditation for the game. When we arrived at the stadium, he pleaded with me to get him an Aberdeen tracksuit and pretend he was on the backroom staff. Bob was a big lad and I remember saying, "Where on earth do you think Teddy Scott is going to find XXXXL gear to fit you?!?" Amazingly, we found something but Bob was bulging out of it all over the place. It was enough to get him into the Ullevi Stadium. To make the whole thing look plausible, he had to stand at the side of the dugout in the pouring rain while the match was going on.

'When Hewitt scored the winner in extra time, I went charging down the track towards the corner flag to celebrate. I turned round to run back and who jumped into my arms but Bob. As I say, he was a big lad and the two of us came crashing to the ground on the track.

'We didn't get a chance to shake hands with di Stefano at the final whistle. We haven't seen him to this day.

'People often talk about the iconic image of everyone bursting from the Aberdeen dugout when the referee blew the final whistle. What most people don't remember is that Alex fell on his face and the rest of us trampled over the top of him to get onto the pitch. I got threatened with the sack for that!

'There is no question it was a special time for Scottish football, with the achievements of Aberdeen and Dundee United. People talk of Arsene Wenger taking Arsenal into the Champions League for something like 20 years on the spin. But Jim McLean took a provincial club like United into Europe for 18 straight seasons. It was just phenomenal. And we didn't do too badly either.

'I don't think I was in my bed for three days after the final. The celebrations were wild and the reception back in Aberdeen was just unbelievable. There must have been 100,000 people on Union Street as we took the trophy on the open-top bus tour. The stadium was full as well when we got back there.'

The party continued for the Dons as Mick Jagger and The Rolling Stones came rocking into the Granite City.

Knox recalled: 'After we won the Cup Winners' Cup, we were invited to a Rolling Stones concert in one of the theatres Dick Donald owned in Aberdeen. Alex said the players could dress as they pleased but the two of us would have to wear a shirt and tie as we were representing the club. The boys all turned up in jeans and T-shirts – as everyone else in the place did – and they were all dancing in the aisles. Mick Jagger was strutting his stuff and Alex turned to me and said, "I suppose we could maybe take our ties off!"'

Little did he know at the time, but these were to be Archie's final days of his first spell at Aberdeen. He'd return to Scotland to see the Dons lift the Scottish Cup thanks to Black's extra-time goal against Rangers at Hampden. But he'd soon be lured away by the manager's job at Dundee, just as Teddy Scott had warned Ferguson at the height of the post-match party in Gothenburg.

He had one more important task before leaving, however, in the wake of Ferguson's infamous televised rant at the end of the Scottish Cup final. Skipper Miller recalled: 'After the 1983 cup final, we relied on Archie to make the manager see sense. He embarked on the famous rant on the Hampden pitch, praising "Miller and McLeish" but hammering everyone else. We'd just won the Scottish Cup to complete a double with the Cup Winners' Cup but Fergie was going crazy. He wouldn't allow us champagne to celebrate and wouldn't even allow the wives and girlfriends to join us on the bus. They had to go on their own bus back up the road to Aberdeen. Fergie said we were a disgrace to our families and our kids with the performance we'd produced in the cup final. He asked us how we could look ourselves in the mirror. It was heading towards major confrontation as the boys were furious – and poor Archie was caught in the middle. Eventually he convinced Fergie to open a bottle of champagne for us. One bottle to celebrate a double!'

CHAPTER FOUR

THE BERMUDA TRIANGLE OF PASSES

HEARTS WERE broken on either side of the border in 1986. Up north, Archie Knox's Dundee would deny Heart of Midlothian an historic Scottish title on a dramatic last day of the season (more of this later). A week later, Alex Ferguson's Aberdeen would heap more misery on the Jambos with a 3-0 Scottish Cup final rout at Hampden.

Down south, The Theatre of Dreams was turning into a personal nightmare for Ron Atkinson as Manchester United ended the season without silverware. Soon the planets would align and the most successful era in British football history would commence at Old Trafford.

But, first of all, two old pals had to be reunited before they could be sent to United.

Archie recalled: 'I'd only been back at Aberdeen with Alex for a few months when we got the chance to go down to Manchester United. Managing Dundee had been great but I felt it was right to go back. I don't know whether it was an ego thing, but I was missing the winning and the success. I remember Alex turning up when I was out training with the guys in the afternoon. My mother had been ill and I thought, "Oh, he's got bad news for me here".

'I ran up to him and his very words were: "We are going to Manchester United". I said, "Oh aye, when's that?" He said, "Tonight".

'Alex said to me that I'd get offered his job as Aberdeen manager when he left for United and he was right – but I was never tempted to take it. How do you follow him? The players were getting older, too, and the team might only have gone on for another two years. Plus the fact that I was getting an opportunity to work at Manchester United, with all the history going back to Sir Matt Busby and beyond.'

United's gain would, of course, be a devastating loss to Aberdeen, albeit Dons' captain Willie Miller believes Archie made the right call. Miller said: 'If he'd taken the job at Pittodrie, Archie's problem would have been the same as anyone else's. How do you follow Fergie? In those days, it wasn't enough to finish second and win the odd trophy. There was pressure on the Aberdeen manager to win league titles and win cups on a regular basis.'

When they arrived at Old Trafford to succeed Atkinson, they were greeted by excited United supporters and a sceptical squad and media. But there were some good wishes, notably in the form of a Telemessage – dated 7 November 1986 – which Archie still possesses to this day. It read: 'Congratulations. Did you check if there was a gymnasium for the Tips Championship before you accepted the job?

'Best of luck in your quest to be the Champion of England, indoors and outdoors.

'Will you still talk to the boys now that you are a big star?

'Regards, Andy Roxburgh.'

The support of the man who'd succeeded Ferguson as Scotland

manager after that summer's World Cup finals in Mexico was appreciated. So, too, was the backing of another Aberdeen legend who had made the journey from Pittodrie to Old Trafford ahead of them. Gordon Strachan, signed by Atkinson two years earlier, recalls the mixture of curiosity and wariness in the dressing room. Strachan said: 'I tried to give them as much support as I could. There were people in the Manchester area who looked down on them because they'd come from Scottish football. I was a lone voice telling people they are excellent at what they do. Archie was completely different from other assistant managers. I don't think the United players had seen a No.2 who was so vocal before. Everyone asked me what they were like. I gave them an idea but, for the first six weeks or so, they were very quiet. It was strange and everyone was asking me what I was on about. But then we saw the true Sir Alex one day at Wimbledon and the rest is history.'

The Ferguson era would ultimately yield an incredible 13 league titles, five FA Cups, four League Cups and two Champions Leagues. He'd raise the European Cup Winners' Cup – his second after the Dons' win in Gothenburg – just days after Archie headed for Rangers to become assistant to Walter Smith in 1991. But as autumn lapsed into winter in 1986, such historic achievements couldn't have been further from the thoughts of dispirited Red Devils' fans.

Archie said: 'When we arrived at United, the team was in relegation trouble. I was still up in Aberdeen when Alex went down at first. The team lost 2-0 at Oxford United in his first game in charge then drew 0-0 at Norwich before I joined him. My first game was also Alex's debut at Old Trafford. We were playing at home to QPR and we were 21st of the 22 teams in the old First Division. John Sivebaek, the Danish defender, scored with a free-kick to secure a 1-0 win. It took us up to 17th place and we eventually finished 11th.'

As Knox and Ferguson laid the foundations for a brighter future, they were also handed the keys to their new home. Even if there was a distinct lack of warning about an exploding oven.

Archie said: 'Timperley was a two-bedroom semi in a housing scheme. We went through the front door, Alex dived up the stairs and got the best room and that was it. It didn't matter a damn because we were hardly ever in the place. We'd be at The Cliff – United's training ground in those days – early in the morning and often at games at night. We both had the same energy and drive we'd had in the early days at Aberdeen and we wanted to make it work.'

They both knew that they'd have to temper the tactics which had worked to such stunning effect in the Granite City. Baseball bats and runs round cricket pitches might work for callow youths, but they were now handling the egos of some of the game's finest.

Bryan Robson was captain of United and England, one of Europe's most highly-rated players and beloved by the Old Trafford faithful. Robson recalled: 'When any new coach or manager comes into a club, the players are always looking to see how good their training is and what the range of training is like. Straight away, from the first few weeks we had under the gaffer, you could see Archie had many and varied training techniques. There was great variation in the training and he made it interesting all the time. Sometimes coaches do the same thing all the time and it can become monotonous. But Archie always varied the work and you quickly realised he was a really good coach. Combine that with the gaffer's great knowledge of the game and you can see why the lads took to them so quickly.

'One of my favourite memories of Archie was before we played Montpellier in the European Cup Winners' Cup quarter-final in 1991. Archie had heard that someone from Montpellier had sneaked in to watch us training at The Cliff. He said, "We're going to have a bit of fun today – let's see what these Frenchmen think of our special warm-up". He then reached inside his tracksuit top and produced a rugby ball. We always started our warm-ups with a game of keep-ball in small boxes on the training pitch. Now Archie had us playing it with a rugby ball. It was bouncing everywhere and the boys were in stitches.

'That's what Archie was like – always great fun to be around. He was deadly serious when he needed to be, but also light-hearted and fun. The boss is right when he says he could have stayed at United and had a great career there. The lads were all disappointed when he went back up to Scotland. We were just starting to have a lot of success at the club again and Archie was a big loss. Like the gaffer says, with Archie's reputation he could easily have been the next manager if he'd stayed with the boss.

'The boss always played the deadly serious one, the hard man. Everything had to be spot-on when he was about. Archie was the light-hearted one and more relaxed with the players. That's the way you have to be as an assistant manager. Sometimes you do get assistants who are serious, too, but I don't think that works as well with the players. You need someone who likes a bit of fun, who takes part in the daft pranks. It works better that way, and that's what Archie and the gaffer had.'

Archie never lifted spirits as much, though, as when he made his United debut – a scoring one – in far-off Bermuda. United had headed for the sun-kissed Caribbean island midway through the new management team's first full season in charge. The trip threatened to spiral out of control with Wales international Clayton Blackmore wrongfully arrested and threats of crowd trouble. Players also missed a late-night curfew and, as Ferguson's temper raged, they were desperate to get the second and last game of the tour over. Archie recalled: 'We went to Bermuda in November 1987 for some warm-weather training and to play a couple of games. We had beaten the national team 4-1 but had suffered some injuries and other problems and had only taken a skeleton squad in the first place. We only had ten fit players for the second game, a bounce match against a team called Somerset Trojans in front of just a couple of thousand fans. Alex said the only thing for it was for me to play at right-back. I wasn't sure as I'd passed my 40th birthday six months earlier. But there I was, making my Manchester United debut, and to cap it all I even managed to get on the scoresheet. It was a goal made in Scotland. I played a pass to Gordon Strachan, he fed Brian McClair and he held it up on the edge of the box. Choccy played it back to me, I cut inside and I sent a left-footer into the top corner. At least, that's how I remember it . . .

'Alex was gutted that I'd scored because he knew I'd go on and on about it all the way home from the Caribbean. And things got even worse for him when one of the lads went down injured and *he* had to come on. The boys decided among themselves that they wouldn't pass the ball to him in the time he was on the pitch. He was absolutely raging as they knocked it about among themselves and declined to pass it to the gaffer. I don't think he got a single touch until the final whistle sounded.'

Skipper Robson was the chief instigator behind embarrassing the boss, and still laughs about it to this day. He explained: 'I still remember Archie's goal in Bermuda. I was playing at centre-back, Archie was at right-back and the boss was on the bench. We were 5-0 or 5-1 up and Archie had scored a cracker to make it 2-0. We had quite a strong side and the boss came on as sub. He went to centre-forward for the last ten or 15 minutes but, as he was coming on, I was shouting to the lads not to pass the ball to him. He kept showing for it and the lads kept it away from him. They were passing it side to side to each other but no one would pass to him. The ball finally went dead after ten minutes and he hadn't touched it. He was roaring, "I know what you lot are up to".

'I think the goal was the highlight of Archie's career – it was a screamer. He loved getting involved in games. On a Friday or the day before a midweek game, after we'd done all the serious work, the gaffer and Archie would love getting involved in a relaxed game. The boss would join in a lot in the early days but he was rubbish!'

Archie's goal is commemorated on the pages of *The Royal Gazette* in Bermuda, dated 2 December 1987. The match report reads: 'The match ended an ignominious tour for United, which attempted to inject some levity into a controversial mid-season tour by starting assistant manager Archie Knox at right-back – and then bringing on 45-year-old manager Alex Ferguson as a striker with 21 minutes remaining.

'Knox, many years removed from his playing career, acquitted himself well – and capped off a solid performance with a brilliant 30-yard goal after beating one man in midfield.

'Jesper Olsen, Brian McClair and David Wilson also scored for United.

'Ferguson's entrance brought some good-natured ribbing from the crowd – but the manager was upstaged by his assistant when Knox glided past a defender and let fly with a 30-yard blast which flew into the top left corner.'

Strachan recalls Archie's spectacular strike as a rare highlight of the tour, and also remembers troublesome trips closer to home. He said: 'The Bermuda trip was nonsense. Archie played right-back, Sir Alex came on as a sub and there was a riot with spectators on the field threatening players. I remember Archie's goal but I'm not sure I had a hand in it. My mind was on the crowd and looking for an escape route if it all kicked off.

'There were some strange trips in those days. Sir Alex, in his wisdom, took us up to Cumbria before we played Coventry City in an FA Cup fourth round tie at Old Trafford in 1987. They'd not been at United long and it was the Coventry team who would go on to win the FA Cup later that season when they beat Tottenham at Wembley.

'We were staying at Windermere and I remember getting the chef to put out a menu which read "As many cow pies as you want for Desperate Dan". Archie was known as Desperate Dan. He wasn't pleased by the nickname and wasn't pleased by the menu either!

'We ended up being caught up in bad weather, it took us three hours to get to Old Trafford for a home game and we lost 1-0. We didn't do it again.'

Strachan would leave for Leeds United in 1989, a move which ultimately saw him land an English league title ahead of Sir Alex. He explained: 'My world, Sir Alex and Archie-free, had been shattered when they arrived at United. As much as I love them – and I love them to death – it wasn't right for me. It was going over old ground and I had heard it all many times before.'

United's pulling power around the globe saw them invited for money-spinning trips to Malta and Japan as well as Bermuda. Like Strachan, Archie had reservations over some of the excursions – especially when he was left alone to deal with the squad. He explained: 'Looking back, some of the trips we went on were ridiculous. But we were Manchester United and everyone wanted to see Manchester United. We were in Malta for a friendly around the time of the Bermuda trip, a trip organised by a big supporters' club on the island. We were winning 5-0 and a boy from the supporters' club came to our bench and asked us to instruct the players to stop scoring. We explained that it wasn't quite that easy but they were worried that the Maltese team would be embarrassed. I think we ended up winning 7-0 but that was only the start of the problems because Alex needed to dash back home early and the players dashed away for a night out.

'When it came to breakfast time and getting together for the trip to the airport, we realised we were minus Paul McGrath.

The big man was a terrific player but he liked a night out, too, and he'd been waylaid somewhere during the night. We left his passport behind for him in the hotel and headed off to the airport as I pondered how I would explain this turn of events to Alex. But somehow the big man managed to get himself and his passport to the airport just minutes before we headed home.'

Losing a key player would have been one thing. Injuring another one – in the shape of star striker Mark Hughes – was quite another. And, despite that stunning goal against the Somerset Trojans, Archie would soon be invited to put away his boots for the safety of the players. He laughed: 'When I first went down to United, I was still only 39 and I'd take part in the training games if we were short of players. I went on one Friday morning – the day before a big game – and ran into Mark Hughes, breaking one of his ribs. Of course, he couldn't play the next day. It was horrendous. I took some awful abuse from Alex for that and he banned me from training.

'I loved competition, no matter what form it took, and so did Alex.'

The fire which burned in the bellies of Knox and Ferguson convinced them that they'd have to make changes at Old Trafford. Their first signing would be Viv Anderson, an England international and two-time European Cup winner with Nottingham Forest. A lifelong United supporter, Anderson had been released by the club as a kid before his career was rescued by Brian Clough at the City Ground. Throw in the fact that the right-back roomed with Robson on England trips and he was never likely to say no.

Anderson recalled: 'Bryan phoned me when Alex and Archie were appointed. I roomed with him with the England team and we were close friends. He said they'd got a new manager – a guy called Alex Ferguson. I replied, "Who's he?" – but as soon as I met him and Archie they won me over.

'I signed for United at the same time as Brian McClair but I came first in the alphabet so I always say I was their first signing. I'd been offered a new deal at Arsenal but I'd always been a United supporter and I'd had a year there as a kid. It was in the days when you could look across to the first-team pitch and watch George Best, Denis Law and Bobby Charlton.

'They'd let me go and told me I'd not make it. I went back to Nottingham, got a job for a week then signed for Forest. The chance to go back to United was something I had to consider. If I hadn't, I'd have been 60 and in a wheelchair and wondering "what if?"

'I met Alex and Archie for two hours and they convinced me to sign. I was just sold on their passion for the club. We'd just bought a new house in London and I had to go back and tell my wife we were moving again. But it was worth it. They wanted to make Manchester United a success again and they wanted to bring in the players to do that. They already had big-name superstars like Norman Whiteside and Paul McGrath, but they very quickly put their stamp on the place.

'If the gaffer ever wanted to take training, we'd say no and say we wanted Archie. That was the respect he was held in. The things he brought to training were things we'd never done before. He'd make you think and would sharpen your brain as well as your legs.

'The thing that shone through with Alex and Archie was their desire to win and their shared love of football. They were a new voice, a fresh voice, a refreshing voice for United. The players bought into it straight away. They instilled the belief that United could win things again. Their methods and the way they would talk to you were great. They didn't mess about. They were going to make a success of it at United and you had to go with them.'

Anderson and Robson had been in the England side which lost 1-0 to Scotland at Hampden in the 1985 Rous Cup. Ferguson was Jock Stein's part-time No.2 at the time, just months before the Scotland boss would tragically pass away in the dugout at Cardiff's Ninian Park. Knox had assumed the role of Tartan Army foot soldier and was determined not to let Anderson forget the result. Anderson, who'd eventually leave for Sheffield Wednesday just days after Knox headed for Rangers in 1991, couldn't believe it. He said: 'Archie taught me to sing "Flower of Scotland". I still know the words and all the "When will we see your likes again". He's a lovely man, a big football man. Any time I see him, even now after all these years, we have a great chat about the game.'

Archie was just thrilled to have Anderson on his side after clashing with him in one of his first games as No.2 at Old Trafford.

He recalled: 'Viv was a great lad, although I didn't think that the first time I had an encounter with him. We were playing at home to Arsenal just a few weeks after we first went to United. They were a good team. George Graham was in charge and I think they were on a long unbeaten run and top of the old First Division. Robson was injured and Alex had asked Norman Whiteside to go into midfield and stir a few things up. He had a horrendous tackle on Paul Merson then David Rocastle retaliated and got a straight red card before half-time.

'In those days, the tunnel at Old Trafford was in the middle of the main stand and much tighter than the big one in the corner nowadays. As we went up the tunnel at half-time, I was surrounded by a gang of Arsenal players including Viv and Tony Adams. They accused me of getting their player sent off by jumping up and down and shouting at the referee for a red card. I said it was nothing to do with me. Eventually, they all got pulled away from me and, as I tried to get into our dressing room, a policeman said to me, "You should have belted one of them – I'd have let you off with it".

'We won 2-0 – Gordon Strachan and Terry Gibson scored the

goals – and it wasn't too long until we had Viv on our side.'

In came Anderson and McClair while Hughes returned from Barcelona and United also landed a defensive colossus. Steve Bruce would lift the first three titles of Fergie's reign plus three FA Cups, one League Cup and two European trophies. He would serve the club with distinction for almost a decade and be regarded as one of the club's best-ever buys. But his move from Norwich City almost fell flat after a premonition which still sends a shiver down Archie's spine. He said: 'When Steve was undergoing his medical to sign for United, I was sitting with his wife, Janet, and trying to make polite conversation. For some unknown reason I blurted out the words "And what do you think you'd do if Steve fails the tests?" The sentence had hardly left my mouth when Alex called and told me he'd failed the medical because of a problem with his knee. I couldn't see how that could be possible. He'd played 250 games for Norwich, for God's sake, and never had an issue. I thought I'd jinxed the deal and was terrified about what I'd tell Janet.

'We needed to get something sorted out and eventually we had another look at him and just decided to sign him. If it had been up to the medical people, Steve would never have been a Manchester United player. Not a bad decision by us in the end!'

CHAPTER FIVE

LIFE IN THE OLD TRAFFORD FAST LANE

FROM THE day their car crashed at Stonehaven several years earlier, Archie Knox had always been wary of Alex Ferguson's driving. But had Greater Manchester Police now been alerted to his fast and loose interpretation of road traffic regulations? So the Manchester United boss believed after losing out on a 'race' with his No.2 to the club's training ground.

Knox recalled: 'We'd sometimes go together from our house in Timperley to The Cliff, but there were occasions when we'd travel separately and see who could get in first.

'We left at 7.30 one morning and were both on the motorway. These were the days long before four lanes on the M6 and M60. We'd take the Salford turn-off and go past Old Trafford to reach The Cliff. There were two lanes at the cut-off and I could see Alex in front of me.

'I thought I'd be cheeky and take the inside lane to get past him. He spotted me in his rear-view mirror and tried to manoeuvre to stay ahead of me. But he was so busy watching me that he ran into the car in front of him. It wasn't major, just a wee bump.

'Of course, it was enough to delay him so I got in first and told Brian Kidd all about it. We came up with the idea that, when Alex finally got into his office, Kiddo would phone and pretend to be the police. I was in Alex's office when the phone rang. Kiddo said, "Mr Ferguson, this is Manchester traffic police. We have had reports of an incident at the Salford turn-off this morning. It's been alleged that you ran into another car while talking on your mobile phone. We'll have to come out to interview you".

'I could hear Alex saying, "That's absolute fabrication. I wasn't on my phone. It wasn't even a smash, it was just a little bump".

'He said to me that I'd need to back him up and say he wasn't on his phone. I just said that I hadn't seen anything.

'We kept him going all day, pretending to watch out for the arrival of the police. When we eventually got back to the office, Kiddo called again and put him out of his misery. He went off his head!'

Ferguson's real driving ambition was to haul the Red Devils out of the malaise he'd discovered when he and Knox first arrived in November 1986. They pulled United into the top half of the old First Division table in their first six months at Old Trafford. Brian McClair and Viv Anderson became the first signings of the Ferguson and Knox era as they carefully overhauled the playing personnel. Scotland striker McClair, who joined from Celtic, said: 'I went down to look at houses a couple of weeks before I actually signed for United. I had long hair and a beard at the time and I remember Archie and the manager telling me that I'd better not look like that when I was paraded at the press conference after I signed.

'I'd not met Archie before but I remember him laughing – he was always laughing – when I was told to shave off the beard. I'd only met the manager once before, on a flight to Nice for the Golden Boot awards a few years previously. The role of the assistant is that of a buffer between the players and the manager.

Archie enjoyed the banter but was always quite clear that he was part of the management team. He was great fun. He'd tell everyone that the goal he scored in Bermuda that day was a piledriver – but it was more of a toe-basher.

'They were so competitive with each other. They'd string up a net between the weight machines in the gym and play head tennis. They often got a youngster to referee their contest but one day I got the job and I vowed I'd never do it again. You couldn't please either of them. I think Archie won but it ended with both of them shouting and screaming at me. I had these two big, red faces coming at me and the pressure was intense. It was just too difficult to ref them.'

Head tennis at The Cliff had replaced Tips at Pittodrie as the method of choice for releasing pent-up tension. Nothing improved the management's mood, though, more than results on the pitch – and they were improving. Their first full season in charge saw United soar to runners-up position in the league, albeit nine points adrift of champions Liverpool. Knocking them off their perch would take a little more time. Eight wins and two draws in United's final ten league games stood as a warning of better times ahead at Old Trafford.

McClair recalled: 'The two of them reinvigorated the club and Archie was a massive part of that. In those early days, they were always at The Cliff – in their hats to keep out the cold. Archie had done a lot of coaching with the young players at Aberdeen and he had a really good way of dealing with the young players at United. He gave them praise when they needed praise, and he'd give them a row and a bollocking when they deserved it. It wasn't a surprise that he created such a good relationship with the young players who were coming through at United.

'I remember once we were caught in a tropical storm when we went on a trip to Japan. We couldn't train outside but the gaffer and Archie found a tennis court which was sheltered from the rain. They decided they'd have two teams – Archie's team and the gaffer's team – and we'd play a game of head tennis. Archie's team won the first game but, being ultra-competitive, the gaffer decided it was to be best of three. He turned his back to get on with the play but Archie whispered to his team to leave the court and get on the bus. They were a good 20 yards away before the gaffer turned round and noticed what was going on. He shrieked, "Knox, get them f***ing back here or you're sacked". Archie came back onto the court laughing his head off because he'd got the reaction he wanted from the gaffer. He had to tell his players to deliberately hit the ball into the net and let the gaffer win or we'd have been there for hours.'

McClair appreciated their humour and the manner in which they built morale and strengthened the spirit within their squad. But there were also times when he – or one of his team-mates – didn't enjoy the methods if they were on the wrong end of them. McClair said: 'The year Jim Leighton signed for United, we were training in pre-season and Archie decided we should go on a 12-minute run. It was a warm day and I was comforted by the fact that Jim was about 50 yards behind me, albeit he was trying his best. Archie didn't think I was going flat out, though, and when he sounded the whistle and everyone stopped he shouted "McClair, keep running". I had to run past everyone else and keep going to the point furthest away from the dressing room when he blew his whistle again. I'd become the only person who had ever done a 13-minute "12-minute run".'

Knox raised demands on the United players with punishments meted out if they failed to meet his high standards. He recalled: 'There was a park at Littleton Road, close to The Cliff, and I'd send the players over there to do laps if they were late for training. They were told that they had to be on the training pitch for a 10 a.m. start. If they weren't there on time, it would be off to Littleton Road. It would be hilarious to watch some of the players screeching into the car park and jumping straight out of their cars and dashing for the training pitch. It looked like Lewis Hamilton and Sebastian Vettel racing in on some days. That car park was a dangerous place at times. The players who were there on time would laugh when they'd hear me tell the latecomers "You're three seconds late – off you go".

'The late ones would accuse me of using a cheap, inferior watch. Paul Ince would just call me names.'

McClair acknowledges that the unforgiving nature of Knox's training was simply intended to raise standards on match days. But he recalls the way in which United's hard-working No.2 would grow exasperated with some of his colleagues. 'Graeme Hogg was a young player coming through at United and famously marked Diego Maradona in a European game one night. We'd play two-touch in training and Graeme would drive Archie daft because he'd always take three or four – or even more – touches of the ball. Archie would be really patient with him for a while. He'd say, "Two-touch, Hoggy. Remember, it's two-touch".

'But one day he finally cracked and shouted, "Right Hoggy, you're all in" – and he'd moan, "I'm wasting my time here. This is beyond my coaching abilities!"

'It could be hard but it could also be fun. Those were the high standards which Archie and the gaffer demanded of everyone.

'Archie once told me and Gordon Strachan a great story about a sports scientist he'd worked with. The lad had approached Archie after a training session and told him the players were working too hard and were in "the red zone". Archie replied, "Imagine we're playing the last game of the season and that we need a point to stay up. Their striker is through on goal but our left-back can come inside and can catch him and stop the goal that would relegate us. Then suddenly, he pulls up and says he can't go on because he's in the red zone". The sports scientists looked perplexed. Then Archie said to him, "You'd better find another colour above red for them".'

Ferguson lapsed into his own red zone one morning in the summer of 1988 as details of his interest in Norway captain Rune Bratseth somehow leaked into a Sunday newspaper. Little did he realise the source of the story was close to home. Or, in actual fact, close to a drinks tent at Royal Lytham and St Annes Golf Club. Knox revealed: 'Kiddo and I were guests of my great friend Ken Schofield at the Open at Royal Lytham but play was rained off and abandoned after only two or three holes. We all ended up in hospitality, two or three different places like the Guinness tent and a few other bars. We eventually ran out of money and were heading off the course when we heard a commotion in the Bollinger champagne tent. Kiddo wanted to go in but we didn't have a bean between us. He said it wouldn't matter as someone would buy us a drink. Sure enough, we bumped into Jim Mossop – the sportswriter from the *Sunday Express* – and he took pity on us.

'Even in those days, it was £25 for a bottle of Bollinger in the tent but Jim offered to give us the money for two bottles in exchange for a story he could use at the weekend. At the time, Manchester United were keen on signing the Norway defender Rune Bratseth from Werder Bremen. My lips had been loosened by a glass or two, so I slipped Jim the story of United's interest in Bratseth.

'I'd forgotten all about it until my phone went when I was still lying in bed the following Sunday morning. Alex's voice boomed, "Have you seen the *Sunday Express*? They've got a story about us and Bratseth".

'He went on, "They've even labelled it as a world exclusive. I don't know how they get hold of these things". Alex was still going on about it when myself and Kiddo were back at the club on the Monday morning. It was several years later that I finally plucked up the courage to tell him that I may have let it slip to Jim at the Open.'

Bratseth never did sign for United, but the pain of missing him was soothed by the arrival of keeper Leighton from Aberdeen, defender Steve Bruce from Norwich City and the return of striker Mark Hughes from Barcelona.

The likes of Lee Sharpe and Mike Phelan would follow, but United were beset by inconsistency and could only finish 11th at the end of the 1988/89 campaign.

But the summer of 1989 marked momentous times at Old Trafford, both on and off the field of play. Ferguson and Knox reacted to the disappointing league finish by buying Gary Pallister, Neil Webb, Danny Wallace and, of course, Paul Ince. If Ince's seven-figure arrival from West Ham United was controversial, though, it paled into insignificance when set against an incredible takeover bid for the club itself.

Property magnate Michael Knighton announced plans to purchase the controlling stake of Manchester United chairman Martin Edwards for £20 million. Backed by former Debenhams chief executive Robert Thornton and Stanley Cohen of Parker Pens, the one-time Coventry City apprentice pledged a £10m redevelopment of Old Trafford and transfer cash for Ferguson and Knox.

It seemed the perfect deal for everyone, with Knighton keen to strike a bond with the United support from day one. Knox recalled: 'I remember the first day Michael arrived at Manchester United. I was with Kiddo, Nobby Stiles, Eric Harrison and Jimmy McGregor at the training ground. Martin Edwards brought him in to meet the staff and introduced him as the new owner of Manchester United. Michael went round the room and shook the hand of everyone. His first words were "Brian and Nobby, it's an honour to be in the same room as two United legends". The rest of us never got a mention and we'd tease Kiddo and

Nobby that they'd be sure to be kept on when the rest of us were sacked.

'We were at home to Arsenal on the first game of the 1989/90 season. We actually won the game 4-1 and played really well. Before kick-off our kitman, Norman Davies, came up to me and told me that the new owner wanted a full set of kit. I said, "Well, Norman, he's just bought the club so you should probably give him a full set of kit".

'Norman replied, "Yes, but he wants to put it on and go out to warm up with the team". That was all well and good, but Norman had the easy job. He only had to hand the kit to the new owner – I had the tough job of going to tell the manager what was going on.

'"That'll be f***ing right," was Alex's response. Alex used to say that Michael had "confidence to burn". But the next thing any of us knew, Michael was out warming up in full United kit. He took a ball into the centre circle and kept it up all the way to the penalty box in front of the Stretford End – then smashed it into the net. He looked up at the Stretford End with his arms outstretched in celebration. The fans were cheering and giving it big licks – it was unbelievable.

'A couple of weeks later, we were playing Derby County at the old Baseball Ground and the place was jam-packed. In fact, there were possibly too many people in the ground and some of the fans were spilling onto the track before kick-off. Michael appeared from nowhere and started pushing out his hands to the supporters like Moses parting the Red Sea. It was quite a scene.

'But things started to go wrong after that, the deal never went through and he ended up taking over at Carlisle United.'

Knighton's dream fell apart when partners Thornton and Cohen withdrew their support and he was unable to conclude the deal on his own. A seat on the United board and 30,000 shares were taken by Knighton as part of the final agreement with the club. But he resigned three years later in order to buy Carlisle United and finally fulfil his ambition of owning a football club.

Twelve months earlier, Manchester United had floated on the Stock Exchange with a valuation of £47m. Seven years after that, Rupert Murdoch's £680m bid for the club was accepted by the PLC board but blocked by the Monopolies and Mergers Commission. And in 2005, United were sold to the Glazer family – the club's current owners – for a sum in the region of £790m.

Such lofty figures would have seemed barely believable at the time of Knighton's bid – or the time of Ince's £1m signing. The England midfielder had sparked a major furore by posing for a photograph in a Manchester United shirt *before* his move from West Ham had been completed.

Some players might have kept their heads down at that stage and allowed the controversy to blow over. Ince wasn't most players. Knox recalled: 'I'll always remember the day he came to sign for United. There had been a lot of hype about the deal and a bit of bad blood from West Ham fans because he'd been pictured on holiday wearing a Manchester United shirt when the deal hadn't been completed.

'Alex was on holiday and I was at the stadium to welcome Incy. He arrived with his agent, Ambrose Mendy, in a massive stretch limousine. They'd driven it all the way from London – a real Billy Big Time!

'He used to call me "Jock Bastard". I didn't take offence, though, as I quickly found out he called everyone from Scotland "Jock Bastard". But I got on so well with him and, of course, I helped him out years later when he was manager at Blackburn Rovers.'

If Knox and Ince quickly struck a bond which endures to this day, the same could not always be said of the relationship between player and manager. Knox added: 'Incy came marching onto the training ground at The Cliff one morning and announced to me, "I'm going to shoot that other Jock Bastard".

'I said, "You can't do that Incy because you've told me that you're going to do it and, if you do it, I'll know it's been you."

'But I was quite intrigued so I asked him how he planned to go about this daring attack on the manager of Manchester United. There was a little enclosure at The Cliff and he said he'd stand behind it and wait until he saw Alex looking out from his office window at the training.

'I asked where he planned to shoot him. "In the head" came the reply. I said, "You'd be better going for the shoulder and just wounding him".

'By the time we'd finished our discussion over the relevant merits of his plan, he'd forgotten why he'd fallen out with Alex in the first place and we just got on with training.

'We played a game at Norwich around that time and Alex decided he wanted to try Ince at sweeper. We were 3-0 down after 20 minutes and his days as a sweeper were over there and then. But he was a great lad and he'd give everything.

'We had a game that season when Incy got hurt just a few seconds into the second half at Old Trafford. He got the ball smacked right into his bollocks. Our physio, Jimmy McGregor, was nowhere to be seen but his bag was at the front of the dugout so I had to run on. When I reached Incy, he was still writhing around on the floor. And his pain levels increased when he looked up and saw me.

'He said, "What the f**k are you doing here, Jock Bastard?" He quietened down with a magic sponge straight into the source of his pain.'

From that 4-1 opening-day victory over Arsenal when Knighton impressed on the pitch, United would win just one of their next seven league games. They would end the campaign in 13th position, the lowest final placing of Ferguson's 27-year reign at the club. Outsiders claimed the pressure was mounting on the management team with Edwards and the board reportedly unhappy at the results and form. Legend has it that Mark Robins' winner in the FA Cup third round tie against Nottingham Forest at the City Ground spared Ferguson and Knox from the sack. But Knox has a different version of events in a dramatic run which took United all the way to the FA Cup final against Crystal Palace at Wembley. 'The Robins story wasn't true at all. I can remember coming off the bus at the City Ground and Alex saying to me that Martin Edwards had said to him that "no matter what happens today, you will still be our manager".

'I think people recognised what was going on and the steps that were being taken to get Manchester United back to the top again.

'But I can remember being 0-0 against Hereford United away at Hereford in the fourth round with four minutes to go and the Hereford boy was right through on Jim Leighton. Someone in the crowd blew a whistle and the Hereford boy stopped. Then someone, Mick Duxbury I think it was, got back and stopped him. We went right back up the park and Clayton Blackmore scored the winner for us.

'I think we had already established in our minds that we were going to be successful, we just needed to get over that first hurdle.'

Newcastle United, Sheffield United and Oldham Athletic were also conquered on the way to Wembley, with McClair scoring against them all.

The see-saw final against Crystal Palace, which ended 3-3 after extra time, is still remembered as one of the most dramatic of the modern era.

McClair also recalls the bizarre scene of United going ahead with an open-top bus parade *before* the midweek replay. 'I remember we had to go round Manchester on a bus after the first game, which had ended in a 3-3 draw. Archie and I just sat at the back waving at people in the high flats. We had a competition and awarded ourselves a point if someone waved back at either of us.'

Ferguson didn't wave much that day, with his mind moving towards leaving out Leighton for the replay and bringing in Les Sealey. It proved the right call with Sealey keeping a clean sheet and full-back Lee Martin emerging as the unlikely matchwinner. But Knox believes it was the toughest call of Ferguson's reign and one he did not entirely agree with at the time. 'I would have gone with Jim again, there's no doubt about it. I thought the goals in the first game could have been prevented by the defenders so I came out on Jim's side on that occasion. But Alex said, "No, we need to make the change". It was fair enough – you go ahead with that and it was proved right at the end of the day.

'That is just what happens in football. Managers have to come up with these big decisions and throughout his career Alex hasn't got many of them wrong. You can't argue with that although you can put up your own case at the time, as I did. I don't think you would have lasted with Alex if you didn't have an opinion.

'The players all understand that these things can happen. Yes, they are bitterly disappointed and it is a major setback to them at the time. But you have got to get on with it. The only thing you are guaranteed in football is your disappointments. If you lose your place, get an injury or whatever, then you are gutted but you can't allow it to fester. If you are going to be one of the top players, you have to get over it and get ready for the next bit of your career.

'Winning that FA Cup final, albeit after the replay, was the big turnaround if you like for United and for us. We had put everything in place with the local scouting and stuff like that to stop Manchester City getting all the local kids. Now we'd got a trophy, some silverware to show for our efforts. The only thing

I regret from the day was not getting a video or photograph of me dancing on the platform with Sir Matt Busby afterwards. We were getting the train back up to Manchester, I think it was from Euston or King's Cross, and we had a great time.'

Knox's own time at United would be over inside the next 12 months as Rangers lured him back to Scotland just days before another trophy success – the European Cup Winners' Cup final victory over Barcelona in Rotterdam – and with a sixth-place finish in the league in sight.

McClair recalled: 'It was the best post-final party ever after the 1991 Cup Winners' Cup. I'd a conversation with Mick Hucknall, a big United fan, and boldly told him Simply Red's next album wouldn't be good as their debut "Picture Book". The album was called "Stars" and sold 3.4 million copies in the UK. Oops.

'When we all got up to dance to "Sit Down" by James at the party, Paul Ince thought it would be a good idea to take his shirt off and throw it away on the dance floor, until he saw his wife glaring at him and had to scamper after it.

'I think I was last to bed at 6 a.m. and first up at 7 a.m. with Bryan Robson and a friend. We toasted the birth of our sons Liam and Cameron – who were born on the same day a few weeks before – with Buck's Fizz.

'But I missed Archie and it didn't surprise me that he'd gone to Rangers. I'd actually asked him when Walter Smith got the manager's job at Ibrox if he'd be joining him. I knew that he and Walter got on well and it was obvious that someone of Archie's undoubted ability would be treasured. United made a great effort to keep him from a financial point of view but he decided the lure of Rangers was too strong and I wasn't surprised at all. He phoned me to say he was going, which was a nice touch, and I wished him all the best. He had been great for United.'

CHAPTER SIX

YOU WIN NOTHING WITHOUT KIDS – OR KIDDS

ON THE face of it, this was football's sliding doors moment. Ryan Giggs scoring his first goal for Manchester United on the same day – 4 May 1991 – that Archie Knox stepped into the Rangers dugout after quitting Old Trafford.

Giggs' effort in the derby against City, the club he came so close to joining as a schoolboy, deflected into the net off Colin Hendry and put his name in lights for the first time.

By stark contrast, Knox was enduring an ignominious debut as Rangers crashed 3-0 at Motherwell to cast a cloud over their title ambitions.

To those on the outside, it would have appeared that the departed coach had missed the emergence of a kid who would become a United legend.

But nothing could be further from the truth.

Giggs may forever be synonymous with 'The Class of '92', the legendary group of home-grown starlets who burst through from youth team to first team to prove to Alan Hansen that you *can* win something with kids. He recognises, though, that the seeds of that team's success were sown many years previously. And Knox was central to it all. 'The first time I met Archie I would have been a 13- or 14- year-old boy,' recalled Giggs. 'The first thing I would have thought about him was that he was an extremely scary man. For his part, Archie must have thought in those days that I was a bit of a mute. All I could manage when he spoke to me was a gulp and a "Yes" or an "OK". I was a bit in awe of the fact that the Manchester United assistant manager was talking to me.

'I should also say that I was nervous because I found his accent hard to understand at times. He is from even further north than Dundee and I would spend a lot of energy concentrating on making sure I was following exactly what he was saying. As I got to know Archie better, I realised that as well as being a tough man he was also very protective. He had a good heart and cared about us young lads. He would come to The Cliff on Tuesday and Thursday nights to watch us train as kids, something that would happen rarely these days.'

Knox recalls youth development and talent recruitment being at the top of the agenda when he arrived at Old Trafford with Sir Alex Ferguson in November 1986. They'd built their success at Aberdeen on home-grown youngsters and wanted to snatch the best in the north-west – or even further afield.

Giggs, raised in nearby Salford but chased by City from an early age, was one of their main targets. Knox recalled: 'The Class of '92 were all in the system before I left United in '91. They had all signed their YTS contracts.

'But getting them all to commit to United was a far cry from the way it had been when we went to United five years earlier. City were getting all the best young players when we arrived at United. We knew that we couldn't allow that situation to continue or we'd be in trouble.

'In the first couple of weeks, we got a big map of the area and stuck it on the wall in Alex's office. We brought in all the scouts and divided the Liverpool and Manchester area into sections on the map. If City, Liverpool, Everton – or anyone else – signed a good young player from that scout's area, they had to answer to us. It was unbelievable managing to pull it all together.'

Giggs was the diamond at the bottom of the mine. He'd been in City's system as a schoolboy and looked to be headed towards a full-time contract at Maine Road. But Knox and Ferguson embarked on an unprecedented campaign of persuasion, perseverance and downright pestering to get his signature on a contract.

Archie said: 'We signed Ryan for United on his 14th birthday. There has always been much play of the fact he was snatched from under the noses of City. But we were so determined to get him because he was one of only two players I've ever seen who, at just 13 years old, I knew would go to the very top of the professional game. One was Ryan Giggs. The other was Wayne Rooney.

'Ryan had used his dad's name, Wilson, when he was younger. His dad had been a professional rugby league player at Swinton and other clubs. His parents had separated, though, and it was just his mother at the house when we went to sign him.'

By the time they'd won the race to sign Giggs, they were almost part of the family and would even be served meals by the winger's mum.

Sir Alex recalled: 'We were at Ryan's house every week because he was with City and we were determined to get him to sign.

'When we left after our tenth or so visit, his mum, Lynne, asked if we'd be back again the following Thursday. It was becoming a regular trip. She had even started to make our tea for us.

'Ryan is very dead-pan. He would make a good poker player. We were not getting any response from him. He would just sit there dead-pan. Little did we know he was desperate to come to United. If we'd known that, we wouldn't have spent so much time and energy doing what we did!'

Even after signing for United, Giggs – who would go on to play no fewer than 963 times for United in a stellar, one-club career – struggled to make out the instructions delivered in that gruff Angus accent by Archie.

Knox laughed: 'Ryan was terrified of me in those early days. I remember him doing a crossing and finishing drill, during which the boys had to constantly change their positions. He ran behind me at one stage and quickly mouthed to Kiddo, "Where do I go now? I couldn't understand anything he told me".

'He was a great lad and a great player. It was wonderful to watch him fulfil all that potential I'd seen when he was 13 or 14 years old. We've all seen him score so many great goals since then and he turned into a remarkable player for Alex and for United.'

Giggs gathered 13 league titles and two Champions Leagues among 35 major honours in a quarter of a century at United. Even among The Class of '92, the local lad stood above all others as the most crucial signing of the modern era for Manchester United. And he believes those early days when Knox and Ferguson were changing the face of the club laid the foundations for much of that success. 'Archie and Sir Alex were a perfect partnership. They were hard-working and they knew exactly what they wanted. Later, when I got into the first team I remember Archie's preseason runs. We would do two laps of Littleton Road, where The Cliff was in Salford. Archie would be at the front. He was fit and strong even compared to us young lads. Because I had known him when he would come to watch us with Eric Harrison and Jim Brown, my transition to the first team as a teenager did not seem that daunting.

'He was part of a great time in Manchester United's history, when Sir Alex was making the changes that meant we would break through and win the club's first league title in 26 years in 1993. He helped the club on the road to what it has become today.'

To this day, Archie believes the way United handled the integration of The Class of '92 was vital to their development. Yes, they were top-class kids – David Beckham, Paul Scholes, Nicky Butt and the Neville brothers among their number. Even some of the lesser lights, such as Robbie Savage and Keith Gillespie, would go on to have outstanding and rewarding careers for club and country.

But they all had to learn the value of the shirt just as much as the value of their pay packet.

Archie added: 'As I say, I have only seen two players in my entire life that at 14 years of age you would put money on to be top players – Rooney and Giggs. All the rest, even Scholes, Butt, Beckham, the Nevilles – and Phil captained England's Under-16 schoolboys when he was 14 – you wouldn't have known 100 per cent for sure. We tried to get permission from the FA to play Rooney in Everton's first team when he was 15. He was that good. We would never have played him week in, week out at such a young age. But he could easily have coped in the Premier League at that age. We didn't get the permission and, of course, we had left Everton by the time he got his debut under Davie Moyes at 16.

'Back in the United days, though, all those guys signed YTS contracts – Beckham and the whole lot of them – for £26.34-a-week. That's what they were getting, every one of them. No difference. If they signed the professional contract at 17, they got a fiver put in their bank or kept for them and another fiver expenses a week. That was their lot.'

Of course, after Archie left United, the majority of The Class of '92 became central to Ferguson's glory years. Gary Neville, writing in his own autobiography *Red*, shared the views of team-mate Giggs on the influence of Archie. 'Archie would pay us visits and, occasionally, the manager would as well. We'd be practising and Archie would come in.

'You felt like standing to attention as soon as he walked through the door. He'd put on these passing sessions and speak to us in a Scottish accent so thick most of us couldn't understand a word he was saying.

'Until we screwed up – then you'd hear every word loud and clear.

'The intensity was incredible. Pass, pass, pass. Get it wrong and you'd be called out to do it again.

'It was tough, physically and mentally. There was to be no larking about. Do it right or do it again.

'Drive your passes. First touch. Control the ball. Pass. Move.

'We were learning the courage and skill necessary to take the ball under pressure and move it on quickly and precisely.

'Everything had to be done at speed. I can still hear Archie barking at me not to "tippy-tap". It was a hard school.'

Whereas Archie instantly recognised Giggs' skill, he was just as quick to admire the attitude and work ethic of right-back Neville. He knew from an early age that the defender, who'd go on to captain club and country, would fight and scratch his way to the game's summit. 'Gary was like a handful of other lads I've worked with in my career. To be honest, I admire them as much as any – simply for the work they put in to reach the level that they did. Back at Dundee United when I was playing and coaching, we had Billy Kirkwood, Derek Stark and John Holt. In later years at Everton, we had lads who came through the ranks like Tony Hibbert and Leon Osman. These guys all had talent but, by their own admission, they had to work hard to make the most of their careers. They were good pros and part of their success was down to the fact that they were willing to work hard and make sacrifices.

'Gary was a worker but those lads in his United team all worked – they were made to work. They were always reminded that if you wanted the trappings of being a footballer you couldn't live the same life as your mates. If you want to go out all the time with your mates that's fine, but you'll have to give up the dream of being a player. To make the grade, you had to make the sacrifices. The smart ones realised that from an early point and knuckled down. Gary was one of the smart ones.'

Arguably the smartest move made by Knox and Ferguson in their early days at United was bringing back Kidd to the club.

He'd been the home-grown teen who won the 1968 European Cup final against Benfica at Wembley alongside Bobby Charlton, Denis Law and George Best.

He had played for Arsenal, Everton and England – not to mention rivals Manchester City – but had been lost to the game's frontline until Knox called for his return.

Archie recalled: 'Brian was working with Salford Council doing some kind of community work. He was on £12,000 a year. I said to Alex that we had to get him on the staff because he knew everyone who was involved in football in Manchester. We brought him in to help with recruitment and scouting – and he turned into the Pied Piper.

'Getting hold of Brian was the biggest difference of all because he knew everyone right down to those running the Sunday boys' teams.'

It proved a masterstroke as Knox and Ferguson found the final piece of their scouting jigsaw. Together, they'd start attracting all the best kids in the area to United. It was the first bell for The Class of '92. Kidd recalled: 'Archie never got the recognition he deserved for those young boys coming through. I have always said that. Other people got the praise and the kudos but Archie was right up there with what he did to give us a chance to sign them.

'When they first started to try to get the youth policy going again, Archie was always there at evening training sessions for the kids. He had a great rapport with them, all of them from the group who went on to become household names to others who still went on to earn a good living from the game. The idea was that, even if they couldn't make it at United, we wanted to give them good principles so they could have decent careers. With me being a Manchester lad, I knew the school teachers and the Sunday league managers. I always had a belief that locally, within a 25-mile radius of The Cliff or Old Trafford, there was decent talent. They just needed a chance and someone to believe in them. That's where Archie came along. He'd be there four nights a week. He'd be there on Sunday mornings, even though he was so heavily involved with the first team. He would make himself available and I can vividly remember him following me to Sunday league games and standing on the sidelines of these little pitches. The work he put in has never been properly recognised but, then again, he's a modest, humble man who doesn't seek publicity.

'He was terrific for Fergie with the first team but also crucial in working to uncover that rich vein of talent. You can talk about Giggs, Beckham, Scholes, the Nevilles, Butt – the list is endless.

'Fergie was instrumental, too. When they came into United at first, they felt the scouting set-up wasn't for them and something needed to be done. They brought me back in and, of course, I had empathy for the local lads because I'd come through the system at United.

'I can remember my mum and dad telling me they'd worried about me when I first went to United at a young age. I'd not really thought like that before. So we made sure we pulled together a system where the parents and the kids were involved together and everyone felt part of it.'

Beckham's parents were among those wooed by Knox as he sought to convince the London schoolboy to commit his future to the north-west.

Archie recalled: 'When we played in London, we'd bring

David and his parents and sister to the team hotel for a meal the night before the game. In the morning, I'd get picked up by the late Malcolm Fidgeon – the talent spotter who found David – and we'd go to watch him playing for his school team before I'd dash off to our first-team game that afternoon.

'In those days, David wasn't the player he eventually developed into. He was a dribbler and quite a small lad. Of course, he developed into a tall lad and his game was all about use of the ball, crossing, passing and working hard.

'United's wide players had to work harder than anyone else in the team as they had to get up and down the pitch and cover their full-backs. If you couldn't handle it, you weren't in the team. I'd see the likes of Scholes, Butt and the Nevilles on Saturdays or Sundays back then. I'd go round with Kiddo to watch their games.

'We brought in players from further afield at Christmas, Easter and all the school holidays. Kiddo would take the local ones and I'd take the ones from further afield. We always made sure they had at least one training session when the first-team lads were involved with them.

'I remember Nick Barmby coming over from Hull and being involved with us for a while. He was a talented lad. Robbie Savage was there, too. He was a centre-forward in those days and the quietest boy you could ever meet. He's not half changed over the years!'

Kidd would later become Ferguson's assistant when Knox headed for Rangers. He'd also manage Blackburn Rovers in the English Premier League. In more recent times, he's been at the side of Roberto Mancini and Manuel Pellegrini as City have won titles. He has also been retained on Pep Guardiola's staff at the Etihad as City – famously dubbed the 'noisy neighbours' by Ferguson – continue to make big sounds alongside their traditional rivals towards the top end of the EPL.

But he's sure none of his personal success as a coach or manager would have been possible without that intervention from Knox more than 30 years ago. 'Archie is one of my best friends in football. He gave me so much help and advice and embraced me helping out with the first team at United as well.

'I was really upset when he left to go to Rangers, both from a professional and a personal point of view. But I knew that he wasn't going to any little club, he was going to Rangers and he was going back up to work with his friend, Walter Smith.

'There's real warmth about Archie and he's so sound and genuine as a person. He's a very loyal person, too.

'We had great times and great nights out. We'd go round The Shambles in Manchester and have a fantastic time. These were the days before Twitter or social media and Archie was such a sociable guy on a night out.

'We'd go to a little place for Christmas nights out which didn't have a drinks licence so you needed to take your own wine. One night, we'd been for a few drinks and then decided to head for a bite to eat. Archie, of course, took the wine. On the way out, he lost his balance and knocked over a bundle of chairs. As everyone knows, he's a big fella. The next morning he asked, "Do you think anyone noticed what happened?"

'I said, "I think there's a chance – there were people sitting on some of the chairs at the time".'

Not content with rearing the best youngsters in the land, Ferguson and Knox also set out to buy emerging talent. They'd been tipped off to the progress of Lee Sharpe, a winger who could play on either flank and had made a first-team debut for Torquay United aged just 16.

Archie remembers the late-night dash to land the kid and keep him from the clutches of their top-flight rivals. 'We went down to watch Lee in a Friday night game against Colchester United at Plainmoor in April 1988. Alex always knew people who knew people and we had been tipped off about this 16-year-old kid down there.

'The game was a 0-0 draw but we saw enough in 90 minutes to convince us that we had to sign the lad. We were heading for London the next day as United were playing in the Football League Centenary Trophy at Wembley. It was a special event to mark 100 years of the Football League. Believe it or not, the games lasted just 40 minutes each. We beat Luton and Everton before losing to Sheffield Wednesday in the semi-finals. They lost to Brian Clough's Nottingham Forest in the final. But it wasn't an entirely wasted weekend because we had managed a terrific bit of business in the early hours of Saturday morning. Cyril Knowles, the old Tottenham defender, was manager of Torquay but Alex didn't want to intrude too much at his club. After the game, he sent me in to speak to Cyril and ask if it was all right to come in and discuss a bit of business. Cyril agreed and, as the Torquay directors were still inside the ground, we very quickly got down to business.

'As luck would have it, Lee's parents had also been down from the Midlands to watch the game and had headed off to join him at his digs. We managed to get hold of them, brought them back to the park and the deal was thrashed out at one o'clock or 1.30 in the morning.

'The only downside was that United booked Alex and me into a hotel used by Saga Tours and we were nearly late for Wembley the next day as we'd had to queue behind coachloads of pensioners to get our breakfast.'

Sir Alex recalls the face-to-face negotiations with Knowles which ultimately convinced him to do the deal for Sharpe. 'I remember we drove Cyril down to the beach and didn't let him out of the car until the deal was done. He'd been a fine player for Tottenham and I knew if we didn't do the deal that night he'd be on the phone to Bill Nicholson and try to get Lee to White Hart Lane.'

Ferguson and Knox celebrated getting their man, but another Scot in Torquay was left crestfallen by the sudden and dramatic turn of events. David Caldwell, later appointed director of football at Albion Rovers, shared digs with Sharpe as teenage hopefuls. He had smashed home two goals in a league clash with Halifax just days before the scouting mission from Old Trafford. No sooner had he returned to his digs after the latest match than Knox appeared on his doorstep.

Caldwell said: 'Archie turned up at the flat with the Manchester United secretary, and our manager was there with the Torquay secretary. I thought to myself, "I've made it!" But they just swept me out the way and asked if my flatmate Lee Sharpe was in! Sir Alex was at the match to watch him.

'I went to get him out of his bedroom where he was on the phone to his girlfriend he had just split up from and he came down to speak to the guys. He came back to tell me he had been offered a five-year contract and asked me what he should do. I told him, "Sharpie, it's Manchester United, just sign!"

'Once the group had left he asked me if I thought his girlfriend would go back with him. I told him he was about to sign for Manchester United so not to worry too much about that!'

Sharpe went on to have almost a decade of success with United, landing ten major trophies and a PFA Young Player of the Year award.

Knox said: 'Before I went to Rangers, I remember Lee scoring in a League Cup semi-final second leg against Leeds United at Elland Road. We'd won the first leg 2-1 and his goal sent us to Wembley where, unfortunately, we'd lose to John Sheridan's goal for Sheffield Wednesday.

'I ran to celebrate Lee's last-minute goal and got smacked in the face by a steward. I didn't hang around to see if I'd get smacked again – I just went straight up the tunnel!'

CHAPTER SEVEN

RED FLIGHT AND BLUE

IN FEBRUARY 2017, Manchester United posted figures to the London Stock Exchange predicting annual revenues of £540 million. Four months earlier, Rangers had reported losses of £3.3m from a turnover of £22.2m. The numbers scarcely stand comparison.

Rewind quarter of a century, though, and the Red Devils were powerless to retain their coveted assistant manager in the face of Ibrox financial muscle. Graeme Souness had ended his five-year reign in Govan, lured away by the romance of a return to his beloved Liverpool.

Walter Smith was promoted to the manager's office atop the famous marble staircase and instantly targeted Archie Knox, his close friend and one-time Dundee United team-mate, to be his No.2.

Alex Ferguson wanted Knox to stay at Old Trafford. After all, United had a European Cup Winners' Cup final against Barcelona in Rotterdam in a matter of days. They'd ended a long wait for silverware at Old Trafford with the previous year's

FA Cup. They were on the brink of unveiling The Class of '92. But the Light Blues' greenbacks spoke loudest. And an era of unprecedented success was about to commence for Rangers.

Sir David Murray, chairman of Rangers at the time, recalled: 'When Graeme and I had a discussion and he said he wanted to go to Liverpool, he originally wanted to stay until the end of the season. I said, "No, I think you should go now", and I spoke to Walter and asked if he wanted to take on the manager's job.

'He said that would be fine and, of course, one of my next questions was who he would ask to be his assistant. I remember there was so much speculation at the time and stories of Ian Durrant and Ian Ferguson going to the bookies to bet on it. But Walter came back to me with Archie's name and the rest, as they say, is history. It was a major feather in the club's cap at the time in the sense that Rangers could take away the assistant manager of Manchester United.'

It was also a massive coup for Smith, who was experiencing his own anxieties over stepping into the Ibrox hotseat to take on his first manager's role. 'Archie had a great relationship with Alex,' recalled Smith, 'and, when I took over at Rangers after Graeme left, I didn't think for a minute he would leave United. Of course, people have to remember that United in those days was completely different to the United of today. But we had a conversation and he said he'd like to move.

'I felt it was important for me to get him. I wanted to show everybody that my job had changed and I was the manager. But, to do so, I needed someone who could come in and immediately take over the training and all those other aspects of the job. It was important I got someone I could trust to do it all – and Archie was that man.'

Typically, there would be no time for Knox to ease himself into his new role. He was thrust straight into the red-hot atmosphere of a title fight. Rangers were on the brink of Three in a Row with just two league games – away at Motherwell and at home to Aberdeen – left on the fixture card. As Knox recalled: 'Rangers were going for their third title in succession and it was vital Walter got off to a good start as manager. But we lost 3-0 to Motherwell which meant we had to beat Aberdeen in the last game of the season at Ibrox. It was a stressful time for everyone at the club, let alone someone who had just arrived.

'The club was building the top deck on the main stand at Ibrox at that time – The Club Deck. When I came in to work on the Monday morning after the Motherwell defeat, one of the workmen spotted me. He shouted down from up high: "Aye, Knox, you've made a big difference haven't you?"

'I was just in the door but already I feared that I would get the blame if we lost against Aberdeen.'

The dugout axis of Smith and Knox would bring seven league titles and countless cups to Rangers. Two years after Knox's arrival from United, they'd move to within 90 minutes of the first-ever Champions League final. They dominated the Old Firm scene for almost a decade and coached some of the greatest players ever to perform in Scotland. But, speaking with the benefit of hindsight, they believe that first week together was crucial to everything that would follow.

'We carried on as normal after the defeat to Motherwell,' said Archie. 'Walter never panicked and he kept things on an even keel. He was always like that – he would never get carried away. That attitude kept the players calm enough, even though there was a lot of hype about that Aberdeen game. Things could have turned out so differently for the club and all of us had we not won the championship that season. But that title win made everyone sit up and realise that here was a good manager, and that Sir David Murray was no fool in appointing him.

'It would have been easy for Sir David to go for a big name

but he realised he had a guy capable of doing the job on his own doorstep. I am sure Graeme backed Walter up to the hilt as well.

'We had a pretty patched-up team for the Aberdeen game at Ibrox on the Saturday. Two or three of our key players were out injured. John Brown ruptured his Achilles during the game after playing with an injection and against medical advice.

'I can remember Maurice Johnston finished up in midfield – but Mark Hateley scored twice and we won the game 2-0. I felt like going back to Ibrox the next Monday and telling that workman, "Well, I did make a difference after all!" But I was just glad we got it over the line for Walter's sake more than my own. It was vital for him to keep the run of championships going.'

Ian Durrant and Ally McCoist had been deemed unfit to start the Aberdeen game as injuries and illness dug deep into the squad, but both played a part off the bench. The sense of relief was matched only by the air of euphoria which percolated around Ibrox at the final whistle. Durrant said: 'I remember Archie's first game at Rangers was the defeat at Motherwell and his second game was that title decider against Aberdeen. What a start!

'It was make or break, not just for that championship but also for the club after Graeme had left for Liverpool. There was a lot of uncertainty at the time about whether or not the gaffer would get the financial backing which Graeme had received. It must have been a gamble for Archie to take on such a challenge. But looking back, it was definitely a gamble which paid off.'

Richard Gough was one of the Rangers stars marked absent from the title decider, but agrees that the win heralded the beginning of a rich era of success. Within six seasons, Gough would be the captain who would lift the historic Nine in a Row title at Tannadice. He would play under Smith and Knox at Everton as well as bringing in the latter as his No.2 during his own brief spell in management at Livingston. 'Archie left Manchester United a week before the European Cup Winners'

Cup final,' he recalled. 'That showed how close he was to Walter. Graeme had brought me to the club from Tottenham. He was very fiery but that suited me as I liked to know where I stood.

'Walter had always been the quiet one. But when Archie came in, he quickly became known as the fiery one and the gaffer was quieter. Don't get me wrong, if you riled the gaffer you knew all about it. But Archie tended to express his emotions and feelings more than Walter.

'We had a very good dressing room. Maybe it's easy to have that when you're winning, but Archie made sure it was good. We'd often go for walks rather than train, especially at the start of the season when the games were coming thick and fast. Archie felt it was more about recovery than training. He wanted us ready for three o'clock on a Saturday, not ten o'clock on a Thursday morning. He knew what we could do and he was great with us. Sometimes he'd just send us for a shower and a sauna.'

The partnership of Smith and Knox sparked from the earliest moment, with the assistant manager certain that that win over Aberdeen was the catalyst for six seasons of unparalleled glory. 'When you take on a club the size of Rangers, it is vital to have success from the first possible moment. Walter continued the success after Souness had left and attracted a terrific level of player, too. When we won that title in 1991, he had the fans on his side straight away. They wanted another one after that which we got the following season and that was us really off and running.'

Murray, who had bought Rangers from Lawrence Marlborough for £6 million in 1988, was a close personal friend of Souness. But the steel tycoon quickly saw the unbreakable bond between Smith and Knox – and knew he'd made the right appointments. 'There was a great synergy between the two of them. Undoubtedly, that was the secret of their success – they were a great duo who played off each other. They worked hard together, they knew each other well and, of course, they had played together at Dundee United.

'When Graeme left, Walter immediately wanted to bring Archie on board and Rangers had the gravitas to be able to bring him from Manchester United in the week they were preparing for a European final.

'I remember they worked so hard and Archie was always on people's backs. He didn't let anybody off with anything.

'I had a great relationship with Archie. Like so many relationships in life and in work, it was built on mutual respect.

'Before we played away games against Hearts and Hibs, we would all have dinner together in Cosmo's restaurant in Edinburgh. There would be Walter, Archie, myself and Dr Donald Cruickshank, who had been the club doctor since the days before Rangers' European Cup Winners' Cup win in Barcelona in 1972. We'd have a meal and wine and we'd sort the world out while the team were staying in the Caledonian or the Roxburghe Hotel. Fond memories.

'Archie is a highly respected guy and a true professional. He made a major contribution to all the success we enjoyed as the Rangers family.'

John Brown had played under Knox at Dundee – and famously scored a hat-trick against Rangers in a thrilling cup-tie. He reached Ibrox three years before his old boss and felt sure Smith had made the correct appointment after Souness's exit. The man affectionately known to Gers fans as 'Bomber' said: 'When I signed for Rangers in 1988, the first phone call I took was from Archie. I hadn't spoken to him since he'd been at Manchester but he called to congratulate me. Things like that mean a helluva lot to me.

'I had so much to thank Graeme Souness for. He signed me for Rangers at a time when Walter was his assistant. But when Archie came in, he and Walter took us to another level.

'The greatest compliment I can pay Archie is to say that I felt Walter and him were a stronger combination than Graeme and

Walter. Together, we won a helluva lot of trophies, we came so close to a Champions League final, we won a Treble and we won Nine in a Row. There were a lot of happy years when Archie got the best out of those boys.

'You couldn't be a shrinking violet in Archie's company. He knew, having been involved in success at Aberdeen and Manchester United, that shrinking violets won't travel far.

'Archie did so much when he came in. He helped Walter unbelievably and was a huge part of the success at the club. He could be tough, but he could also have a pint with you at the right moment.

'I was a Rangers supporter as a boy and first came across Archie when he was playing for Forfar against Rangers in the League Cup semi-final in 1978. He was player-manager and I was struck by how well organised his team were. They gave Rangers a real scare. I was only 15 or 16 but I remember thinking how fortunate Rangers were to reach the final and how well Forfar had played.

'It's no surprise that he's had the career that he's had in coaching and management when you look back at his early work.'

No one knew more about Knox's early work, even before the success-strewn seasons at Aberdeen and Manchester United, than Smith. And he had no one else on his mind when Murray invited him to select an assistant in the wake of Souness's shock departure. 'Archie had great experience by the time he came to Rangers,' said Smith. 'He'd been a manager in his own right at Forfar and Dundee. He'd enjoyed huge success with Sir Alex Ferguson in two spells at Aberdeen and also been at Manchester United.

'I remember arriving at Rangers in 1986 after I'd been appointed as assistant to Graeme and we were competing for the final European place against Archie's Dundee team.

'When we got together at Rangers five years later, we'd sit down and discuss the training we wanted to do. Then Archie would go and do it all. It felt right from the very start.

'People I'd worked with in the past, like Jim McLean and Graeme, had allowed me to go and do that work. Now I wanted to let Archie go and do it. I always felt confident in him doing the job. I could not have had better help from anyone.

'There were aspects of my job, such as dealing with the media and other matters, which had put Archie off a return to frontline management. But I knew he'd be an assistant who would take the pressure off me by going away and doing the other aspects of the job. He was meticulous in his preparations. People talk about "good cop, bad cop" but it was never like that with us. Results told us that the way we operated was working well. From Rangers' perspective, we had a good run together.

'Archie is one of these guys who people outside of football seemed to view as being gruff and having a rough edge. As an assistant, not everyone is going to love you. But the vast, vast majority of players always had great respect for Archie. He didn't stand any nonsense in training and, if he had to sort something out, he'd sort it out without the need to come to me. He wouldn't, and we wouldn't, have been successful if he hadn't been respected by all the players at the club.'

The seeds for the success that was to follow were often sown on the sun-kissed grass of Rangers' pre-season training base in Il Ciocco in Tuscany. As Knox recalled: 'When we went to Ciocco with Rangers, the legendary Italian coach Arrigo Sacchi, for six years in a row, sent his right-hand man to watch our pre-season training. He couldn't believe the training we did from a 9 a.m. start in the morning and then a 5 p.m. bit at night.

'The players had an hour break at lunchtime, then were in their beds from 2 p.m. to half past four and then trained again. These boys then were as fit as anybody.'

Gough, whose personal fitness allowed him to stay in top-flight football beyond the age of 40, credits those lung-bursting sessions in the Italian heat for much of Rangers' success. 'Walter and Archie were such big influences on my career. Their man-management was incredible. People will argue that it was an era when Rangers had the cream of the crop in terms of players, but sometimes the bigger egos are harder to handle.

'It's different at Forfar if you drop a striker when you play against Brechin than it is dropping Ally McCoist for a Rangers game against Celtic. Walter and Archie needed the ability to coach these great players but also handle the players. They could do both.

'Arrigo Sacchi himself eventually came to Ciocco and would take notes at the side of the pitch and marvel at the intensity of the training.

'Archie was a shy man, not one for talking publicly about his work. But that shyness went when he walked into a dressing room – that was a working environment he was comfortable with. He could be loud in a dressing room, a real presence. He demanded high standards, he never settled for second best, he always wanted more. He was a hard-ass.'

The public image of Knox, especially in his seven-year spell at Ibrox, was that of a sergeant major or an ultra-disciplined head teacher. Many of those who worked under him confirm that he had the ability to turn the toughest of players into quivering wrecks. But Smith, not to mention countless of those players, are quick to emphasise the other, softer side of his personality. 'When you get to know Archie, he is never happy with anything. He was always moaning to me about this or that. But that gruff exterior hides a real sense of humour. I don't think he would survive in the manner Archie has through his career if he hadn't had that sense of humour. He created a good environment wherever we went.

'I used to sit in the Main Stand at Ibrox and watch games and, if things weren't going well, I would go down to the dugout. I always knew the first statement Archie would make when I arrived at the touchline. He'd say, "Right, what are *you* going to do?" That meant there were subs in the offing.

'He worked extremely hard to create an environment in the place that is sometimes difficult for a manager to create. Having been as assistant myself, I knew I didn't want to be as close to the players as I had been in the past.

'Anyone who came to Rangers enjoyed playing there and we wouldn't have won so much if they had not enjoyed being there. Archie was charged with that responsibility and I could not have picked anyone better.'

Coaching some truly great players was second nature to Knox after working with Miller, McLeish and Strachan at Aberdeen as well as Robson, McGrath and Whiteside at Manchester United. But his ability to handle the likes of McCoist, Durrant and, later, Paul Gascoigne off the field was just as important.

McCoist said: 'Archie was brilliant at sussing out situations. I'd just come back from an injury when I got a bang on an ankle in my first game back. I was devastated. I had an X-ray at hospital on the Sunday morning, they diagnosed ligament damage and I was out for another eight weeks.

'I came back to the club after the scan and Archie was waiting for me. He could tell how low I was feeling. He said, "Right, there's only one place for us – the pub in Houston". We went down for four or five pints and a curry and we watched the football on the telly.

'When we parted, he said, "Take tomorrow off and the hard work starts on Tuesday". It was just what I needed to lift my spirits.

'I was really lucky that I played under great assistants. It can be an equally important job to that of the manager in terms of dealing with the playing staff. There are not enough Archie Knoxs in the game nowadays. I hate to come across as one of those boys who say it was always better in my day. But Archie called a spade a spade and gave players stick when they needed it. There's not enough of that today and I think young players are mollycoddled.'

Durrant added: 'Archie could be the bad cop sometimes and the good cop at other times. That was the way it was, and it was a man's game. He and the gaffer could cause a bit of chaos in their own right, and I don't think they get the credit they deserve for their achievements at Rangers.

'We had big nights in Europe against elite clubs like Ajax, Juventus, Marseille, Borussia Dortmund and Red Star Belgrade. Some of those teams went on to *win* the Champions League after they'd played us.

'At times, we were beaten by better players but there were times when we were unlucky, too. I scored in Levski Sofia in the second leg of a Champions League qualifier but we switched off with ten seconds to go and it cost us £15 million in terms of reaching the group phase again.

'I don't think the gaffer and Archie get proper recognition for it all. It was an incredible time for the football club.'

McCoist and Durrant did feel the wrath of the management team during one summer in Italy.

Record goalscorer McCoist said: 'We were in Ciocco one pre-season when Archie left his book with all his training drills on a table at breakfast.

'Durrant and I were on it in a flash to steal it. Looking back, it would have created less of a row if we'd kidnapped one of his daughters. He was going daft and his face was tripping him. He came straight for Durrant and me and roared, "I'm not even remotely laughing".

'Of course, we just hit him with the old "Book? What book?" line and denied all knowledge of the theft.

'We kept it going for a couple of hours until Walter eventually intervened and ordered the book's safe return before the real trouble started.'

A first summer together saw Smith and Knox recruit Andy Goram, Stuart McCall, David Robertson, Dale Gordon and

Alexei Mikhailichenko among others. Mikhailichenko, a Ukrainian signed from Sampdoria in Italy's Serie A, brought new challenges for Knox. He recalled: 'Chenks was a terrific player but let's just say he wasn't the most active at times. When we warmed up with little games in the dressing room, he'd just sit at his seat and not even move. One day I encouraged him to warm up but yet again he declined my advice and said, "I'm okay thanks".

'I repeated my encouragement so he stood up, walked over to the hair dryer in the corner of the dressing room and blew hot air up and down his body. He said, "There – I'm warmed up now, Archie".

'Durrant still tells the story of the day Chenks and Pieter Huistra switched wings and I was screeching at them to switch back. Chenks just shouted over to me, "Archie, I cannot go over there. I have blond hair and the sun is shining too strongly".

'The boys had great fun with him and Oleg Kuznetsov on nights out, serving them "Scottish wine" – Buckfast or Lanliq!'

Europe would again prove a thorn in their flesh as McCall's two goals were insufficient to prevent an away goals defeat to Sparta Prague in the first round of the last-ever European Cup.

Continental competition would provide so many highs and lows for Rangers over the next few years, with Knox always keen to impress. Home-grown midfield star Durrant recalled: 'You could always tell it was a European week because Archie had an extra spring in his step. He loved taking on the Marcello Lippis and Ottmar Hitzfelds.

'Archie built an infrastructure at the club by introducing the likes of John McGregor and John Brown to coaching roles after they hung up their boots. He was always conscious about improving the club, building the structure and making things right for challenges at home and abroad.

'It was Rangers' own small bootroom and he wanted it filled

with people who knew the club. It's similar to Pedro Caixinha's appointment of Jonatan Johansson at Rangers now.'

As well as Brown and McGregor, Billy Kirkwood worked behind the scenes at Rangers as a coach. A key player in Dundee United's heyday, Knox has always rated the coaching talents of Kirkwood. He said: 'Kirky was a terrific player and reached the semi-finals of the European Cup with United in 1984. But I've always felt that his ability as a coach and a manager hasn't received the recognition it deserves. He took Dundee United back into the top flight and was unfortunate to lose his job there. He also did well for St Johnstone and Livingston and, of course, is still working at Rangers. He is an outstanding coach in his own right and has brought real qualities to Rangers.'

Bomber, recalling his work under Knox at Ibrox, added: 'Archie had a wealth of knowledge of the game, some of which was gathered on trips to places like Barcelona and Juventus. He'd go away for a week at a time to study the techniques at some of the biggest and best teams in the world. He came back after, say, watching Ronaldo – the original one – in his best season at Barca, before he moved to Inter Milan. He said, "I've just seen a player train for an entire week without touching the ball with his right foot".

'He came back from Juve marvelling at Lippi's tough training sessions, the unbelievable fitness levels and the discipline. He spoke in glowing tones of Antonio Conte, who was playing in the Juventus midfield and, of course, has now won the English Premier League title as Chelsea boss. He loved watching these European greats and was determined to go to any lengths to improve Rangers as a team.'

The 1991/92 title would be sealed by McCoist's goal in a home draw against Hearts in late April.

An early-season loss to Hibs in the League Cup semi-final was forgotten by that championship triumph and a Scottish Cup final victory over Airdrie.

Perhaps even more memorable for Rangers supporters, though, was a hard-fought semi-final triumph against Celtic. Down to ten men from as early as the tenth minute after left-back Robertson was sent off, McCoist claimed the only goal at Hampden with a low shot from the edge of the box which skimmed across the sodden surface.

TV pictures show Knox punching the air with delight while manager Smith tries to calm his players for the inevitable Celtic siege which would follow in the second half.

And only now has Knox revealed the secret behind the success – a half-time trick which cost him all of £5.

He recalled: 'Davie Robertson had been sent off after just a handful of minutes for booting Joe Miller up in the air. Ally McCoist scored before half-time – you can still see my celebrations in the YouTube footage – and I knew Celtic would throw everything at us in the second half.

'I went out before the second half kicked off and grabbed one of the ball boys at Hampden. I asked if he was a Rangers fan and he said "yes". So I gave him a fiver and told him to get the message round his pals. If the ball went out for a Celtic throw in, just leave it until the Celtic fans throw it back. If the ball goes out for a Rangers throw-in, just leave it full stop. I watched him go round all four sides of the Hampden pitch telling his pals not to go for the ball. We needed every advantage we could get and we managed to hang on for the win.

'We beat Airdrie 2-1 in the final, but the semi-final is probably the game everyone remembers best that year.'

CHAPTER EIGHT

THE LAST NIGHT AT THE PROM

A WEEK after Ally McCoist's goal against Hearts sealed Four in a Row, a fresh onus was placed on Rangers' all-time record goalscorer by Archie Knox.

He required two goals against Aberdeen at Pittodrie to claim the coveted Golden Boot as leading marksman in Europe's leagues. To say McCoist's preparations for such a momentous occasion were unconventional would be an understatement. But Knox ensured he would not let slip the chance to make history, even if he'd given him the slip 12 hours earlier.

John Brown recalled: 'We'd won the title and had a Scottish Cup final against Airdrie the following week. The last league game was at Aberdeen. Walter knew if I got booked at Pittodrie then I'd miss the final. He told me I'd not be playing but I could come up the road for a few beers with the staff.

'When we booked into the Holiday Inn in Dyce, Archie and Walter were horrified to discover there was a university ball – a sort of prom – taking place the same night. There were young lassies everywhere and Archie, who was in charge of keeping an eye on everyone, was running around daft. I think he was still going up and downstairs at six in the morning, trying to make sure all the boys were tucked up in their rooms. But, of course, not many were answering their doors.'

McCoist, who had already hit 32 league goals before the trip to the Granite City, would end up not only landing the prize but would also successfully defend it the following season.

On the eve of that personal landmark, however, his mind drifted to catching out Rangers' assistant manager. 'Archie was walking about the hotel corridors trying to look into the rooms through the spy glass on the outside of the doors. I telephoned reception and pretended to be Goughie. I said, "It's Mr Gough here. I'm a little concerned that there is a large man on the second floor trying to look into all the rooms". The next thing we knew there were two big security guards up on the floor to deal with this large man. He was shouting at them and telling them who he was. We were inside the rooms killing ourselves laughing.'

Gers skipper Gough – the real one, not the one on the phone – still chuckles at recollections of their last night at the prom. 'Archie was always clever enough to give boys like McCoist and Durrant an extra bit of leeway because he knew what he'd get back.

'He gave Gazza an even bigger bit of leeway in later seasons because he knew he could be a crackpot – but also knew he could win games on his own. He treated him differently and it was superb man-management.

'The gaffer and Archie could shout and bawl at me and they knew it would just make me more determined to prove them wrong. But they also knew that if they shouted and bawled at Gazza, they risked losing him.

'When we went up to Aberdeen that day, Walter and Archie went into town for a bite to eat and, unusually, left us to our own devices. When they came back, Archie was checking to make sure we were all in our beds. He was trying to look through the peep holes.

'I was in Durranty's room and the call was made to reception to complain that this stranger was trying to look into guests' rooms.

'The next thing we knew, those big security guards had arrived and were trying to huckle Archie out of the place. He was shouting, "I'm the assistant manager of Rangers, y'know!" but the lads were having none of it. It was hilarious.'

McCoist added: 'The next day, Walter had given the teamtalk and left the dressing room. Archie slammed the door shut behind him. He read the riot act and told us we were all a disgrace. He said, "I know you were all at that prom and all bevvying."

'He said if we didn't perform and score a couple of goals then he'd tell Walter and we'd be in bother.

'After 15 minutes, Alexei Mikhailichenko played a ball in to me, I nutmegged Stephen Wright and stuck one in Theo Snelders' top corner. It was one of the best goals I ever scored for Rangers.

'Nobody ran towards me to celebrate – they all ran towards Archie in the dugout and celebrated in front of him.

'By the time I got there, he just patted me on the head and said, "Aye, not bad – but I need another one from you".'

The 1991/92 season bedded Knox in alongside Smith, with the arrival of the likes of Andy Goram, Stuart McCall, David Robertson and Mikhailichenko pivotal to ongoing success.

Scotland midfielder McCall was drafted in from Everton for £1.2 million on the night of the Champions League signing deadline. He'd never met Knox before – but soon realised the lengths to which the Gers No.2 would go to ensure he got the job done. 'Archie was the first person I met when I first came to Rangers. He picked me up at the airport and took me to David Murray's office in Edinburgh to sign the contract. I didn't know him at all, but I knew he'd come to watch me with Alex Ferguson when they were at Aberdeen and I was a kid playing for Bradford City against Halifax.

'I signed the contract in Edinburgh but I needed to get back to Ibrox for the medical so I could be registered for Europe before the midnight deadline.

'Archie was hurtling down the road. I could see the two lanes were narrowing into one due to roadworks, but Archie didn't seem to be slowing down. He hit one cone, then a second, then a third. There were cones flying everywhere and I was sh***ing myself. But it summed Archie up. He had to get the job done – in this case getting me to Ibrox – and he wasn't too bothered how he did it.

'Archie never had a problem with you if you gave everything. I've seen him be ruthless, but I've also seen his great humour – he'd use whatever he had to get the best out of you.

'Rangers was a great place to be in those days. The relationship that Archie and Walter had with the players was terrific. The bond was remarkable and has lasted to this day. If there is ever a reunion, Archie's is the first name on the sheet. Normally, you'd keep the staff at arm's length but Archie, Walter and Davie Dodds were a huge part of the camaraderie which was built up at the club. Off the field was as exciting as on the field in those days, and it was all down to Archie, Walter and Davie.'

McCall didn't take long to be lured into the head tennis circuit in the gym inside the stadium. The competition would go on for hours with Smith and Knox ready and willing to take on all-comers. But getting back out of the gym – even if you had an important date to make – wasn't always easy.

McCall explained: 'I still smile when I think back to a day at Ibrox when Davie Dodds and I were playing head tennis against Archie and Walter. It was lunchtime in the dressing room gym – and Davie and I were winning. It was first to three and we got there first. Archie then insisted it be extended to first to five – and we got there again. By this time it was nearly two o'clock but Archie was desperate to win and demanded we play a few more points.

'The sweat was blinding me and eventually I had to stop and

say, "Right, it's quarter past two and I need to go."

'Archie shouted, "What do you mean? Where are you going?"

'I said, "In an hour and a half, I need to be in Callander as I'm getting married." I nearly missed my own wedding because I was beating them at head tennis.'

McCall was a goalscorer in the League Cup final win over Aberdeen as Gers sealed a domestic Treble in 1992/93. The Dons were also beaten in the Scottish Cup final, while Five in a Row was secured with a nine-point gap over the same side.

It was the surge to within 90 minutes of the first-ever Champions League final, however, which separated this season from the norm. Danish champions Lyngby were defeated 3-0 on aggregate in the first round to set up a Battle of Britain with English champions Leeds United for a place in the inaugural group stages. These were ties which would grip the entire nation, with Smith and Knox determined to win the day over Howard Wilkinson's side.

Inspiration came in the form of criticism from the English media, while there was no shortage of help from unlikely quarters. Knox recalled: 'We still trained up at Anniesland in 1992 and in the days leading up to the Leeds game, this man approached me at the side of the pitch.

'He said, "Archie, I don't want to interfere but have you watched *Match of the Day* to see how Leeds have been playing?"

'He introduced himself as Stuarty Daniels of the Kinning Park Loyal Rangers Supporters' Club and promptly warned me about Eric Cantona. He said, "If anyone goes near Cantona in the box, he'll go down spread-eagled". To emphasise his point, he spread his arms out wide.

'We won the first leg 2-1 at Ibrox with Ally McCoist scoring the winner after we'd fallen behind to an early goal from Gary McAllister.

'Rangers fans were banned from Elland Road for the return leg and we expected a rough reception from the Leeds support.

'As the team bus was drawing up towards the front door of the stadium, I could see one lad standing right in front of us in a Leeds scarf, Leeds hat and Leeds top. As the bus came to a halt, he pulled up the Leeds shirt to show a Rangers shirt underneath. He then saluted the bus. Yes, it was Stuarty Daniels of the Kinning Park Loyal.'

There was seldom a dull moment when Rangers arrived at away grounds, with bus driver and kitman Jimmy Bell a central figure. As Knox recalled, 'I was fortunate to work with so many great people over the years at Rangers. Campbell Ogilvie, the club secretary, and Laura Tarbet in the office were great with me. My great friend Bob Reilly, the commercial director, used to wind up me and Walter if we'd lost a game – really just to raise our spirits. I remember Bob sticking his head round the door one morning after a European defeat and muttering the words "tactically naïve". I dashed out after him and managed to catch him down the tunnel and haul him back by his tie!

'Bob was one of the first people I met when I went to Rangers. He arranged a club flat for me [Bonni Ginzburg's old one] and a club car [a second-hand one].

'Jimmy Bell is up there as another of the great characters at the club. He's still there after all these years. He was in charge of the music on the bus to away games and always seemed to time our arrival at grounds just as Tina Turner's "Simply the Best" was blaring out of the sound system. It didn't matter if we were at Celtic Park, Pittodrie or wherever. He'd put his window down and turn the music up – and it didn't always make for a great reception.'

The trip to Elland Road was the first time Knox had been involved in a Battle of Britain in Europe's blue riband competition since Liverpool took Aberdeen apart in 1980. It was a defeat which still irked both him and Alex Ferguson, a former Rangers player and by now boss of Leeds' great rivals Manchester United. Gers star Durrant, who'd scored the only goal in the second leg against Lyngby in Denmark, vividly recalls the build-up to the visit to Elland Road. 'Archie always had a great rapport with Walter, just as he'd enjoyed with Sir Alex at Aberdeen and United. He would always look for articles in the press in which people had written us off. He'd pin them on the dressing room wall. John Sadler, who was Chief Football Writer at *The Sun* in London, had written off Rangers ahead of the Battle of Britain against Leeds United in the first-ever Champions League. He said Leeds would batter us and there was a line in the article about "sending the Jocks back up the road". There was more stuff about how Rangers think they could cope in the new English Premier League but they couldn't.

'This was perfect for Archie. It was like someone had wallpapered the dressing room by the time he'd stuck up all the offending articles.

'We won both legs and the first person into the away dressing room at Elland Road after the second leg was Sir Alex. His Manchester United team were battling a strong Leeds team at that time and he loved the fact we'd turned them over.

'Archie knew the Scotland-England thing would rile us up. He was very diligent in everything he did – even selecting the right newspaper cuttings. I remember thinking at the time that it must have been a big decision for him to leave United and come to Rangers because they were beginning to win things again at Old Trafford.'

Gers were on a winning streak, too, with some of the more unorthodox methods of Smith and Knox proving hugely beneficial to morale and team bonding. Durrant added: 'Goughie came out with the famous line that "The team that drinks together, wins together" – but if we'd all drank as much as people believe, we'd all be dead by now.'

Centre-back John Brown confirmed: 'The ways of raising morale were legendary – and it wasn't always a pint or two. It could be pie and beans at ten in the morning or a round of ice cream sodas.

'Archie had studied Leeds and told Goughie and myself to hold a high line when we defended against them. He felt that Cantona and Lee Chapman didn't have the pace to run in behind us, so we could squeeze the play up. Of course, it worked to perfection and we won home and away. Sir Alex was in the dressing room afterwards. Leeds were their big rivals at the time and he walked round shaking all of our hands.'

Gers were plunged into a tough group with Marseille, Bruges and CSKA Moscow, with the winners claiming the prize of a final place against AC Milan in Munich's Olympic Stadium.

Scott Nisbet, a home-grown player who had been converted from striker to right-back, was the unlikely matchwinner against Bruges at Ibrox with a spectacular, deflected shot from distance.

Nisbet was a hugely popular member of the squad, with Knox fondly recalling his influence. 'We once prepared for a cup final with a nine-a-side practice match on the pitch at Ibrox. Of course, the place was deserted and the stands were empty – but the tannoy suddenly crackled into life. A voice announced, "Attention, attention – an emergency situation has arisen within the stadium. Big Nizzy is on the ball".

'Of course, it was McCoist, He'd slipped away from the side of the pitch and got hold of the microphone at the public address system!'

Durrant had struck the other goal in the home win over the Belgian title winners on Nizzy's glory night and he also earned a point in the white-hot atmosphere of Marseille's Velodrome.

But the campaign would end in heartache with a goalless draw at home to CSKA leaving McCoist in tears and Rangers' dreams in tatters. Brown said: 'The 1992/93 season is down as one of the best in the club's history and rightly so. I am very proud to have been a part of it all. There was a work ethic about that team and a never-say-die attitude which served us well and took us so close to the final. Even in France, after Durranty had equalised, we had chances to win it. If we'd played on for another ten minutes we would have done.'

Basile Boli, who would move to Ibrox a year later, scored the only goal for Marseille in the final – with the French champions banned from defending their historic crown amid match-fixing allegations.

The following season would see Durrant and McCoist score in a League Cup final victory over Hibernian. Around the same time, Knox was embroiled in the scariest incident of all his foreign trips in football. He can still look back and chuckle at the escapades in Valencia, Poznan and further afield. But this was no laughing matter. 'I was on a scouting trip to the Holland v England game, a World Cup qualifier in Rotterdam in October 1993. It was the night Ronald Koeman scored for the Dutch and ended England's hopes of reaching the finals in the USA. It cost Graham Taylor his job. It was also the most terrified I've ever been at a football match.

'I was trying to get to the turnstile to enter the stadium but got pushed back against a wall. All of a sudden, there was shouting and roaring. At first, I didn't know what it was about then I saw English and Dutch supporters charging at each other and throwing stones, bricks, anything they could get their hands on. The police stood back for a while and let them get on with it. I was cowering with my hands over my head as the stones hit the wall above me. There was nowhere for me to go and they were now right next to me. This went on for ten minutes and I was petrified that I'd be hit by a brick or mistaken for an English or Dutch fan and clouted. It seemed to last for ages.

'Eventually, the police brought in horses and charged at the fans. It created a gap and I just ran as fast as I could to get away from it. It was truly scary.'

Back home, another league title – the sixth in succession – would land at Ibrox, albeit back-to-back Trebles would be denied them by Craig Brewster's historic Scottish Cup final winner for Dundee United.

Almost two decades after Smith and Knox had failed to win the final as United players, and with Jim McLean now retired from the dugout, the Terrors would thwart Rangers.

Levski Sofia's last-gasp winner in the Champions League qualifier prompted a signing spree and a renewed bid to crack Europe. Boli was signed from Marseille in June 1994 and, one month later, an even bigger name arrived on the Ibrox scene. Brian Laudrup.

Boss Smith recalled: 'It was mentioned to us that Brian may be available as he'd finished a loan spell at AC Milan and didn't want to go back to Fiorentina. Archie had watched him recently and told me not to hesitate to go for him. I'd heard of the Laudrup brothers but Archie had seen Brian close up and said we had to go for him. That's when I had to take over and go to the chairman, David Murray, and meet the player to put the wheels in motion.'

Durrant added: 'Archie watched football anywhere and everywhere. He'd think nothing of getting on a plane to Milan then coming straight back after the game.

'Archie was brilliant at one-liners. He used to go to games with the club's chief scout, Ewan Chester, and would always wind him up saying he was "looking for the new Ronaldo" all the time.

'Archie had great contacts and it was down to him that the club managed to land Laudrup in the first place. He was at a game and a scout he knew happened to mention that Laudrup was available. It was a throwaway remark but Archie kept pressing him. David Murray became involved and a deal was struck at £3 million. It was just coincidence that Archie was at that game and met that scout. That's how simple it was but maybe it was his hard work which had brought him to be in the right place at the right time.'

It proved a tough baptism for the expensive newcomers, with another Euro exit at the first hurdle against AEK Athens.

The League Cup campaign was also ended before August was out, surprisingly at the hands of Falkirk despite a Laudrup goal.

There surely could be no questioning the quality of continental acquisitions who, between them, had won the Champions League and European Championships. Or could there?

BBC Scotland reporting icon Chick Young had what has been variously described as the 'audacity', the 'temerity' or the 'idiocy' to ask the question of Smith.

What followed was an exchange which to this day remains a YouTube sensation – and ends with an intervention from Knox which brings a tear to the eye. Young said: 'It was the morning after the AEK Athens defeat at Ibrox and the BBC had sent me to get a follow-up interview with Walter. He was particularly grumpy that morning, perhaps unsurprisingly, and the interview was filmed by cameraman Billy Frew, who sadly died from cancer a few years ago.

'We were shooting down the tunnel at Ibrox and I started by suggesting that the players hadn't been good enough. I mentioned Basile Boli and Brian Laudrup – but Walter was having none of it. He knew if he swore then we couldn't use the clip, so he kept swearing. I only needed 20 or 30 seconds of usable footage for a piece for *Reporting Scotland* that night, but it wasn't happening.

'All of a sudden, Archie emerged up the tunnel and Walter said something like, "You need to hear some of his f***ing questions". Archie was in silhouette as he came up the tunnel then, with perfect timing, he appears into the light and offers to shove the microphone up my a**e.

'By that point, the camera is shaking because Billy is laughing so hard. Even Walter had started laughing.

'Eventually, he calmed down and said some usable words so I could go back to the office.

'In those days, the interviews were done on tape – just like old cassettes. You'd cut them up to get what you needed and the rest would be recycled in the bin. I thought the footage of the attempts at an interview was priceless so I kept it in my bottom drawer. At Christmas '94, the BBC produced an in-house video of out-takes and asked us if we had anything to put in it. In those days, the tapes never left the building and there had never been any leaks.

'A while later, I was out in Marseille doing a feature on Trevor Steven when I got a call from a reporter on the *News of the World*. He said there was grainy VHS footage of an interview between myself and Walter Smith which was doing the rounds in the pubs. He wanted to run the story so I explained the circumstances. Fast forward ten years and, coincidentally, I was back in France when I got another call from the *News of the World*. This time they told me that the video was running up a spectacular number of hits on YouTube.

'My first question was, "What's YouTube?" and my second was, "What's a hit?"

'It was explained to me and I phoned Walter to explain it to him. Apparently, it had received 500,000 hits at the time and I joked about whether we'd get 10p from each of them. Walter said that would be great and we could donate all the proceeds to charity. I said, "You can do what you want with your proceeds . . ."

'The *News of the World* did a second story and, from then on, it's been a standing joke between us all. The story has followed me around for nearly a quarter of a century.

'Archie and Walter were, and still are, pally with me. Archie is off his trolley. I was with him for a beer not so long ago and he managed to sneak a note into my pocket which read, "I'd still stick that microphone up your a**e!"

'The Variety Club put on a tribute dinner for me recently and the evening started with the video on a big screen. Archie was there to see it. If I hadn't wanted it shown, I had full control to throw it in the bin all those years ago. But I kept the tape as I thought it was hysterical. I think it's had two million hits now and it has gone round the world. More importantly, we've had even more laughs about it than we've had YouTube hits.'

Despite a Scottish Cup defeat to Hearts at Tynecastle later in the 1994/95 season, Rangers would win a seventh straight title with Laudrup overcoming his sticky start to be crowned Player of the Year.

Durrant added: 'Archie was meticulous in the way he set up training. These were the days long before Rangers had their own training ground. We were everywhere in those days – West Scotland Cricket Club, Partick, Jordanhill. But you always had to match Archie's standards. If he thought you were slacking, he'd bring a halt to it, tell everyone to get back in the cars to Ibrox and he'd bring us back to start all over again at two o'clock. That's Laudrup, Gazza, everyone. We'd be sent back for falling below Archie's standards and told to train again. He'd had those standards at Aberdeen and Manchester United. If you fell below them, he'd treat it as an act of disrespect.

'Archie put demands on you but he was always there for you, too. There were a few times in my career when I needed him to be there for me – and he always was. He comes down to watch our games at Dumbarton nowadays and will hand the manager, Stevie Aitken, a three-page report when the game is finished.

'When you look back on the last generations of Scottish football, Archie must be one of the most significant figures. I nearly got the Queen of the South job a while back and, if I had, I was going to take Archie down with me.'

Durrant insists the high esteem in which he holds Knox is mirrored all around the senior game in Britain. 'Archie would work us hard. I think we were six or seven straight summers at Ciocco and even the likes of Arrigo Sacchi came to watch us train. He couldn't believe the work we put in. Mind you, I couldn't believe it either and there were times when you felt your lungs were going to explode in the altitude.

'Sacchi couldn't speak a word of English and the gaffer and Archie certainly couldn't speak Italian, so he didn't come along for the conversation. But they all seemed to understand the football and, despite everything he'd won in the game, he came back year after year to study our training.

'We had a real rivalry with Aberdeen for a few years around that time. They were enjoying a resurgence for the first time since Sir Alex and Archie had left for Manchester United almost a decade earlier. But any time you met the likes of Stewart McKimmie – the Aberdeen defender – on a Scotland trip, he'd always ask how Archie was getting on. It was the same with Brian McClair, who had been with him at United. Archie was always held in the highest regard for his coaching.'

That universal respect for Knox took a temporary dip one day, however, as Rangers faced Falkirk at the old Brockville. McCoist was chasing another Golden Boot but a minor injury had convinced Smith to leave him among the substitutes. The striker takes up the story, one which fortunately ended with the protagonists smiling the next day. 'My face was tripping me that day at Falkirk because I wasn't 100 per cent fit but I was challenging for the Golden Boot and I wanted to play.

'Walter didn't start me and, to make matters worse, when I did get on I missed a couple of chances to score. After the game, Archie said, "The subs will be in tomorrow". I'd taken the complete hump by this stage and replied, "I'll not be f**king in".

'The conversation then went along the lines of Archie saying, "Aye, you'll be in" followed by me saying, "I'm telling you right now, I won't be in".

'The next thing, he's in my face and I'm in his face. I pointed at my jaw and said, "I won't be in tomorrow – and there it is if you want to have a crack at it". We ended up being pulled apart and I was thrown into the shower to cool off. I was still in the shower when Walter walked in. He had his hands in his pockets and said, "What's the matter with you?" I said, "I'm not playing, I'm injured and I've missed a couple of chances".

'Walter asked if I'd calmed down and I said that I had. He said, "That's good because you're f**king in tomorrow".

'When I turned up at Ibrox on the Sunday morning, Archie had pinned a note above the dressing room door which read "Welcome Coisty". He was standing there with his hand outstretched and said, "Good morning, I'm so glad you could make it". It was fantastic.'

Knox recalled: 'I'm pretty sure McCoist only played for a few minutes at the end of the game. After the game, I said to the players that the unused subs and the ones who'd hardly played were to come in on the Sunday. I wasn't happy with the way he'd spoken to me so I jumped into the bath after him. What followed might best be described as a good, old-fashioned stramash – handbags.

'Walter had been out speaking to the media and came back into the dressing room to ask, "What the f**k is going on?"

'But McCoist was terrific around the club – and so popular. After home games at Ibrox, I'd make sure to leave with him as he would be mobbed by autograph hunters on Edmiston Drive and I could slip away unnoticed to the car park.

'In later years, when Marco Negri was playing and scoring goals, it was often the case that McCoist and Durrant would be on the bench. But if we were struggling, I'd turn to the two of them and say, "Right, let's start the karaoke session". As soon as the pair of them stepped out to warm up, the whole place started singing and the atmosphere completely changed. They had an amazing effect on the supporters. They could give the whole place a lift, even when they weren't playing.'

CHAPTER NINE

GAZZA:
FRIEND, GENIUS, ROAD SWEEPER

ARCHIE KNOX has struck up a rapport with more players than he'd care to mention. Many of those relationships endure to this day.

With Paul Gascoigne, it was so much more.

When Gazza pitched up at Ibrox in the summer of 1995, Rangers manager Walter Smith tasked his No.2 with looking after this flawed genius. To some, it would have been akin to an invitation to herd feral cats. But Knox embraced it to such an extent that, over the course of the next three years, he became a father figure to Gazza. A mentor, a counsellor, a rock.

Ian Durrant is only half joking when he says the Rangers assistant manager was a 'babysitter' for the England international midfielder. But Knox wouldn't have changed it for the world. Indeed, he'd do it all again for one of the most enigmatic talents ever to pull on a Light Blue jersey.

Durrant recalled: 'Archie had a lot of responsibilities at the club, but one of the most important things he had to deal with was Gazza. The gaffer had too much on his plate to worry about him. We used to take turns to watch him, it was a babysitting job. He was nuts, but whenever he heard Archie's voice you could see the expression change on his face. Archie knew how to treat Gazza and always kept him on his toes. He knew how to get the best out of him.'

When Smith and Knox discussed the possibility of signing Gazza after his turbulent time in Italy's Serie A with Lazio, they were under no illusions about what they'd be taking on. From burping into TV microphones and wearing comedy breasts to singing on *Top of the Pops*, the extrovert Geordie was one of the game's best-known and most controversial characters. All that mattered to the Ibrox management was what he could provide on the pitch as they edged ever closer to their Nine in a Row dream.

Off the park, however, many of their fears were confirmed after Smith flew to Rome to talk Gascoigne into the move.

They'd met briefly the previous year during a holiday in the United States. Now was the moment to place that relationship onto a more formal footing. It soon became apparent to all, though, that Gazza didn't do formal.

Knox said: 'When Walter first went to sign him, he was in the grounds at the back of his house in Rome on a quad bike trying to run down his friend, Jimmy "Five Bellies" Gardner. He'd give him a start and then chase him on the bike.

'Walter had been thinking about signing him and asked me what I thought about the move. Before I could answer, he just said, "I know what you're going to say about the other stuff, but should we sign him for the team?"

'I said, "yes" and that was it.

'Gazza had class on the pitch. Brian Laudrup and Gazza could do fantastic things on their own. They could produce something from nothing. Gazza's goal against Aberdeen when we won Eight in a Row in 1996, running from halfway and holding off all those defenders, was simply staggering.'

So, too, were many of the No.8's exploits off the pitch. Smith knew he required someone with a steady and disciplined hand to oversee his blue riband signing. There was only one man for the job.

Smith said: 'We'd read in the English papers that Paul was coming home and he'd been linked with a return to Tottenham or a move elsewhere. He was recovering from a broken leg at the time. I'd met him on holiday the year before but I didn't really know him. Archie knew him from his days at Manchester United when Paul was beginning to emerge at Newcastle and, later, Tottenham. Archie had come across him a few times and when we discussed the possibility of making a move, he encouraged me.

'I doorstepped him in Italy and that was that. Archie's input in the Laudrup and Gascoigne deals was a big influence.

'I rang Gascoigne's doorbell in Rome and this voice said, "Who is it?" I told him who it was and he said he'd come down. The next thing I knew, he was arriving on the quad bike. He said, "What are you here for?"

'I said, "I'm here to see if you'll sign for Rangers".

'He said, "Okay".

'I said, "What do you mean?" and he just replied, "I said I'll sign for you".

'And he did, even though he had plenty of offers from elsewhere.

'It was always going to be a challenge, mainly in the kind of boyish aspects of it. But when you take Paul Gascoigne, you take him knowing what you're taking. There's no use complaining about it afterwards. You sit down and say to the rest of the guys, "Look lads, we've brought him in. He'll probably get away with a bit more than the rest of you but he'll win us football matches".

'He was never bad. It was always stupid things, it just happened to him. It would just come into his head and happen. The repercussions were always left to me but I must say Archie handled him fantastically and kept him out of my road for the majority of the occasions.'

The majority but, unfortunately, not all. Gazza's brushes with officialdom at Ibrox remain the stuff of legend.

With Durrant, Ally McCoist, Andy Goram and others already in the dressing room, it hadn't been the quietest of working environments prior to summer 1995. But Gascoigne took it to a whole new level. Knox remembered: 'Gazza loved going into the Plaice Café on Paisley Road West for bacon rolls and tea after training. If we did a light session at Bellahouston, we'd walk down to the café so the lads could relax. Quite often, we'd walk back to Ibrox from there.

'One day we arrived at the café and there was a council worker outside sweeping the street. He had the old-fashioned brush and cart and was wearing the bright yellow council-issue jacket and a hat. Gazza decided it would be better if the boy joined the rest of the players for rolls and tea – and he'd do his job for half an hour. The next thing we knew, Gazza was wearing the full council gear and was out working on the street. He was sweeping up the pavements, picking up litter and putting everything into the big bin on the cart. People were going about their daily business on Paisley Road West and walking past him, never thinking for a moment that this street sweeper could be Paul Gascoigne.

'Another day, we came out of the café and were ready to walk back to Ibrox. Gazza decided he wanted to catch a bus and stood at the bus stop on Paisley Road West. The next thing we knew he was on the bus in his training gear and football boots – waving to us as the bus passed us by. The bus driver dropped him off outside the front door at Ibrox and he was back long before the rest of us. We asked how he'd paid the fare but he just said the driver had let him off with it. That was typical Gazza.'

The one-time Newcastle and Tottenham star had just turned 28 when he returned from Italy. He was at the peak of his on-field powers. He had already graced a World Cup semi-final and FA Cup final and scored a stunning goal in the Rome derby to endear himself to the Lazio supporters. Such was his quality that the club record fee of £4.3 million which Smith and Knox lavished on him quickly seemed like a bargain.

In only his fifth league game for Rangers, he repeated the feat of Rome's Olympic Stadium by scoring against Celtic in his first Old Firm derby.

He'd seal the title with a stunning hat-trick against Aberdeen at Ibrox on the penultimate weekend of the season.

Without question, Gazza's display against the Dons remains one of the greatest individual performances ever produced by a Rangers player.

'It goes without saying that Archie had a great rapport with the likes of me, Coisty and Ian Ferguson,' recalled Durrant. 'But he also struck up a great relationship with Laudrup and Gascoigne. He was a father figure to them and commanded respect. It sounds strange to believe, given his quality, but Gascoigne was never sure he was playing until Archie gave him a nod in the dressing room. Archie would tell him that this game was one on which everything relied and he could be the man to make the difference for us. He'd instil so much belief in him.

'Everyone remembers the game at Ibrox against Aberdeen when Gazza scored a hat-trick to clinch the title. But what people don't know is that Gazza was begging to come off before he'd scored that great goal with the mazy run. He was shouting over to the bench that he was done, he was so tired. But Archie asked him for one more effort. He could always seem to get another ten yards out of Gazza and, on this occasion, that led to the run and the hat-trick goal.'

Gazza scored 19 goals in 42 games and was named as PFA Scotland Players' Player of the Year and Scottish Football Writers' Association Footballer of the Year.

If only things had been so straightforward off the pitch.

Knox recalled: 'On the day of the 1996 Scottish Cup final, when we beat Hearts 5-1, Jimmy Bell, our kit man and a big presence behind the scenes, came through to me to report a problem. Gazza had no gear. He didn't know where his club suit was and he'd arrived without a shirt and tie or even a pair of proper socks and shoes. Jimmy was sent round the place to try to find a suit for him. He eventually found one, albeit one which was three sizes too big.

'I kept spare clothes in a locker at Ibrox and, luckily, I had a shirt and tie. He even needed socks and pants from someone. We eventually got him fixed up with clothes but he still needed a pair of shoes as all he had were trainers and football boots. I had an old pair of shoes at the back of my locker. They'd been soled and heeled okay but had this horrible big buckle on the front – and they were also too big for him. Gazza being Gazza, he just wore them anyway.

'When we reached Hampden, the boys went out for the traditional walk on the pitch before kick-off and Gazza, typically, started a wee kickabout with the ball boys. In the television commentary, you can hear Jock Brown saying, "There is Paul Gascoigne, he's playing football with the young ball boys in his £400 Gucci shoes". If only Jock knew the truth of it.'

The chaos was only temporarily interrupted by the final itself – a one-sided victory over Hearts inspired by Laudrup and hat-trick hero Gordon Durie. 'After the game, we came back to Ibrox for the celebrations,' recalled Archie. 'We used to have parties for the sponsors and supporters in the big suites inside the stadium. Walter and I were in the manager's room having a beer before the party. It's one of those rooms where you need to enter a security code into the keypad – I think it was four numbers and a letter. The office was locked but the door suddenly swung open and Gazza came in. We immediately asked how he'd got in and he said he'd been watching over our shoulders for days to work out the code!

'He said, "Have you any beers?" We said yes but he couldn't have them as there would be plenty at the party along the corridor.

'But he said he wasn't going to the party as he'd promised some pensioners from Howwood – a village close to where he was living at the time – he'd go fishing with them if we won the cup.

'We said, "But we've got the party here". But Gazza said he'd promised them that he'd join them at the loch after the game. He still had the oversize suit and shoes on but he took some beers away and headed off to fish with the pensioners.'

Cup final hero 'Jukebox' Durie was the butt of arguably Gazza's best-known escapade, unsurprisingly in tandem with team-mate McCoist.

Knox explained: 'The most famous story, of course, is one when they managed to get the keys to Gordon Durie's new car – and they hid two fish in it.

'Gazza and McCoist hid one fish under the driver's seat and another one under the spare wheel in the boot.

'Jukey was moaning about the stink but had been convinced by someone that it was coming from the catalytic converter in the car. It went on for days and he had to drive round in freezing conditions with the windows down as he couldn't bear the smell. When he eventually took it back to the garage, they found a fish under the tyre but not the one under the seat.

'When the boys eventually told him where it was, it had rotted and become stuck among the springs under the seat. I'm sure the car was never the same again.'

Just a month after that cup final triumph with his Rangers pals, though, Gazza turned enemy as England faced Scotland at Wembley in the group phase of the European Championships.

From the moment the Euro 96 draw had set the Auld Enemy on collision course, there seemed an inevitability that Gascoigne would play a decisive role. So it would prove with the clinching goal – past Rangers team-mate Goram – as Terry Venables' Three Lions won 2-0 against Craig Brown's Bravehearts.

Knox said: 'The TV cameras came down to the training ground at the Albion after Scotland and England were drawn together at Euro 96. Gazza was trying to wind us all up. He said, "Scotland isn't even a national team – it's just a mix of sheepshaggers".

'I told him we had a better international record at the time as we'd qualified for five World Cups in a row.

'I gave him a playful slap and, before I knew what was happening, he'd been pounced on by Alan McLaren and Andy Goram.

'He was shouting that we'd not played five good games in the five finals we'd reached – and the home-grown boys at Rangers were tearing into him. Goram warned him that if he scored against him at Wembley and celebrated anywhere near him then he'd be getting it. The Goalie said he didn't care if he was sent-off or sine died, he'd have him. If you watch the TV footage of Gazza's goal, you'll see him run towards The Goalie for a split second and then veer away. He obviously remembered the warning.

'The celebration, of course, is remembered by almost everyone for "The Dentist's Chair" when his England team-mates squeeze the water bottle at him. But it could have been a celebration remembered for other reasons if he hadn't kept away from Andy.'

Back at Rangers, Knox and Smith were willing to ignore a multitude of off-field incidents so long as Gazza maintained his on-field brilliance. He played a significant role in the historic ninth consecutive league title, with hat-tricks against Kilmarnock and Motherwell. He ended the campaign with 17 goals in 34 games, including two in a thrilling 4-3 League Cup final win over Hearts at Celtic Park.

Knox said: 'The night we won Nine in a Row at Tannadice, we ended up back in the old Swallow Hotel in Dundee. The place was mobbed with guests and the boys piled into the bar to get a few beers. I was talking to someone and walked into the bar behind them – and I had a double-take at Gazza. He was standing at the bar having a drink and was still wearing his full kit from the game, even his boots. He'd just come off the pitch at the final whistle, after we'd beaten Dundee United 1-0, and started the celebrations. He'd not even bothered to have a shower or get changed before getting onto the bus.'

Record goalscorer McCoist added: 'Gazza wore his Rangers strip all the way back to Glasgow. The whole place was in absolute uproar. I don't think it was until we reached the Swallow Hotel that we realised the crackpot hadn't bothered to get changed. We were all there in our blazers, trousers and club ties – and there was Gascoigne in his full kit and boots.'

The antics of the England superstar knew no bounds, albeit he did require to be reminded that not everyone around Ibrox shared his sense of humour – or style.

Knox said: 'Gazza was always up to something. Before one Old Firm game, he'd flown a hairdresser up from London and paid him an enormous sum of money for a new haircut. It was like nothing I'd ever seen before. The only way to describe it was as though he had little marbles of hair glued on top of his head. I had one look at it and immediately knew that he'd have no chance of playing the next day unless it was sorted. Walter would have gone mental. Luckily, the hairdresser was still at Glasgow Airport waiting on his flight back to London and we caught him just in time. All the hairdresser could do was cut everything off and try to patch things up as best he could. It still looked ridiculous.

'Then he had his teeth done. He went for these big implants. You've never seen anything like this – he looked like a horse.

He told us later that his father, John, had been up staying with him when he'd had them done. As he was leaving the house to head into training that morning, his dad just said to him, 'Good luck today, son!' To be fair, in a bid to get it over with, he came straight in and stood in the middle of the dressing room to give the biggest grin you've ever seen. The rest of the players absolutely slaughtered him.

'We went to training and I've no idea how they did it but, when we came back, there were bales of hay and bags of carrots under Gazza's peg in the dressing room. He went straight back to the dental hospital that day and had more surgery to have them all filed down. They were better the next morning – but not much better.'

McCoist remembers the moment Gazza unveiled his new teeth – and admitted the midfielder could laugh at his own misfortune. 'I don't think I have laughed as much ever in my life as the morning Gazza came in with his new teeth. He was in first every morning because he couldn't sleep, but this day he was the last man into the dressing room. He swung the door wide open, stood in the middle of the dressing room and dropped his Versace bag on the floor. Then he smiled with these new gnashers. We were laughing so hard that we were holding each other up for five minutes. It was absolutely hilarious.

'He said, "What do you think?"

'I said, "I think you could eat an apple through a letterbox with those boys."

'We had to go to train at the West of Scotland Cricket Club but we made a couple of calls to get a bale of hay and a bag of carrots left at Gazza's peg for him coming back. He had just split up with Sheryl so we thought it would be good to set up a mock wine bar in the dressing room.

'I was to be the glamorous leggy blonde and he was to chat me up with his new teeth in our "wine bar".

'The rest of the players were "mingling" in the wine bar when Gazza came in and approached the table.

'He said, "Hi, I'm Paul. Can I join you in a glass of wine?"

'I said, "By the look of your new Edward Heaths, we won't be needing a corkscrew."

The mere mention of Gascoigne's name still brings a wide smile to Knox's face and those of his former team-mates. One of England's greatest-ever players, he has sadly fallen on hard times since hanging up his boots. But memories of his Ibrox heyday – a spell which Gazza himself rates as the most enjoyable and rewarding of his career – still spark giggles.

Durrant said: 'Gazza had signed a boot deal with adidas and, for some reason, he'd got his hands on a pair of size 16 boots for a laugh. We were back in the changing room ten minutes before kick-off and, of course, Gazza had pulled on these big boots.

'Archie told him to take them off but Gazza replied that it was in the small print of the contract that he had to play in them. Archie was trying to stay calm about the whole thing – until Gazza dashed out of the dressing room with the boots still on.

'He was trying to run up the tunnel towards the pitch – not easy in size 16 boots – and was doing fine until Archie rugby-tackled him to the ground.

'We all rushed out to see what would happen, and it nearly came to fisticuffs. Of course, once Archie convinced him to wear the right boots, he scored two goals in the game.'

The big boots were just a small part of Gascoigne's large wardrobe. He might not have found a suit for the '96 cup final – but fishing attire was never a problem.

Knox said: 'He'd come in wearing his waders after spending all night fishing. If he'd caught anything, he'd bring it in too. Just ask Gordon Durie.

'He was phenomenal in terms of the spirit in the dressing room. It was mayhem every morning.

'When we signed a new player, there was a tradition that they had to stand next to the showers and balance a cup of water on their head. The rest of the boys would soak their socks or jockstraps, tie them up in a tight knot and throw them at the new lad. Of course, they aimed at their face – or other parts – and just pretended that they were aiming for the cup of water. The likes of Alexei Mikhailichenko had never seen anything like this before. But that was the Rangers ritual.'

In that packed summer of '96, Archie and wife Janis were also guests at Gascoigne's marriage to long-time girlfriend Sheryl Failes. The star-studded ceremony in Hertfordshire was attended by football's great and good – with a big-money deal agreed to sell photographic rights to a style magazine. But ahead of the big day, Archie still had to keep an eye on Gazza. 'Janis and I were invited along with the likes of Terry Venables, Bryan Robson, David Seaman and their wives or partners. We all stayed in the hotel which was hosting the ceremony. It was top secret as *Hello* magazine had bought exclusive rights to the wedding photographs and Gazza was getting a right few bob.

'Everyone was having a drink the night before the wedding and I had to grab Gazza at one point and remind him he was getting married in the morning. But, to be fair, he was up fresh and okay for the ceremony.'

For all the chaos which followed Gazza, Knox recalls a warm and generous side seldom seen by the public at large. 'Gazza was great at any of the Christmas parties for children, especially those with learning difficulties. The players would go along for a little while and one of them would dress up as Santa. Maybe they'd stay for an hour or two – but Gazza would be there from start to finish having a laugh with the kids. He was a natural at all that and he loved it. It wouldn't be a case that the kids necessarily knew him. He just loved being in their company and could make them laugh and play.

'I remember we played a European tie in Romania and some fundraisers came into our hotel looking for charitable donations for the local orphans. Gazza went upstairs to his room and – what he was doing carrying this amount of money, I don't know – brought down £600 in cash and gave it to them.'

A young Archie (*centre, front*) with parents Norman and Elizabeth and siblings Jim, Jack, Evelyn, Arthur and Margaret.

Archie's wife, Janis, with daughters Susan, left, and Lesley.

Archie with close friends Bob Hopcroft (*left*) and Bryn Williams.

Janis graduates with her teaching qualification from college in Edinburgh.

Archie carries Susan and Lesley on a day trip to the seaside.

Archie tries to rouse his Forfar team as extra-time approaches against Rangers in the 1978 League Cup semi-final.

A brief break during training with the Loons at Forfar Academy.

Forfar Athletic squad with Archie (*front row, second from left*).

Working on a loft extension at 16 Kinnettles Terrace, Dundee – the first-ever Knox family home.

Dundee United squad including Frank Kopel, Walter Smith and Hamish McAlpine.

Managing to pinch the ball from Celtic's Kenny Dalglish while playing for Dundee United.

Archie enrols for the SFA coaching course at Largs with, among others, close friend and teammate Walter Smith.

Raising the Cup Winners' Cup with Alex Ferguson in 1983.

Not even the rain could dampen the party in Gothenburg.

Archie and brother Jim with the European Cup Winners' Cup after Aberdeen's win in Gothenburg in 1983.

Just some of the silverware Ferguson and Knox won at Aberdeen.

Celebrating a Manager of the Month award at Dundee.

With Alex Ferguson during the early days at Manchester United.

It's all too much for the Manchester United squad at Littleton Road.

Brian Kidd, centre, is welcomed back to Old Trafford by Alex Ferguson and Archie Knox.

Watching Bryan Robson and Peter Barnes in training at United.

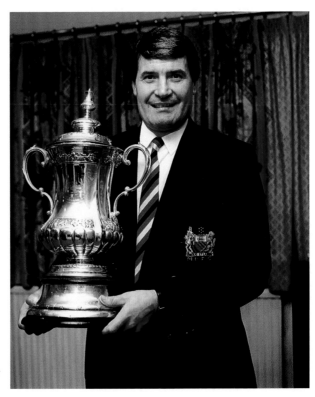

The FA Cup after the 1990 replay win over
Crystal Palace at Wembley.

With Steve Bruce after a United victory.

Walter Smith welcomes Archie to Rangers in 1991.

In the Ibrox dugout in the first day in the new job.

Anguish at Champions League elimination to Levski Sofia in 1993.

Trophy joy with Walter upstairs at Ibrox.

Archie and Paul Gascoigne celebrate Eight in a Row in 1996.

A reunion with Sir Alex Ferguson. *SNS Group*

Archie with great friends Craig Brown and Alex Smith. *SNS Group*

Aberdeen's 1983 heroes back together with the trophy.

Walter Smith and Sir Alex Ferguson join Archie at his 70th birthday celebrations in Dundee in May 2017.

CHAPTER TEN

THE CHAMPAGNE WARM DOWN

THE AFTERMATH of Gazza's title-clinching hat-trick against Aberdeen was almost as memorable as the treble itself.

As Ian Durrant recalled, 'We'd won the league but I think Archie had us back in the next day for a warm down. It became known as "The Champagne Warm Down". Peter Kingston, who was chief of catering at Ibrox for many years, became heavily involved in this ritual. He'd secrete away bottles of champagne in each of the corners and would stash some plastic cups with them. We'd jog to the corner and have a cup of champagne, then jog to the next corner and have another one. It was a great jest.'

The architect of this unusual training session was, of course, Archie Knox. And he knew it would win universal approval among the Rangers squad. 'After we won the title, I asked Peter to lay out ice buckets at the four corner flags of the pitch with the champagne in them. His staff were also to lay out a table with trays of glasses. I'm sure Peter and the girls at Ibrox thought I was daft.

'We still had the Scottish Cup final to come so we needed a bit of a warm down. But the boys also needed to relax. When we reached the corner flag, we'd have a glass of champagne. Then we'd run between the goals to the next corner flag and have another one. The morning consisted of us going from one corner to another and sipping away at the champers. It was great.

'It helped keep the atmosphere up at the end of a long season. But I'm not sure the likes of Brian Laudrup had ever seen players drinking while they were training – it was beyond belief.

'We had some great times with Peter and his staff at Ibrox. I remember him coming in one day and asking if we could score a goal around five or ten minutes before half-time as it would mean increased sales at the kiosks of £5000 to £10,000. He was deadly serious.'

Unwinding was crucial for the squad as they sought to cope with the pressures of pushing towards Nine in a Row while again trying to make an impact on Europe. To that end, trips to the Plaice Café were viewed as almost as important as the hard yards at Bellahouston or West of Scotland Cricket Club. Even the long arm of Glasgow's finest was employed to bring some levity at the end of a tough week for the Rangers squad.

Knox recalled: 'If we were training at Bellahouston, we'd often go over to the Plaice Café on Paisley Road West for bacon rolls and tea. We were in there one day when two police officers pulled up in a squad car and came in for a cup of coffee. I don't know who – but it was probably Durrant – sneaked up to them and asked if, for a laugh, they would pretend to arrest Davie Dodds. The idea was that they'd lift him for alleged non-payment of parking fines. The two policemen came up to him, read him his rights, the whole lot. They asked him to accompany them to the station at Govan where he'd be charged. Davie was protesting and saying he'd never had a parking fine in his life. The boys were all cheering. They put him in handcuffs and escorted him down the stairs into the back of the police car and drove away. We were all standing at the window waving at him – and he was shouting that he didn't do it! They took him to Govan police station and went through the whole rigmarole before they told him it was all a big joke.'

The legend of the Plaice Café even stretched to Turin ahead of a Champions League clash against Juventus in autumn 1995.

Ally McCoist recalled: 'We were playing Juventus in the Champions League but we had so many injuries we could hardly put a team together. A TV crew came over from Italy to study us but Archie took us to the Plaice Café for bacon rolls and tea instead of training. There were 15 of us sitting in the café with this TV crew filming us. I'm not sure Alessandro Del Piero and Fabrizio Ravanelli prepared in the same way.'

Rangers gathered just three points from a tough Euro group featuring Juventus as well as Borussia Dortmund and Steaua Bucharest. But the title was gathered with newcomers such as Derek McInnes, signed from Morton, helping them to Eight in a Row. McInnes wasn't always so sure he'd savour success, though, after missing his own debut through suspension.

He explained: 'I was about to sign for Rangers from Morton but there was a hoo-ha over the fee and the move was delayed. My final game for Morton was against Dundee and I picked up a booking which put me over the old disciplinary points threshold and landed me a one-game ban. Rangers had problems with injuries and they wanted me in to make my debut against Aberdeen at Pittodrie. The first time I met Archie, he came in and said, "You kept that f***ing quiet – you're no use to us now", and he stormed back out.

'I had a great time at Rangers under the gaffer and Archie. The games of head tennis with the two of them were legendary. They'd grab the young boys to referee for a couple of hours and the lads would be petrified to give a decision against either of them. Barry Robson tells stories of him and Barry Ferguson taking in tea and toast to the gaffer and Archie on a tray. Barry says Archie would slap him round the head and he could do nothing as he was holding the tray!

'We lost 4-1 to Ajax in the Amsterdam Arena in the Champions League in my second season at the club. The lad Dani had scored twice by half-time and Gazza had been sent off. All week we'd worked on Stuart McCall marking Dani. At half-time, I was sitting next to Stuarty in the dressing room. Gazza was in the toilet by this stage and the gaffer was trying to make adjustments to play the second half with ten men. The whole time, Archie was standing behind the gaffer shaking his head and growling at Wee Stuarty.

'I could feel Stuarty desperate to say something but, as soon as the gaffer stopped talking, Archie looked over and said, "You had one job".

'Stuarty had an ice pack on his knee but picked it up and threw it at Archie, moaning, "How can I man-mark someone when we're down to ten men?" Archie stepped forward and the two of them were at it.

'Looking back, we should have known how it would go after our light training session in the stadium on the day of the game. One of the Ajax groundsmen was hovering around and a clearance was booted over in his general direction. He flicked the ball up with his steel toe-capped boot and volleyed it straight back to Archie's feet.

'Archie said, "If the groundsman can do that, we've no f**king chance!"

'I found Archie absolutely brilliant to work with. He was demanding of the players but I loved his training. We never had a lazy day. Archie knew that a large part of the success at Rangers was keeping the very good players happy and he was good at that. Training was competitive – everything meant something. He wanted you to train the way that you played. It could be fiery and there could be arguments, fights and scraps. But that was what he wanted from everyone.'

Knox was no stranger to a scrap, and the players agreed that it was better to settle differences and move on rather than allowing them to fester.

He recalled: 'There were plenty of battles in those days – arguments and full-blown fights. People will have their own opinions about whether that was the right way to run a dressing room but it's the way it was back then. Every pre-season I'd have a fall-out with Andy Goram. Walter and I would be at the front of the runs and he'd be at the back. I'd have a go at him and he'd have a go back. He wasn't pleased by the demands, but we knew it was right for him.

'I fell out with Nigel Spackman in pre-season early on, too, because he wasn't impressed with one of my routines. He was told if he didn't like it then he could go back to Ibrox and train on his own. It was one of my first days at the club.

'I always felt that I had to lay down a marker to the players. If you didn't do that, you were leaving yourself open.'

John Brown had experienced Knox's methods at Dundee a decade earlier and was a fan of the way he ran the dressing room. 'If it all kicked off, Walter and Archie would just stand to the side, have their cup of tea and wait until it had all calmed down again. They would let the steam go out of the situation and then deal with the team afterwards.

'McCoist and Gough were at it all the time. That's just because they were winners. They would battle with each other all the time. We all had our run-ins with each other but you shook hands at the end of it and got on with it. It was all about what happened on a Saturday. It was about getting the points at the end of the game.'

One of Knox's personal disputes ended with him facing SFA charges after a row with legendary referee Brian McGinlay.

He recalled: 'I still have the photograph of the bust-up with Brian. It's not my proudest moment. Donald Findlay, who was on the Rangers board at the time, insisted on representing me when we went before the SFA Disciplinary Committee at Hampden. Dougie Smith, who'd been a team-mate of mine at Dundee United back in the day, was chairman of the committee. We used to call him "The Skip".

'Donald spent 45 minutes speaking to the committee as if they were the guilty men. I'd been charged with swearing at Brian but Donald questioned each and every one of them as though it were them who'd shouted at him. I didn't get a chance to say a word before Dougie asked us to leave the room for the committee to consider their verdict. Dougie came back in and said, "It's the decision of the committee to censure you for your remarks to Mr McGinlay".

'Then he paused and added, "Severely, by the way".

'Given some of the punishments and touchline bans which had been handed out by the committee, not to mention fines, I think Donald and I both treated it as a victory.'

Rangers were used to victories in those days as superstars such as Gascoigne and Laudrup dovetailed with the home-grown core of players. Another highly rated overseas star, Romanian striker Florin Raducioiu, might have been added to the squad but for a crazy mix-up at the start of the 1995/96 season which left Smith and Knox unusually red-faced.

Knox said: 'Walter and I flew out to Barcelona to watch the player in a La Liga match between Espanyol and Racing Santander. We reached the hotel reception to check in and I went to sort the rooms while Walter asked the concierge what time the kick-off was in the Espanyol game. He replied, "Uno-zero". Walter said, "No, it can't be one o'clock as it's past one o'clock already. What time is kick-off?"

'The concierge then reached behind the desk to produce a newspaper and point at the Espanyol match report. Neither of us speaks a word of Spanish but it very quickly became very apparent that the game had been played the night before and we'd missed it.

'Walter was blaming me and I was blaming him. Then we agreed we should blame the scout who'd tipped us off. Walter began to make arrangements to get us home as quickly as possible. Then he said, "Archie, I'm going to make an executive decision. We're going out". The next thing we were sinking beers on the Ramblas and watching the Barcelona game on Spanish TV.

'We came home as planned the next day and, fortunately, David Murray never followed up on the success or otherwise of the scouting mission. It was a year or two before we felt confident enough to tell him that we'd wasted his money on a wild goose chase.'

Smith confessed: 'I took full responsibility for it. I just wish there had been someone else to blame. I don't think I mentioned it to the chairman until much later.'

More travel chaos would befall Knox a year later as Rangers were plunged into a hazardous Champions League qualifier against Alania Vladikavkaz in a far-off corner of Russia.

Chief scout Ewan Chester embarked on the initial spying trip, with Knox accompanying him on the follow-up mission.

It developed into a *Planes, Trains and Automobiles* adventure which would have sent Steve Martin and John Candy into gales of laughter.

Chester recalled: 'Whenever we had a draw for Europe, Walter had me primed to go out and watch the opposition. I was on holiday in America and saw in a Sunday newspaper in New York that we'd been drawn against the Russian champions. I came back to a voicemail that the club needed my passport to arrange a visa to head over to watch Alania. I went out twice – the first time on my own and the second time with Archie. I flew to Moscow and then boarded a domestic Aeroflot flight to Samara, where Alania were playing a league game.

'It was like going back 50 years. They were the kindest people but they had nothing. Every taxi was a Lada and the interpreter spoke in a clipped BBC English accent.

'I flew back on the team charter to Vladikavkaz. We nearly crashed and we circled three times before landing in a lightning storm.

'It was amazing to think this team from 40 miles from the Chechen border had won the Russian title ahead of all the big Moscow teams.

'The hotel had torn curtains and cold showers. I was living on cheese and biscuits.

'All I could think about was bringing Ally McCoist, Richard Gough, Paul Gascoigne and Brian Laudrup to this.

'On the second trip – with Archie – we flew from London to Moscow, where we stopped at the British Embassy and had a lovely western hotel. But Archie couldn't believe the "wacky races" as he called them across the ten-lane highways in Moscow.

'The Aeroflot flight down to Vladikavkaz was incredible. We were sitting round a table as if we were on a train and were facing one man – and his dog. We faced them all the way down to Vladikavkaz, with seatbelts optional. The man was huge and was guzzling brandy. He was offering it to us and wasn't the type of man to refuse his hospitality.

'When we landed, we had to walk across the tarmac and it was full of potholes. I'm not sure Archie could believe what he was seeing.

'We were supposed to be there for five days to watch a tournament involving Vladikavkaz, Botafogo, Valencia and Auxerre.

'On the way home, we shared an Aeroflot plane with the Valencia squad back as far as Moscow. But there weren't enough seats. Valery Karpin, a famous Russian international, was one of the last on board the flight and didn't get a seat. It was like a

Glasgow bus with Karpin and one of his team-mates standing in the aisle for the entire journey.

'I wouldn't have had my career without Archie. We'd have a few beers on these trips and I'd learn so much from him. We must have done our job all right on that trip as we won 7-2 over there and 10-3 on aggregate to reach the group stage.

'On the way back home from Moscow, we were demob happy. We had a glass or two of champagne on the BA flight and we were glad to be going home.

'But the final leg of a marathon 18-hour journey – the flight from London to Glasgow – threw up more problems. Archie was in the window seat and I was in the middle. We were just desperate to get back up the road. A Rangers fan, who had been down at a race meeting near London and was celebrating some success, sat in the aisle seat. All the way home, he'd chat away about the game at Ibrox against Vladikavkaz on the Wednesday night and how we'd do.

'When we finally landed in Glasgow, he stood up, shook Archie by the hand and said, "All the best for the game, Walter."

'I took great pleasure in telling McCoist and the rest of them about that the next day. But in all seriousness, I couldn't make up the debt I owe Archie for my career.'

Not all foreign travel led to such chaotic scenes for Knox, however, as close friend and former midfield dynamo Durrant recalled. 'Archie was a great buffer for Walter. He always knew about the nights out and knew what to tell the gaffer and what not to tell him. If he felt we'd overstepped the mark the night before, he'd get the message across by running us even harder in the morning.

'Archie was the best motivator I ever worked with. A lot of the stuff I use in my coaching now is based on things he taught me. He was often the go-between, too. The gaffer was great but, at any club, you need someone to act as that link between the players and the manager. It could be chaos. It was usually Coisty and I in the midst of it, but Ian Ferguson was often involved and Stuart McCall could be a mischievous bastard as well. Gary Stevens could do his bit, too, and there were nights out when Richard Gough thought he was the Scarlet Pimpernel.

'Nine out of ten times, Archie would be in the middle of it. He liked a night out and still is great fun to be around.

'We had an annual trip to Monaco. It was something which Graeme Souness had started and, fortunately, Walter had decided to continue. You can imagine us Glasgow boys out there in Monte Carlo. You need a few bob in your pocket to drink over there. We found ourselves drinking with some multi-millionaires on a £30 million yacht in the harbour. I'm still not too sure how it came about. But there was a karaoke machine on the boat and the next thing we knew Archie had the microphone in his hand and was belting out Bill Haley.

'We'd have an annual golf day at St Andrews, too, and Archie would bring down some of his old pals from Dundee. He loved the bonding sessions and always looked upon them as a good way to integrate the foreign boys with the local lads. He loved the celebrations if we'd won a trophy, too, and used to insist on Jimmy Bell taking the team bus down Paisley Road West after a cup final or if we'd clinched a title away from home.

'He used to send the security folk off their heads but he'd love seeing his picture in the Bellrock, the Grapes or the District – the big Rangers pubs.

'In a way, it helped the boys find out what it meant to play for Rangers. Then we'd end up back at Ibrox with Archie on the karaoke.'

CHAPTER ELEVEN

LAUDRUP NEVER HEADS THE BALL

RICHARD GOUGH in floods of tears, Paul Gascoigne wearing his kit in the pub and Brian Laudrup scoring with a header. The final episode of Rangers' Nine in a Row charge featured scenes which few fans would have predicted. A place in the history books was assured with Laudrup's goal against Dundee United at Tannadice on 7 May 1997. But the real foundations were laid with a clean sweep of wins over Celtic in a season of dramatic twists and turns.

Archie Knox recalled: 'Rangers would easily have been in the top three or four teams in England at that time. I have no doubt about that. Remember, we beat Leeds United, the champions of England, home and away a few years earlier.

'Rangers were attracting a very high level of signing. You could never disregard a team that had the level of player Rangers had in those days. The team had goals in it, an abundance of ability, outstanding midfielders, exceptional defenders and a great goalkeeper. It had the likes of Gascoigne and Laudrup, goalscorers like Mark Hateley and Ally McCoist, midfielders like Stuart McCall, defenders like Gough and John Brown and a great keeper like Andy Goram. That team had everything.

'Celtic had good teams as well. We just held the upper hand in that Nine in a Row era. We knew we were getting pushed the whole way by Celtic and that kept everybody on their toes. We knew if we had a bad spell that Celtic would capitalise on that. Every Old Firm game we went into treating Celtic as equals. That is the way we dealt with it. There was always pressure on us to perform. There could be no mistakes at home or away.'

That pressure reached unprecedented heights as Rangers sought to match the Nine in a Row achievement of Jock Stein's greatest-ever Celtic side. Seven straight league wins at the start of the season, culminating with a derby triumph over Celtic at Ibrox, was the perfect start.

Gough and Gascoigne scored against the Hoops, with the captain recognising the importance of the victory. He said: 'The crucial part of the season was winning all four league games against Celtic. They had strengthened with the likes of Paolo Di Canio, Jorge Cadete and Pierre van Hooijdonk.

'There had been times near the start of Nine in a Row when they only finished third or fourth in the table. They were experiencing the kind of problems that Rangers are going through at the moment. There were different moments when our biggest challenge came from Aberdeen or Hearts or Motherwell. But this was a very strong Celtic team – they'd only lost one league game the season before – so taking 12 points from them was vital.

'All the games against Celtic that season were close. I scored with a header from a Jorg Albertz corner in the first one and Gascoigne scored as well, but only after John Hughes hit the bar with a header. Laudrup scored the winner at Celtic Park and we needed two late goals from Erik Bo Andersen, after he'd come off the subs' bench, to win the New Year game at Ibrox.

'Brian Laudrup got the winner in another close game at Celtic Park to ensure we won all four games – and that made all the difference at the end of the season.'

Durrant had always savoured the derbies against Celtic – and was always desperate for tickets, too. He recalled: 'In Old Firm week, Archie had this incredible habit of being able to get his hands on gold-dust tickets for the game. As local lads, it was always me, Coisty and Ian Ferguson who had most requests and we had to try to get as many tickets as possible for the derby game. Archie referred to us as the "rabbits" in Old Firm week as we'd always be scurrying around looking for tickets. And he loved taunting us with them.'

Laudrup's winner at Celtic Park in November 1996 thrilled the Rangers fans who had managed to secure tickets by whatever means. But the key fixture of the season was undoubtedly the one back at Ibrox on 2 January 1997 – the night Bo Andersen wrote his name into Rangers folklore.

Smith and Knox's plans for the game had been wrecked by injury and illness to several of their key performers. Despite Albertz's early free-kick flying low into Celtic goalkeeper Stewart Kerr's bottom corner, the hosts were pushed onto the back foot. When Di Canio equalised for the visitors in the second half, it seemed as though the pendulum was swinging decisively towards Celtic.

But the Rangers management gambled by withdrawing fans' favourite McCoist and Australian international Craig Moore to allow for the introduction of strikers Peter van Vossen and Bo Andersen. The Danish striker scored twice in the last seven minutes to provide three vital points – and the fresh impetus to push for that historic title.

Bo Andersen recalled: 'I had been promised a start in that game but I had been sick all week. Richard Gough and Brian Laudrup were also ill and they missed the match. I had the flu and a bad fever but on the day of the game I felt a bit better. Richard and Brian didn't make it but when we met at Ibrox, Walter Smith asked me how I was feeling. I told him that I couldn't play 90 minutes. I didn't feel well enough to do that. I said to Walter, "Use me as a substitute to finish the game".

'At half-time, Archie came to me and said, "Erik, you have to be ready. You have to go on and score two goals".

'I said, "Yeah, yeah – that would be fantastic but it won't be easy."

'It was such a difficult game because Celtic had a good team and they were on a great run. They had players like Di Canio, Cadete and van Hooijdonk. Celtic had spent a lot of money and they were really challenging us for the league title. They wanted to end our run and, if we had lost that game, it would have been really close in the run-in to the end of the season.

'At 1-1 in the game, Walter put me on and I scored twice to give us the win. It is one of the best feelings I have ever had in football – I felt like I was in heaven.'

Durrant recognises it would have been hellish to have come so close without landing that record-equalling ninth title. And he'll forever remember the intervention of Bo Andersen, in the midst of a run of seven straight league wins, to keep Celtic at arm's length in the Old Firm title fight. 'Andy Warhol spoke about everyone having their 15 minutes of fame – and that night was Erik Bo's moment. There was a flu bug going round the place and I always look back on that night as being crucial to Nine in a Row. Jorg Albertz had scored with an exocet of a free-kick but Celtic came back into the game and we needed those goals by Erik Bo.

'If Celtic had won that night, the whole dynamic of the league would have changed and we might not have won it. I think it was one of those big games at Ibrox when Archie would tell the ball boys to "disappear" once we were winning and we were trying to hold on!'

Laudrup scored again at Celtic Park to seal a fourth derby win of the campaign, and repeated the feat to clinch the title on an historic night at Tannadice.

Gough said: 'My tears that night were a mixture of joy and relief. I don't think people truly realised the pressure we were under. The weight of expectation was so heavy. We hadn't done well in the Champions League that season because so much focus was on matching Celtic's record of nine consecutive championships.

'I remember going to a fans' event after we'd clinched the eighth title. I walked in the door and everyone was going mental. A big Rangers fan pulled me to one side and said, "Great win, big man – but you'd better not f*** it up next season." That was the pressure already put on our shoulders and there were times during the season when we really felt it.

'I said before the season kicked off that it was a campaign of 36 cup finals. That was the mantra. By the time we reached Tannadice for the penultimate game, we just wanted it done. Maybe that explained my tears on the pitch. But it was worse in the dressing room – there were quite a few in tears. The older ones, who had lived with the pressure for a few years, really felt the emotion that night. We had got so close and knew that if we missed out, we'd never get another chance at it.

'We had one game left after the Dundee United match – away to Hearts – but we were so desperate to get it done and get over the finishing line at last.

'From the sixth title onwards, people had been talking about Nine in a Row. Now we'd finally done it.

'It's funny the things you remember about different seasons. I remember scoring five goals, which was a lot for me. I remember having trouble with my calf muscle late in the season and I remember having the chance to clinch the title at home to Motherwell, only for Owen Coyle to score and beat us. I even remember going to Tannadice without the likes of myself, Andy Goram and Mark Hateley because of injury.

'I wind up the boys and tell them that I actually won ten championships, as I got my first with Walter and Jim McLean at Dundee United in 1983. I won it across the road at Dens – but Tannadice was always a special place for me. I even made my Rangers debut there. The night of Nine in a Row, I felt my career had gone full circle. It felt strange but it also felt right for it to happen up there.

'I think it felt the same for Walter and Archie, who had both spent so much of their careers with Dundee United. If we couldn't win it at Ibrox then Tannadice was the next best place for the three of us. That said, I didn't particularly enjoy watching the game. I'm not a great spectator and it was a pretty nervy night for us all.'

Knox would later be shocked by Gough's tears and Gazza's decision to go all the way home in his full kit and boots. But the manner of Laudrup's historic goal was arguably the most surprising element of a night which will live with him forever.

Knox said: 'I can't ever remember Brian heading a ball in a game never mind scoring a header. He just absolutely refused to use his head. His face told the whole story after he'd scored that night. It was like he was asking: "Did I just score with my head there?"

'I don't know what he was doing through the middle anyway. That was McCoist territory.'

Tannadice would be the pinnacle for that Rangers team, with the bid for Ten in a Row ending in disappointment a year later.

By that stage, Smith and Knox were already set to exit Ibrox with a new era planned by David Murray under the management of Dick Advocaat. There would be no place in the Dutchman's team for the vast majority of the men who'd created history under Smith and Knox. The era ended with Scottish Cup final defeat to

Hearts in May 1998. It wasn't the way any of them had wanted to bring down the last curtain. But John Brown believes that side will never be usurped in the hearts of the Rangers fans who witnessed the glory years. Bomber said: 'The best thing about being part of the Nine in a Row era was the family atmosphere at the club. Everybody was tight and we worked our backsides off for each other. If a couple of boys were not playing too well all the players got behind them and tried to help them recapture their form. That came from the management because they were able to get the best from the players.

'Graeme Souness and Walter – and then Walter and Archie – knew what to say and do at the right times and all the players looked up to them. Don't get me wrong, if you stepped out of line or you weren't pulling your weight you were quickly told but there was mutual respect there.

'We had a togetherness that nobody could break and I think that was the key to our success and winning Nine in a Row. During that era, we enjoyed ourselves but when we got onto the training pitches or started to prepare for games we changed and focused on what we had to do. We played hard but worked even harder and we would never have been as successful as we were had that not been the case. The extra hours you put in will always benefit you in the long term.'

Alan Stubbs, who would later play under Smith and Knox at Everton, was in the Celtic side which failed to stop Nine in a Row. But he enjoyed more success the following season when the Hoops prevented a record-breaking tenth consecutive title heading for Ibrox.

Stubbs recalled: 'Rangers had a fantastic team at that time. Celtic were rebuilding again under Tommy Burns and then under the other managers. Tommy put the foundations in place and we managed, under Wim Jansen, to stop Rangers doing Ten in a Row.

'It was huge for us. We were the underdogs in the Ten in a Row season and, if we were honest, we felt Rangers had more quality in their squad. Rangers were bringing in great European players in that era. They were buying as big as many teams in the English Premier League.

'The rivalry will always be there no matter what characters are involved, even nowadays with Brendan Rodgers. People in England don't realise the magnitude of something like Celtic v Rangers. There can be ignorance around it south of the border. When you're in that bubble in Glasgow, it's as big as anything. For us to have beaten Rangers to that title was great. Because of the rivalry and history of the two clubs, it was an enormous achievement for Celtic to stop Ten in a Row.

'It was a fantastic season but there were times when it wasn't nice for either side. The pressure in the build-up to games could be difficult. You could cut the atmosphere with a knife. It was electric, it was hostile and you felt it could go off at any moment. I'd never experienced anything like it – but I couldn't say I didn't enjoy it. I loved those Old Firm games.

'The Old Firm game had that recipe of fear, intensity and exhilaration. Players either rise to meet it or they crumble. Even now, some top players in England ask me about those games. They are intrigued by them and say they'd love to go to one.'

Ironically, the start to the 1997/98 season had looked promising for Rangers after Smith and Knox sparked an Italian invasion. Lorenzo Amoruso, Sergio Porrini and Rino Gattuso all arrived at Ibrox, along with striker Marco Negri. Negri hit 23 goals in his opening ten league games before falling foul of a mystery eye injury which blighted the rest of his stay.

Knox recalled: 'I'd gone over to Italy to watch a striker called Filippo Maniero, who was scoring goals for Verona in Serie A at the time. I knew Sven Goran Eriksson and I went to watch his Sampdoria team train while I was in Italy. I went to Parma, too. I stood and watched Lilian Thuram train on his own at Parma after the rest of his team-mates had gone home. All they did was feed him balls and he'd find a target with a pass. Time and again he'd practise it on his own. Two years later, he'd win the World Cup with France and score both goals in the semi-final win over Croatia.

'I always told young boys coming through about the dedication of Thuram and what it took to become a professional at the top level. Sven understood it all and had a great set-up at Sampdoria. He knew I was over to watch Maniero – but he had another target for me. He told me to go to Perugia because they had an out-and-out goalscorer there called Marco Negri. That was that.

'It wasn't always great, even in those opening weeks when he seemed to score every time the ball went to him. At half-time in a game at Ibrox, I asked him to start running the channels and making himself available to take passes from the full-backs.

'He replied, "Archie, have you watched me play before?"

'I said, "Of course, I have."

'He said, "Well, you know I no do that". And that was that!'

Gers had endured mixed fortunes when importing strikers, with injury also hampering the progress of young Chilean frontman Sebastian Rozental.

Knox recalled: 'I'd been over to Chile and watched Sebastian. I'd actually gone over to watch Ivan Zamorano in the first place. We quickly found out that Zamorano was bound for Italy and Inter Milan, so we went after Rozental instead. Lazaro Rozental had a whisky-importing business in Chile but he also worked as his son's agent. When they came over to Scotland to sign the contract with Rangers, Lazaro brought a friend with him. The friend was Manuel Pellegrini, who would later win the English Premier League title as Manchester City manager. Manuel was out of coaching at the time and was running a five-a-side complex in Santiago. He was out of football but he was still a football man. He wasn't involved in the Rozental deal but he was close friends with Lazaro. He watched us train and he also watched us play head tennis. Walter and I used to play in the home dressing room and it could go on until 5 p.m. It was mayhem. I don't think Manuel had seen anything like it!

'He's a good guy and I've met him a few times since then. He certainly knows the game. Looking back, it's surprising he was out of the game for so long when he came over here.

'I've met Lazaro and Manuel again. We had dinner together in Barcelona when we were over for a game. I saw Manuel a couple of seasons ago at the England v Scotland game at Wembley. And I spoke to him when I was down at the Etihad for their Champions League group game against Viktoria Plzen.'

The Ibrox head tennis challenges didn't diminish, even during the battle for that elusive tenth title. Knox said: 'It was Tips at Aberdeen but head tennis at Rangers. We'd play in the area at the mouth of the tunnel or in the dressing room with a net strung up. We'd play pairs with Walter and I facing a couple of the players. There were days when we'd still be playing late in the day. They all wanted to take us on – McCoist and Durrant, Bomber, even Alexei Mikhailichenko. They loved it.

'John Greig came in one day and wanted a game but it wasn't his turn. He went next door to the gym instead and that's where he suffered his heart scare. We were oblivious to it all as we were still playing head tennis in the dressing room.

'We used to get the young boys to referee. The likes of Barry Ferguson or Barry Robson would be dragged in – and they hated it.

'We just failed to win Ten in a Row that season. It went down to the last game. We were up at Tannadice against Dundee United but the result didn't matter because Celtic beat St Johnstone.

'I think the edge was taken off our play because everybody knew Walter and I were leaving and a lot of the players were leaving, too. That was a wee bit of a regret.'

Gough had actually left in the wake of the Nine in a Row success, jetting out to America's MLS just 24 hours after lifting the trophy. 'I announced in the October that I'd be leaving. Looking back, maybe I should have kept it quiet. As it turned out, I came back the next season after injuries to Lorenzo Amoruso and Alan McLaren. I actually found the Ten in a Row season easier because there seemed to be less pressure now we'd matched Celtic's achievement. We should have won Ten, too, but we fell away in the last two or three games, drawing with Dunfermline and losing at home to Kilmarnock.

'I'd agreed to leave for the US as soon as the title was won so I was away the day after Tannadice. But we celebrated way into the night after that win over United, first at the Swallow Hotel and on the bus on the two-hour journey back from Dundee and then in a club in Glasgow. They're great memories.'

Durrant believes Smith and Knox left a rich legacy in the form of emerging players and the signings they made in the summer of 1997. 'Young players came through like Barry Ferguson and Charlie Miller. They also brought a young Craig Moore from the Australian Institute of Sport during their time at the helm. Barry used to take the tea to the gaffer and Archie and he'd hate it. In the morning, you could hear him talking about "that bloody Knox". But Archie became aware of it and started his own surveillance, which ended when he and the gaffer caught Barry saying it on tape. Archie was going about the place like James Bond.'

Alas, Advocaat failed to get the best out of Gattuso, who would return to his homeland and win almost every medal in the game – including the 2006 World Cup. But the little Italian firebrand left behind warm memories and brought some laughter in his brief spell at the club.

Ewan Chester, the chief scout under Smith and Knox, recalled: 'Rino arrived without a word of English and the boys had a great time winding him up.

'Tiny, who worked in the kitchen at Ibrox, wanted to help settle him in and was always making him pasta. There was a little serving hatch and, after we'd eaten, it was a routine to walk past and shout in, "Thanks ladies".

'This one day Rino, who had been eating lunch with Ally McCoist, decided he wanted to thank them for making his pasta. He walked up to the hatch and said, "Ladies . . . er, ladies . . . er, ladies". He was clearly trying to get something out in English. Then he splurted out, "Ladies . . . that was f***ing shite." The boys had put him up to it and were rolling about laughing.'

CHAPTER TWELVE

WISE OLD OWLS AND A FALLING TREE

Nil Satis, Nisi Optimum. The words have been inscribed on Everton's club crest since the famous club was founded in 1878. The Latin phrase translates as 'Nothing but the best is good enough'. It's a motto which resonates with every Toffees fan. It's a message which Archie Knox eagerly grasped on his arrival at Goodison Park in the summer of 1998.

The trouble was, some of his new colleagues thought he embraced the words a little too literally. Dave Watson, the club's FA Cup-winning captain three years earlier and a Blues legend, recalled: 'Archie used to harass the groundstaff at our training ground at Bellefield. He ordered them to make sure all the pitches were perfect and the cones were all straight. He used to hammer them.

'One night, gale force winds brought down a big tree on one of the pitches. The groundstaff got in early and put a pair of Archie's tracksuit bottoms below the tree trunk, so you could just see the "AK" initials sticking out. They placed his top on the other side of the tree as if it had landed on him – and they all stood smiling to get their photo taken. It was a great laugh and Archie took it in good fun when he came in.'

Knox still laughs at the memory: 'In the winter, lots of leaves would fall on the pitches at Bellefield and I'd warn the groundstaff that I wanted them off before the first team trained on it. They'd be raking leaves when I arrived in the morning. Robbie Gillespie was one of the lads there at the time and the worst moment of his day was when he saw my car arrive in the morning. His highlight was when I left at night!'

Good humour was not always in ready supply at Goodison as Knox and Walter Smith wrestled with tough challenges they'd scarcely known in Scotland. Instead of battling for championships and cups, they fought to steady a great name in the grip of off-field uncertainty and financial disarray. Smith, who had never worked in England, recalled: 'Archie was a massive help to me at Everton. I'd only worked for two clubs, Dundee United and Rangers, and had been fortunate to enjoy a decent level of success with both of them. Archie's career had taken him to the likes of Forfar in the lower divisions and also to clubs like Dundee. Even at the start at Manchester United, he had experienced a different side of things with Sir Alex Ferguson. The experience he had amassed at all those clubs proved invaluable to me in dealing with many different scenarios at Everton.

'It was really tough and we went through two different periods when the club was close to administration. We went a year and a half without an owner and, if it hadn't been for chairman Sir Philip Carter and chief executive Mike Dunford, Everton would have been in even more trouble than they were. It was an up and down period for us, as it was for the club.'

It was a period of flux on Merseyside which demanded the nous of two wise old Owls. Luckily for Everton, they snatched them from the claws of Sheffield Wednesday.

Archie recalled: 'After leaving Rangers in the summer of 1998, we were on our way down to Sheffield to sign a deal. Everyone knew we were leaving Ibrox and Walter had been doorstepped at the World Cup finals in France by the Everton owner, Peter Johnson. We hadn't heard any more from him after that initial chat but, all of a sudden, Wednesday's chairman Dave Richards wanted to do a deal with us.

'We were driving to Sheffield to sign when Peter phoned Walter to say he'd like to offer us jobs and could we go down to Goodison the next day. We stopped the car at Carlisle for a cup of tea and a blether. We'd said to Dave Richards that we'd go there. But we both knew there was no comparison between the two clubs in terms of size or potential. I said, if it was up to me, I'd take Everton. Walter agreed, but how would we tell Dave that we weren't coming? We didn't just want to phone him so we continued the journey to Sheffield and told him face to face. We apologised and said there had been a hiccup as we'd been offered another job and wanted to at least speak to the other club about it. Of course, they weren't best pleased.

'We drove back up the road – Walter to Helensburgh and me to Houston. It was quite late but Walter came back to pick me up again at 6.30 the next morning to drive down to Everton. It hadn't been the most pleasant few hours but we got down to Goodison, were officially offered the jobs and signed the contracts there and then.'

Everton required four wins in five games in a nerve-shredding run-in to finally stave off the threat of relegation at the end of their first season at Goodison.

The scale of the cash crisis was laid bare when star striker Duncan Ferguson, who'd played under Knox and Smith at Rangers, was flogged to rivals Newcastle United. These were problems which they'd never experienced at Ibrox – and they had to fight hard to keep their heads above water.

Smith said: 'Everton is a great club and, when you look back now, while we had a battle on our hands we enjoyed it down there. We couldn't have gone to a better club but, equally, couldn't have gone at a tougher time. But we would have been in far more trouble if Archie had not been at my side to influence things when we needed him to do so. My coaching and management upbringing hadn't given me experience of a position where we were struggling and having to buy and sell players and turn over the squad so regularly. He was a massive help.

'There was a time when we were doing well and had managed to bring in the likes of Marco Materazzi and Olivier Dacourt. But Duncan Ferguson was sold, the chairman put the club up for sale and there was a fair amount of turmoil. I don't think I would have got through it without Archie at my side.'

Everton had bright young things emerging from Bellefield's school of excellence. Even falling trees couldn't disguise that fact. But they weren't ready for the unforgiving environment of the English Premier League, so Knox and Smith opted for some old hands. They married Watson, a respected former England international, with Rangers' Nine in a Row captain Richard Gough. Both aged over 40, they were – and remain to this day – the oldest defensive pairing in English top-flight history. But it was a stroke of genius.

Knox recalled: 'When we went down to Everton at first, they'd just handed new deals to Michael Ball, Francis Jeffers, Richard Dunne and Danny Cadamarteri. They had won the FA Youth Cup under Colin Harvey and had all been rewarded with contracts on much bigger money. Danny seemed to arrive for training in a different car every day. What a boy! I had to try to get my point across to all the young lads that they should always be thinking about how they could improve their game, not just thinking about the trappings the game could offer them. Whether they agreed or not, we couldn't throw them all in at once so we brought in Goughie to play alongside Waggy [Watson].'

A 13th place finish was only one position higher than the previous campaign, but relegation had never been on the agenda this time. Not a bad achievement considering the £8.3 million transfer spend was less than half the sum which had been recouped in sales.

Watson, now working on Rafa Benitez's staff at Newcastle United, recalled: 'Archie and Walter had done a great job at Rangers and brought a wealth of experience to Everton. They had respect as soon as they came into the place because of their past achievements. It was great to work with them. I was part of the staff as a player and as a coach at that time and it was great for me to work with them. I saw at close quarters the passion both of them had for the game.

'Archie was first in and last out every day. He'd go to a game at night or would watch one in his little den at home. Football was his life 24/7.

'He had a way of dealing with people – and it wasn't cuddling them. He'd be in their face if he needed to be and it could be brutal at times. I remember the day Alex Nyarko was confronted by a fan who punched him when we lost 4-1 at Arsenal. The lad had struggled with the language barrier and had said that he wanted to leave Everton and go back overseas. After the game, you could see he was feeling really sorry for himself in the dressing room and looking for sympathy. Archie broke the ice by saying, "If I could have run quicker than that fan, I'd have punched you first!" You can't buy that kind of thing.

'Marco Materazzi hadn't been at the club long when he was short with a pass back and a striker nipped in to score against us. He sat on the ground at the side of the pitch – not far from the dugout – with his hands on his head and started crying. He was just a young lad at the time. Archie walked down towards him.

I hope Marco wasn't looking for words of consolation because Archie said, "Get up and get back on the pitch you soft get!"

'We had lots of good fun but, if the team lost at the weekend, Archie couldn't get over it until we played again and won again. The defeats really got to him and he found them hard to get over.'

Gough, of course, found the differing demands of Rangers and Everton equally unusual. Like Knox and Smith, he'd swept all before him in an era of unprecedented success in Scotland. Now he found strikers sweeping towards him at a rate he'd barely witnessed in his two decades north of the border. 'Everton was different for us all and I quite liked the freshness. But I did find the expectations strange to deal with.

'We went to Old Trafford one day to play Manchester United and Don Hutchison said to me as we got off the bus, "We'll be lucky if we only lose 2-0 today". I couldn't believe his attitude and I told him so.

'The game had just started when John Collins went down the wing and crossed for Francis Jeffers to score. As we ran back, I went past Don and told him I was right.

'By the end, we'd lost 5-1 and Ole Gunnar Solskjaer had scored four. Big Don certainly had a point.

'We'd been used to having to win every game at Rangers, but this was different. As a defender, I was actually defending more than I'd ever done. But the expectation levels were odd for us at first.'

But amid the relative mediocrity of the 1999/2000 season, one result shone like a beacon of hope for every Toffee.

Liverpool 0 Everton 1. 27 September 1999.

It stands – to this day – as the last time the Blues tasted success across Stanley Park.

Archie said: 'It's incredible to think back to that win in 1999. It's still the last time Everton defeated Liverpool at Anfield.

Kevin Campbell scored right at the start and it was a really bad-tempered derby game. Francis Jeffers was sent off in the second half along with the Liverpool goalkeeper, Sander Westerveld. Liverpool threw on a young Steven Gerrard and then he was sent off, too, near the end and it finished ten against nine.'

Gough protected a clean sheet in a famous victory – and enjoyed arguably his greatest day in Everton blue. 'David Weir and I were the two centre-backs that day. Walter and Archie had brought David down the road from Hearts. I remember being interviewed before the game by the *Liverpool Echo* and they were asking how I'd cope against Robbie Fowler and Michael Owen. They must have been about 15 years younger than me – at least – but I said I was sure I'd be able to hold my own. They asked how I'd cope in my first Merseyside derby but I thought 50 Old Firm games would stand me in good stead. In the end, we were fine. I actually enjoyed the challenge and it's great to look back and remember the way we won.'

Smith recalled: 'I think Gough was nearly 40 – a great advert for Everton's youth policy! If you're away to Liverpool you are going to have to defend well and we did.

'The weirdest thing was when Kevin scored at the Kop End. I spotted plenty of Everton fans jumping up around the Kop celebrating. You would never get that in an Old Firm derby. That was my abiding memory – the Reds and the Blues sitting together all around Anfield.

'Historically, Everton don't beat Liverpool away very often so it remains a special result for the blue side of the city.

'We still beat them on a few occasions at Goodison and shared some thrilling draws but Liverpool usually came out on top because Steven Gerrard influenced so many derbies. He rose to the occasion with Jamie Carragher and Robbie Fowler. Their local lads always drove on the other quality players around them at Anfield.'

Knox and Smith were driven by a shared desire to disprove the doubters and lead Everton through a period of transition.

But a 16th place finish in the league and cup defeats to Tranmere Rovers and Bristol Rovers were hard to take.

Ferguson returned from Newcastle and Paul Gascoigne, who had worked wonders under the guidance of Knox and Smith at Rangers, was also brought on board. Weir, who'd spend almost a decade at the club before being reunited with Smith at Rangers, recalls the importance the management placed on team-building. 'Archie could put the fear of God into you. But you would go away for pre-season training and he would also be laughing and joking, really funny and good-natured. He kept the whole place going with his humour and light-heartedness. He was really fun to be around.

'We used to go to Ciocco with Everton, just as he had done with Rangers a few years earlier. Archie's first job of the day was to get everyone into the swimming pool for 7.30 a.m. The boys – and I include Gazza in this – hated it. But Archie treated it as his duty and a little tester for all the players.

'Walter and Archie were quite hard on Gazza but they needed to be to keep him in line – as much as was possible. Gazza was probably past his best by the time he came to Everton but he still had a real respect for Archie and Walter. I wouldn't say they easily kept him in tow, but they kept him in tow more than most other people could manage.

'We didn't have to stay in the swimming pool for too long on those mornings in Ciocco but you'd see Archie throwing boys into the ice-cold pool and having a great time.

'But as the season wore on, especially the seasons when things weren't going as well as we'd have liked, Archie would get angrier and more confrontational at times. He could go from laughing and joking to pinning people up against a dressing room wall!

'Bellefield was a small training ground and you could hear Archie everywhere you went. He has a big personality and you could hear him right round the place, whether he was talking to the kitchen staff or the first-team players.

'I saw a different side to him when I worked with him again with the Scotland team. He had been out of the game for a while before he returned to the international set-up with Walter. They were great friends and it worked well. It was different for Archie because you only had the players for a certain period of time and you almost had to pander to them. In a club environment, the context is different. You had to be on your toes at club level because your livelihood was at stake. With Scotland, he was definitely more relaxed whereas, at club level, he was full-on all the time.'

Incoming transfer business at Everton tended to be successful, even if it wasn't always reflected in results on the field. Thomas Gravesen, Gary Naysmith and Alan Stubbs were three astute acquisitions for Knox and Smith as they scratched and scrapped to improve the squad. Naysmith, another Scotland international defender who – like Weir – had been recruited from Hearts, recalled his arrival. 'I'll always remember Archie's first words to me when I signed for Everton. He told Danny Cadamarteri the same thing. We were playing a game and were under a bit of pressure. He told us that at times like that some players can go missing. Archie told me, "Naysmith, be a do-something player – don't be a do-f***-all player". Those words always stayed with me!

'He was great for me, he signed me. I actually got my move to Everton based on Archie because he'd seen me in the Scotland set-up.

'Archie was assistant manager to Craig Brown. We'd been in Croatia and I'd played well, and I was close to signing for Coventry City. Archie went back to Walter and said he should sign me. Walter would have known me from my days at Hearts but Archie was key to the move.

'The day I went to sign, Archie turned to me and said, "Right Naysmith, I don't want to put any pressure on you but the only other player I've ever recommended he sign was Brian Laudrup".'

The likes of Nyarko and Materazzi might have melted in the face of Knox's fire, but Naysmith felt it was an approach which helped him beyond belief. 'A lot of the players at Everton weren't used to someone like Archie, someone who told you it like it was. He might have shouted at you but the next day it was all forgotten about. I like that because I'd come up with that at Hearts with Jim Jefferies and Billy Brown. For me, I preferred to be told if I'd played well or played badly. I get on great with Archie and still see him to this day.

'Archie knew I wasn't the most talented of players but he also knew I'd give him a shift. I played full-back, wide midfield, central midfield. I was liked by him because I'd give 100 per cent. There were better players on the ball but he knew what he'd get from me and I think he respected that. Even when I went to Aberdeen towards the end of my career to play for him and Craig again, he would put me into the team for those reasons.

'Archie was old-school. He worked you hard but didn't mind you going out as long as you did the business on match days. I think a lot of that is missing from the game nowadays. I just have really good memories of playing under him.

'We were down at Watford one day and Archie had words with Stephen Hughes, the former Arsenal player, and jumped a skip to try to get to him. Walter had to send him into the shower to cool down. That was just his passion. He could slaughter you after a game then the next day he'd say, "How are you – did you have a nice night last night?" And everything would be forgotten. I genuinely liked it like that.'

The arrival of Stubbs, a lifelong Toffee who had faced Knox

and Smith in the heat of Old Firm battles in Scotland, added another dimension. He knew his beloved club was experiencing hard times after so much success in the 1980s and 90s, but couldn't resist the lure of pulling on that famous blue jersey. 'I was an Everton fan and this was an opportunity I feared I'd regret for the rest of my life if I didn't take it. I played under Martin O'Neill at Celtic and he was a very animated character. He was a little bit like Walter and Archie in that way. Walter was calm more often than not. Archie was the flip side of that and was usually the animated one. There were times at Everton when he was like a caged animal. He'd give people a rollicking, but that was normal at that time. Archie was a passionate guy and you could never fault his enthusiasm. He wanted to win and wanted Everton to do well. But you wouldn't want to be on the wrong end of one of his verbal volleys. He had a wicked tongue on him.

'I don't think Everton saw the best of Walter and Archie because it was a difficult time to be at the club from a financial point of view.

'They had a great balance. I only saw Walter lose it once. They were mostly good cop, bad cop with Archie giving the brunt of the rollickings. In fact, Archie could be the ruthless cop. It felt like he had a baton on the end of that tongue!

'It was a difficult environment for them to work under because the Everton fans can be knowledgeable and demanding. The worst thing for them at the time was the fact that Liverpool were doing reasonably well across the park. It's bad enough for an Everton management team if you're not doing so well – but it's a lot worse if Liverpool are doing better. It's similar to Celtic and Rangers.'

Alan Myers was director of communications for all but a few months of Smith and Knox's Goodison reign. He firmly believes they were denied the credit for the job they did in trying times for the Toffees. 'It was an unforgettable three years. Archie and

Walter came in at a difficult time for the club and they were a breath of fresh air. Just watching the way they worked together was amazing. It was funny to listen to the banter. I used to call them "The Brothers" after a David Attenborough documentary about two lions in the Serengeti which had that title. These two lions used to roam around together and cause trouble for everything else. A bit like Archie and Walter.

'Archie brought a real sense of team to the club. He insisted I went on the team coach to games – something which had never happened in the past – and he made everyone feel welcome.

'We had some memorable Christmas parties, including one when we played a game called "Bouncy Boxing" which was like the jousting from the TV show *Gladiators*. I got to the semi-final and somehow beat Walter – which he wasn't too happy about – but I got battered by Chris Woods in the final.

'Archie was a real Jekyll and Hyde. On the training ground, he'd be a stern, serious, almost unlikeable person. He was so professional. But the moment he was away from the training ground and the serious business, he'd be an absolute gentleman. He would become a real friend, someone you could count on and trust. The difference was palpable and you couldn't believe it was the same person.

'One of my favourite moments came in one of only three or four press conferences he did in all his time at Everton. It was during a transfer window and all the media were desperate to know where Walter was. Archie simply said, "Flu".

'The next day, Everton signed a player from France – I think it was Olivier Dacourt – and the press were going daft. At the next press conference, one journalist said to Archie, "You told us Walter had flu". Archie replied, "No, I said he flew".

'We operated out of Portakabins at Bellefield in those days. I was in one and Archie and Waggy were in another. Waggy was in charge of warming up the players before training and one day decided to run them through my office. Of course, the players knocked all the papers off my desk and caused a general mess. I was furious. I knew Waggy was responsible so I went into his office, knocked all his paperwork off his desk and hid his phone in a drawer. Of course, what I didn't realise was that Waggy would return, do the same to Archie's desk and pin all the blame on me.

'By this time, I was back at Goodison and I started to get a series of phone calls from anxious players. Paul Gascoigne, then David Unsworth called me to say Archie was on the warpath and was in a car with Waggy on the way to get me. With perfect timing, a lady from the club shop – which was directly below my office at Goodison – called to say there was a man with a snooker cue waiting to see me.

'It was with a fair degree of trepidation that I went downstairs – to be confronted by John Parrott, who was delivering a cue for one of the Everton directors! Archie never did arrive. Waggy had eventually confessed to wrecking his desk because he was afraid what Archie might do to me!

'Waggy was left in charge one day for a trip down to London because Walter and Archie had returned to Scotland to attend a funeral. We were at Waltham Abbey before a game against West Ham and Waggy had been warned not to let the lads have a drink on the Friday night. When we reached the hotel, we were told there was a Dick Turpin-themed night on and the hotel would be delighted if we'd attend. There would be complimentary drinks, too. Waggy warned the players of the message from Walter and Archie and how drinking would be frowned upon. I looked in about 10.30 at night to find a live horse in the centre of the room, our coach driver wearing a Dick Turpin hat, the kitman with two "wenches" on his knee and Waggy hiding in a corner. Out of the corner of my eye, I saw Walter and Archie arriving in reception. To say they weren't pleased would be the understatement of the year!

'They were great for the club and Archie taught me the only Scottish saying that I know, "Get tae f**k!"

'The main thing I'll remember them for, though, is the way they cared for the staff and were so kind to the people at the club. They made everyone feel part of the team and they'd have done anything for you. The fans maybe thought of Archie as a hardman but he's anything but that. He's so caring and generous.'

Watson and Myers remain close friends to Knox, as do others who worked behind the scenes at Everton – and on the other side of Stanley Park.

Archie said: 'I met Ray Haughan when I was working at Everton. Ray was a friend of our kitman Jimmy "Jeemie Lah" Martin – a man who claims to be the best kitman in Britain! Ray worked for Cosmos Holidays at the time and he fixed up Janis and me with summer holidays abroad for quite a few years. He has become a great friend and eventually got a job as player liaison officer with his favourite team, Liverpool. He works closely with Jurgen Klopp and is highly regarded at Anfield. I was recently at his wedding to Naiomi and, at the time of writing this book, they were expecting their first child. Let me tell you, Ray was punching well above his weight when Naiomi agreed to marry him!

'I was lucky to meet many great people in my time at Everton. Bill Ellaby, the player liaison officer at Goodison, and his wife Irene's friendship was great and we went out on a regular basis with Walter and Ethel Smith and Dave and Liz Watson.'

Everton were to finish 15th at the end of the 2001/02 season but, two months earlier, the board of directors had chosen to relieve Knox and Smith of their duties.

A 3-0 FA Cup quarter-final defeat at Middlesbrough – an eighth consecutive game without a win – would end a near four-year reign at Goodison. David Moyes would move down the road from Preston North End to continue the Scots' influence in the dugout. And Knox would end up great friends with Moyes, even visiting him in Spain when he bossed Real Sociedad after his brief spell as Sir Alex Ferguson's successor at Manchester United.

Knox recalled: 'I get on well with Davie. One of my daughters, Lesley, lives in Spain with her family and I spend a bit of time over there. I went to see Davie and Billy McKinlay, who was his assistant, when they were at Sociedad and going through a hard time. I'd watch the team train at their training complex, which is built into the side of a rocky hill. It was roasting and there wasn't much cover so I'd lie out in a goal net, soak up the Spanish sunshine and watch them do their work.

'It's odd how things turn out in football. When I was at Dundee, we'd take Billy as a 14-year-old in our weekly sessions for west coast kids in Motherwell. It must have been around 1983.

'Badger was a great player – then Jim McLean stole him for United before we could get his name on a sheet of paper at Dundee!'

Everton and that second crack at the game in England had been an experience which Knox wouldn't have swapped for the world. He and Smith bequeathed Moyes a squad which featured Weir and Stubbs at the back, Ferguson and Campbell in attack. David Ginola was on the flank, home-grown youngsters like Tony Hibbert and Lee Carsley were next off the Bellefield production line. And a 15-year-old called Wayne Rooney, who Knox and Smith had been denied giving a first-team debut by FA red tape, was about to be unveiled to a wide-eyed planet football.

Knox said: 'We had some great times. I don't think there was one moment when we wished we'd taken the job at Sheffield Wednesday. We worked with some great people and brought in some terrific players. We also made some friends for life. We bought Gravesen, a Danish international midfielder from Hamburg, and he went on to play 150 games for Everton. He was a great lad and was still at Goodison long after we'd left. I remember waking up one morning and seeing on the sports news that Everton had sold him to Real Madrid. I couldn't believe it – but I was thrilled for him. I checked my phone and I still had a number for him so I tried to give him a call to wish him all the best at his new club. When he answered the phone, I said, "Is that Thomas Gravesen of Real Madrid?" He replied, "I know, Archie – I can't f**kin' believe it either!"'

CHAPTER THIRTEEN

FRIENDS, FAMILY AND A FLOODED TENT

LIFE FOR Archie Knox began in the little village of Tealing, nestled at the foot of the Sidlaw Hills between Dundee and Forfar. The youngest of six children, he was raised at Tarbrax Farm by farmworker father Norman and mother Elizabeth. 'My father worked on many farms in the area and we moved around to various tied houses on those farms,' recalled Archie. 'When I left school, I went to work with my brother Jack on a dairy up near Forfar. But that life was never for me. It was non-stop work – you were either at the tatties, the berries, the neeps or bringing in the hay on the farm. Every school holiday was taken up by farm work. But it was a good upbringing in terms of teaching you about work. I can remember cutting thistles in a field for the six weeks of my summer holiday. At the end of it, the farmer gave me half a crown – 12 and a half pence. It was worse than slavery!'

Jack was the second of the Knox six, after eldest brother Jim and before Evelyn, Arthur, Margaret and, of course, Archie.

The family moved wherever Norman found work, with his

youngest son finding lifelong friendship – and the beginnings of a football career – when they moved to Dunning in Perthshire.

Archie said: 'That was where I first met Ken Schofield. He lived nearby in Aberuthven and his father – I called him "Didi" after the Brazilian World Cup star – took the local boys' club. We played football in a tiny room in the village hall. We could only manage four-a-side and it was mayhem.

'Ken's dad drove round the farms in the Co-op van. My mother would go out and get the groceries from him. We didn't have a car to go to the shops – not many folk did in those days – so you waited for the local grocer to come to you.

'It's funny when you look back on things now. When I first went to Aberdeen, my mother still didn't have a washing machine in the house so I bought her one for Christmas.'

While Knox would achieve fame in football, his boyhood pal would become executive director of the European Tour for almost 30 years – the man credited with revolutionising European golf and the Ryder Cup.

Back then, however, they were only interested in their next kickabout.

Schofield recalled: 'From the moment Archie came through to Dunning village, we became buddies and remain so today. We went to Auchterarder School together – I was one year ahead – and we attended Aberuthven Boys' Club, which was jointly run by my late father and the head teacher of Aberuthven Primary School. As soon as Archie arrived, it was clear he would be our best footballer at the boys' club and the school.

'We bonded immediately – as did our families – and Archie and my father became real pals, too. My father had been a fine footballer himself. He had signed provisional forms for Bury in 1939 before serving for seven years during and after the Second World War. He ended the war teaching machine gunnery near Comrie and settled in Perthshire with my mother. At that time, he played junior football for Auchterarder Primrose with, among others, Ian Mailer – brother of Ronnie, who captained Dunfermline to their Scottish Cup triumph over Celtic.

'In running the boys' club, he let us play football indoors and outdoors constantly – and Dad played with us. He would line us up at opposite ends of the village hall and would call out the numbers from each team who would play against each other. He called it "ones and twos" – and we loved it!

'Occasionally, he would have his own number and would pitch in. Archie christened him "Didi" after the great Brazilian who played in three World Cups in 1954, '58 and '62 because it was tough to get the ball off the old man. I was normally not able to – unless I fouled him – and I usually did. I think from that time Archie reckoned I was a bit of a clogger and I didn't have Dad's or Archie's skills.'

From those early days in the village hall in Dunning, the friends would progress through the local youth ranks.

Schofield added: 'I played once for the Perthshire Schools team in my last year in 1961/62 and we lost 7-1 against Clackmannan at Alloa's ground. I think Archie played, too, and he certainly played the following year against Dundee Schools at Muirton Park. From memory, the score may have been Perthshire Schools 4 Dundee 7 – and I think Peter Lorimer may have scored five goals for Dundee.'

Knox said: 'I'm sure Lorimer only scored a hat-trick and it ended 5-2! But I definitely played with Ken for Letham Royals Under-16s in Perth. I'd walk a couple of miles from the farm to Aberuthven and we'd get the bus to Perth. We'd play at The North Inch, the big public park in Perth, under the street lights. It was great in the juvenile leagues in those days.'

Schofield is equally nostalgic about those early days, long before the pals became two of the most recognisable figures on the Scottish sporting scene. 'From school football we went to the juvenile and junior leagues. Of course, Archie went on to play successfully as a professional. He deserved that success because he totally lived and breathed the game whereas I realised after being chosen for the County Under-21s to play against the Under-18s – when I was just 17 – that my days were numbered. I concentrated from that moment onwards on my bank exams and then, of course, later went south and moved into golf.

'Throughout the 1960s we became pretty inseparable. Archie was my best man when Evelyn and I married in 1968 and, a year later, I was Archie's when he and Janis married in Musselburgh. Their wedding was the same day Tony Jacklin won the Open Championship – and it was suggested the best man's concentration may have wavered at various times during the day!

'Archie and Janis went on to have two beautiful daughters, Susan and Lesley. We, too, are blessed with two beauties and our eldest is, yes, Susan Lesley! That just about sums up the closeness of the families. And all in our family feel fortunate to have known Archie for the long haul. He is a wonderful man and a true friend.'

Years later, when Knox had moved into management and Schofield was running European golf, there were many reunions to play at the tour's Wentworth headquarters.

Schofield said: 'Archie started to make his way in management – notably of course with Alex at Aberdeen – and although I was then living in the south we would stay in touch. It didn't – and never has – mattered if we miss a year or more in speaking or meeting. We always carry on as if it had just been yesterday.

'I was thrilled when we watched the Dons win the European Cup Winners' Cup in Gothenburg and saw them have so much unprecedented success domestically against strong Rangers, Celtic and Dundee United teams.

'I can remember him moving to Dundee for those three years and coming up to see him in his office at Dens Park. After that, he moved to join Alex again and the rest, as they say, is glorious history. He had success at United and then with Walter at Rangers and later Everton. When Walter and Archie left Everton before the end of the season in 2002, they arranged to visit the Masters at Augusta. I was still at the European Tour and, of course, we met up at Augusta Country Club. Much wine was consumed. Although, again from memory, not quite as much as during the Saturday of the 1988 Open at Royal Lytham. That day the rains came and play was quickly washed out. Archie had arranged to bring Brian Kidd to the golf and we met up in my field office and embarked on champagne and wine followed by more and more.

'The great Seve Ballesteros won that Open from Nick Price on the Monday. We were just about recovered by then.

'I think the first time Manchester United were down for a Cup Final at Wembley, Archie brought Alex out to Wentworth. We had lunch but from memory Alex had just had an appendix op, so we didn't play. But from that moment on, Alex has always been there for me, just as with Archie.'

Knox added: 'I remember Ken had us down at Wentworth for a charity game in aid of the CLIC charity for children suffering with cancer and leukaemia. It was the day after the World Matchplay Championships had finished and we were playing off the same tees with the same pin positions on the greens. At the second hole, I hit one of my best-ever drives and followed it with an absolutely cracking three wood. I was so pleased with myself until Ken pointed out that my second shot was just short of where Thomas Bjorn had hit his drive the day before.'

If golf wasn't going to be Archie's bag, his football career never looked back after those early days with Ken and Didi in Dunning. 'I moved on to Errol Juniors and it was from there that I signed for Forfar Athletic,' he remembers. 'They didn't even have a manager in those days and the players were signed by the committee. Jake Young became the first manager, then Dougie Newlands who'd been in Scotland's provisional squad of 40 for the 1958 World Cup finals in Sweden. He was followed by Ian Campbell, whom I'd known from his days as a PE teacher at Kingsway Technical College in Dundee. Ian was such an enthusiastic guy. I became great friends with Ian, his wife May and his family, Colin and Lesley, over the years.'

While playing for school and juvenile teams, Knox always made sure he was free to watch his beloved Dundee on Saturday afternoons. Dad Norman would take Archie and big brother Jim to watch the Dark Blues in their greatest era of success. They won the Scottish League title under legendary manager Bob Shankly – brother of Bill – in 1961/62, reached the semi-finals of the European Cup a year later and lost the Scottish Cup final another year on. 'My father, Jim and myself only missed one game home and away when Dundee won the championship. I was at every one of the European Cup games the following season – the 8-1 win against Cologne, Sporting Lisbon, Anderlecht and AC Milan in the semi-final. There were crowds of 40,000.

'I can still reel off the team from the time – Liney, Hamilton, Cox, Seith, Ure, Wishart, Smith, Penman, Cousin, Gilzean and Robertson.

'I was maybe ten years old when my father first took me to watch Dundee at Dens Park. I was behind the goal at Muirton Park in Perth the day we won the league with a 3-0 win over St Johnstone. They were great days for a young lad, watching Paul Van Himst with Anderlecht and Cesare Maldini – Paolo's father – with Milan.

'One of the best teams I ever saw at Dens, though, was about a decade later when Twente Enschede beat Dundee in the old UEFA Cup. Dundee had a very good side, including the likes of Gordon Wallace and Jocky Scott, but it was the era of Dutch "Total Football" and Twente were outstanding.'

Knox, of course, would step into Bob Shankly's shoes by managing the Dark Blues many years later. But he wasn't the only one of the four brothers who managed to make a career in the game. 'Jim played for Raith Rovers and played with me at Forfar Athletic later in his career. I remember him causing an awful rumpus at Forfar one day when the team was announced and I'd been left out. The committee picked the team in those days and he gave them pelters. He was a bit volatile that way.

'Jim also played at Coventry City with the likes of John Sillett and George Curtis, who later led them to the FA Cup final win at Wembley against Tottenham in 1987. He won the FA Vase at Wembley in 1983 as manager of VS Rugby with his son, Steve, playing in the team.'

But none of the other Knox siblings – nor best pal Ken Schofield – were on the scene when Archie met the love of his life.

He revealed: 'I had been on holiday at Butlin's in Skegness with my pal, Jim Coutts, and we were heading back up the road to Dundee. Jim was friends with Janis's grandparents and we stopped in at Edinburgh to visit Mabel and Willie. Janis was there and we had a night out with them. It went from there and I used to go through to Edinburgh all the time after that. The actual holiday had been a disaster but maybe it was destiny that it took us to Edinburgh and I met Janis.

'I'd bought my first car, a Mini, and we were going to drive to Skegness in it. But the engine blew up before we left. Jim had a Morris Minor with a six-volt battery and the motor just burned oil. We had to stop every 50 miles to top it up. It finally exploded on the way home and we took it to a scrapyard where the scrappie offered us £12 – exactly the sum we'd each spent in Skegness. That was enough for us to go on a camping trip when I eventually got my Mini repaired – but it was no more successful.

'We'd pitched our tent on a slope and woke up in the morning to discover all of our clothes in a puddle at the bottom of the tent. I had to drive the Mini home wearing nothing but my pants. If we'd been stopped by the police, I think we'd have got the jail.

'The only successful part of that holiday was meeting Janis. It transformed my life and she was a truly wonderful wife and mother. She had trained as a teacher and kept teaching after we were married, whether we were living in Dundee, Aberdeen, Manchester and even after I came back up the road to Rangers.

'Janis was amazing. There was never a question about us moving or a complaint that the girls were switching schools again.

'My father had been exactly the same as me in terms of moving to where the work was. He had umpteen jobs and I took all the travelling from him. The only regret I have in my career is trailing my family all over the place. I'm now living in my 28th house. The kids were in about ten different schools. It couldn't have helped their education and it must have been difficult going into new schools and having to make new friends.

'When Janis taught at Whitfield Primary in Dundee, she had a class of 45. I can remember there were nights when she'd come home in tears due to the stress of it all. But she'd also tell great stories from the kids in her classes and some of the stuff they'd said or written in their jotters. There was one wee lad who, when asked to write down what had happened at the weekend, wrote "My dad has run away with Winnie the Clippie".

'Janis worked and had to look after the kids because I was never there. I had very little influence in my kids growing up – apart from giving them a row if they had misbehaved. I'm just glad they have turned out the way they have – but it was all down to their mother's efforts.'

Archie and Janis grew close to the families of his former team-mates Bryn Williams and Bob Hopcroft. When he first headed for Dens Park as Dundee manager in 1983, he even lodged with Bryn and wife Margaret for a spell. 'I'd spend a lot of hours at Dens and I'd often return looking for a bit of solace or comfort – maybe in the shape of a pint. They threw open their doors to me and were so generous. But Bryn was training for a marathon and was off the drink.

'I'd known Bryn since he played with Hoppy and me at Forfar. He'd actually come through at Dundee United. Hoppy and I still kid him on that he was the only left-back who never put his head on the ball. He was a smart-looking guy and didn't want his face injured!

'But Bryn certainly showed commitment in those days when he was training for the Dundee marathon – and did it in two hours and 42 minutes.'

Bryn said: 'I remember taking the call from Archie when he got the Dundee job and was leaving Aberdeen. He asked, "Do you have a bed for the night?" Six months later, he still seemed to need that bed.

'He was a good lodger because he spent most of his time at the club. He put in an incredible amount of hours.

'When he wasn't there, he was dragging Margaret – his "surrogate" wife at the time – round houses he was viewing in Dundee.

'I think we were a stabilising influence on Archie at the time because he'd taken a big step up to return to management on his own. We had a great time together and we did manage a couple of pints now and again. I wasn't completely off the drink!

'On the day of the marathon, the Lord Provost of Dundee – Jim Gowans – had asked Archie to come down to the finishing line. I was certainly surprised to be greeted by the city's provost and the manager of Dundee when I reached the end. I tell folk if it wasn't for Archie staying with me, I'd have done 2:39!

'Archie also offered my sister, Bronwen, a job working for him at the club and she had the time of her life there. Margaret's auntie, Audrey, was also employed as a cleaner and she'd be forever warning the players not to walk into Dens Park in dirty boots or put sticky fingerprints on the brass she'd just polished.'

Bob Hopcroft added: 'My time at Forfar overlapped with Archie's and, although we're great friends, we didn't play together too often. I do remember him scoring a couple of hat-tricks, though, and coming to the attention of St Mirren when he first moved away.

'I think he maybe earned Forfar a wee bit more than I did when I went to Brechin. But his friendship has been far more valuable over the years. That said, we did need to be separated by our former manager, Ian Campbell, at half-time in a game against Montrose. For the record, Archie was talking a load of rubbish – but he went on to make a decent career out of it!'

Archie's two daughters, Susan and Lesley, still vividly recall their vast number of house moves during their primary and secondary school days. They went from Aberdeen to Dundee and back again – on several occasions – and also spent time at schools in Manchester and Glasgow.

The Knox family's travels became almost second nature and the girls adapted accordingly. They look back with no regrets and realise that, as their dad worked round the clock to ensure success at his various clubs, their mum always provided the required support and guidance at home. Their only regret was not having their mum around to enjoy her four grandchildren – Anna, Olivia, April and Archie.

Janis sadly passed away in Strathcarron Hospice in Denny on Christmas Eve 2006 after a long battle with illness.

Susan and Lesley fondly recall their mum and how devoted she was to bringing them up the best way possible – and also remember the happy times spent together in their many houses up and down the country. Being involved in the football community wasn't always ideal. Susan remembers Lesley being spotted by Alex Ferguson smoking on a night out in Manchester. Unknown to Lesley, Alex felt duty-bound to report the incident to her dad. It was discussed at Manchester United's training ground the next day. Archie left immediately and Lesley's smoking career was over before it had started!

Archie recalled: 'The best part of the whole story was when Alex said to me, "But don't tell Lesley it was me who told you".'

Both daughters made the time to support their dad whenever possible and were regulars at many grounds all over the country, enjoying the many highs and a few lows along with the rest of the fans. It would be fair to say that, for a number of reasons, following Rangers during the 1990s proved costly for Archie as every league title triumph and cup final appearance involved a new outfit for both Susan and Lesley. Mind you, it was a sacrifice he was always happy to make.

Lesley now stays in Spain with husband Nigel and kids April and Archie and runs a successful fish and chip shop in La Cala.

Susan decided to stay in Glasgow where she lives with husband Andy and daughters Anna and Olivia and where she has carved out a career in the food industry.

Archie now spends the majority of his time not dealing with high-profile football players but running an on-demand taxi service for two teenage granddaughters!

CHAPTER FOURTEEN

NEVER MIND THE BUZZCOCKS – BE A LOON

THE LITTLE piece of paper would no longer be of sufficient size to chronicle all his achievements in the game. But it was one of the most important notes in Archie Knox's career. His first contract extension, signed by Forfar Athletic and Knox on 29 July 1969, promised 'six pounds when playing, four pounds when not playing'. The document – on light blue paper not dissimilar to the colour of the Loons' famous shirts – added: 'Loss of earnings from ordinary employment will only be paid for midweek matches.'

Given that Knox was combining part-time football with a full-time job as a surveyor with Bett Builders in Dundee, there was real significance in that final line. It marked a pay rise for the promising midfielder and ensured Forfar would earn a decent fee when he was lured away by St Mirren a year later.

His first deal, signed as an 18-year-old in 1965, had paved the way not only for more than 300 appearances in two spells at Station Park – the most he played for any one club – but also for all the success which was to follow from Pittodrie to Ibrox, Old

Trafford to Goodison and beyond. It ensured a lifelong bond with the Loons, albeit both parties always knew that Station Park would never be big enough to contain Knox's ambitions.

Knox recalled: 'I had great times at Forfar – as a player, a coach and a manager – and the club is still important to me. I had five years there as a young part-time player and it gave me a great grounding for what was to lie ahead.

'I went to St Mirren in 1970 after the manager Alex Wright sent his No.2, Willie McLean, to watch me score three goals against Montrose at Links Park. The deal was for the massive fee of £2,500. I suppose it was good money for Forfar in those days.

'I used to get a lift to Queen Street Station from Iain Munro, who went on to play for Scotland at full-back, and I would get the mail train back up the road to Dundee. It was horrendous. I was part-time and I'd get home from training at 1.30 a.m. and be back up for work at 7 a.m. There was one midweek night when I drove down in my Triumph Herald to meet the boys to travel to Stranraer for a game. I was on Castle Street in Paisley, on the way to Love Street, when I encountered a big lorry at a set of traffic lights. This huge steel rod – about three inches thick and eight feet long – came flying off the lorry. As it crashed down in front of me, I ran over it with my front wheels but it flew up under the car. It caught the back axle and ripped the entire back off the car. I was sitting in the middle of the street on two wheels! The lorry kept going and the police weren't interested. And I still had a game to play that night. St Mirren sent some people to help me get the car off the road and I got a lift down to Stranraer. All this for just £12-a-week. But, looking back, I was probably lucky that the rod didn't fly through the windscreen and hit me.'

Knox would keep up his fitness with lunchtime training sessions at his beloved Dundee, where he first met Willie McLean's brother Jim.

He recalled: 'Jim would take me for extra training. I think it was to keep himself fit as much as anything. He used to do the running with me.'

On leaving Dens to be appointed manager across the street at Dundee United, McLean quickly tied up Knox's signing – handing back St Mirren the £2,500 they'd paid for him. 'I was happy to come back up the road. I didn't miss that mail train one little bit at midnight. As a Dundee supporter, it didn't seem strange to sign for United. What will seem strange to some people is that, in those days in Dundee, you supported both teams to an extent. I had been to all Dundee's big European nights with my father and brother. But I'd also been to Tannadice to watch United play Barcelona in 1966.'

Jim McLean, by now building on the firm foundations laid by Jerry Kerr at United, embarked on a Dundonian dynasty. In later years, it would bring him into direct competition with Knox and Alex Ferguson in New Firm derbies. It would also yield the 1983 Scottish league championship and an appearance in the 1987 UEFA Cup final.

His first brush with success, however, was the 1974 Scottish Cup final against Jock Stein's Celtic at Hampden. 'Jim had organised a full-scale practice match on the pitch at Tannadice before the cup final,' remembers Archie. 'I think his intention was to give a run-out to the boys he was going to start in the final against Celtic. But he had to abandon the game because there were so many people flying into tackles. They were kicking lumps out of each other – some really vicious stuff.'

United's trip to Mount Florida had sparked a fresh enthusiasm for football on Tayside, with the *Dundee Evening Telegraph*'s Scottish Cup final preview on 2 May 1974, including pen pix of the squad:

Walter Smith – 'Walter was surprised to find himself in the

United party for their Fairs Cup game in Barcelona. He knew he had no chance of playing but it was a great thrill for a teenager. It turned out to be quite a costly trip. Walter left a valuable camera in a taxi and never saw it again.'

Andy Gray – 'When in his last year at school, the careers officer asked him what he wanted to be, Andy promptly replied, 'A professional football player.' The careers officer responded: 'Well, I can do nothing for you!'

Archie Knox – 'Unlucky to be a cartilage victim in the last year and took some time to make his comeback. But packs a real wallop in his boots and scored many a valuable goal for United.'

Alas there was to be no goal for Knox in the cup final. 'I missed a sitter that day – it still haunts me. You were looking at a Celtic team with Billy McNeill and Kenny Dalglish, so we were up against it and ended up losing 3-0. But it could have been an equaliser.'

He may not have scored at Hampden but, of course, the national stadium would later be the scene of cup glories at the side of Alex Ferguson and Walter Smith.

Smith said: 'We became team-mates at United when Archie arrived from St Mirren. It was Archie who got me to go down to Largs to start doing my coaching badges. He'd been there the year before and had enjoyed it. I had been taking the Dundee United 'S' Form signings on Monday nights but hadn't studied for any coaching qualifications. By the time I returned to do my 'A' licence, Archie was already on the staff at Largs after impressing Andy Roxburgh.

'Jim McLean had a huge influence over the majority of players at that time, when you consider how many of them went into coaching or management. Jerry Kerr had been hugely successful but when Jim came in we saw more of the modern variety of training. It was great. We were not the best players. I say that not with a sense of modesty but because it's a statement of fact. We had a good attitude and Archie was more a forward-going type of player whereas I was more defensive.'

Knox agrees that he presented more of a goal threat from the United midfield in those days.

He laughed: 'I think Walter scored three goals in a 17-year playing career and I always wind him up about how prolific he was in front of goal. One of those goals was in the derby against Dundee at Dens Park when he was wearing a pair of white Hummel boots. George Fleming also had a pair but he was a cultured midfielder whereas Walter was more of a destructive player. Walter had a cheek wearing white boots but there is a famous photograph of him celebrating his goal against Dundee by kissing the boot!'

If Knox and Smith ever had any on-field shortcomings, they more than compensated for them with their coaching prowess. And Knox believes they both learned from one of the greats in McLean – even if it didn't always seem so at the time. 'I was taking the reserves at United before I went back up to Forfar. I'd suffered a pelvic injury which had ended my season and Wee Jim asked me to help out. I was only 28 and there could be some good players in the reserve team at that time, the likes of Frank Kopel, Paul Sturrock, John Holt and Alex Rennie.

'I remember going down to Ayr and losing 2-0. Wee Jim hauled me in and demanded to know "Did they not try?"

'I was only part-time at United and was still working for Bett, the Dundee housebuilder, to top up my money. I went in on the Monday night after the Saturday game and Wee Jim had all the players who'd played at Ayr lined up in the dressing room. He went round them all one by one and made me give my opinion on how they'd played against Ayr. It was the worst ever as I didn't want to drop anyone in it.'

Knox played a handful of games for Montrose after leaving United in 1976, but he was soon lured back across Angus to Forfar. It would prove to be a move which would define his career and set him on the path to dugout success. He'd have problems at Aberdeen, Manchester United, Rangers and Everton – but not the ones the rookie gaffer would encounter in those early days back at Station Park. 'I was playing with Kenny Cameron at Montrose when I got the chance to take the manager's job at Forfar. We had a friendly game against Arbroath and news of my appointment had been announced in the *Dundee Courier*.

'When I arrived at the ground, we didn't have enough players to make up a team and I had to borrow some from Arbroath. I couldn't understand where they all were so I got all their telephone numbers from the club secretary, Jimmy Robertson. When I enquired with one player about his no-show, he said, "Aye, I saw in the paper you'd got the job but I didn't think you'd give me a game!"

'We had an equally sparse attendance at training one night shortly after I started and I had to go through the phone-round again. One lad told me, "Sorry, I couldn't make it – I had tickets for The Buzzcocks". It was the original "Never Mind The Buzzcocks" moment.

'I can't remember the names of these players because, as I'm sure you can imagine, they didn't last long.

'That was the way of it in part-time football at the time, and it was even worse in the juniors when I tried to look there for new players. I'd been tipped off about an exciting young player at one of the Fife Junior teams. Sure enough, I quite liked the look of him. I agreed a deal with his club and started negotiations with him. We could offer him a tenner a week and the chance to put one foot in the professional game. I told him we trained every Tuesday and Thursday night but if we had a game on a Wednesday then we'd only train on a Monday. He said the Tuesday night would be a deal-breaker because he played darts and dominoes in the pub with his pals on a Tuesday.

'I tried to reason with him that he was throwing away a great chance – but he said he'd rather throw arrows and he turned me down!'

Knox's personnel problems would continue as he tried to build a squad capable of challenging for promotion from the bottom tier of the Scottish game. 'We were playing a Tayside Reserve League game up at Pittodrie but we didn't have a fit goalkeeper. Kenny Dick was helping me at the club as my assistant manager. I told him I'd seen this young keeper at a local junior club and sent Kenny to bring him along as a trialist.

'We all travelled to those games by car and just met up at the grounds. When we reached Pittodrie, this stranger got out of one of the cars. I asked Kenny who he was. Kenny said it was the keeper I'd recommended – but I'd never seen this lad before. It turned out Kenny had brought the wrong keeper from the juniors.

'The injury situation was so bad that I was playing centre-half in front of this lad. We were getting humped 3-0 at half-time. I said to him, "Right, if I'm heading back towards you just stay in your goal and I'll pass it back." In those days, keepers could still pick up pass backs. Then I said to him, "When balls are crossed into the box, just punch them away rather than trying to catch them."

'The lad looked straight at me and said, "You f**king think you know it all." I replied, "Maybe, but I do know that you'd not be playing if the right keeper had turned up. And you won't be playing again."

'Kenny Dick helped me so much in those days. He worked for the district council during the day but did so much for Forfar at night. He'd even carry the magic sponge – or he did until one day at Raith, when he needed to treat Kenny Payne, the brother of the former Dundee United player Graeme. He was lying face down on the pitch when Kenny ran over to him. Kenny turned him over to discover a gaping wound above an eye with blood spurting from it. As you can imagine, there wasn't the biggest crowd at the game and every one of them could hear Kenny Dick screeching, "Oh my God, he's cut!"'

Those early teething troubles almost convinced Knox to turn his back on coaching and devote all of his time to his full-time job as a surveyor. But Forfar chairman Sam Smith persuaded him to stick with it – and it was advice which he has never forgotten.

Archie said: "Sam Smith was a huge figure for me in the early days. I'd been at Montrose under Kenny Cameron and there was talk of me going to Forfar to work with Jerry Kerr. I wasn't sure about it but Jerry left Forfar and I was offered the chance to take charge on my own. I was only 28.

'Sam kept me in football. He made sure I didn't have to deal with the committee, other than attending the occasional board meeting. Sam was in charge. In fact, he'd have been perfect for one of the big jobs at the SFA never mind Forfar Athletic. He knew football. He was an auctioneer and had farms in the Forfar area, but he'd played for the club and played for St Mirren as well.

'When I took over at Forfar, I was raw. I'd coached under Jim McLean and I thought his methods of management were the way it should be done. We lost 4-1 at Brechin on a Tuesday night and I went to see Sam the next day. I said that I just couldn't see any improvement and I wanted to call it a day. Sam asked me to have a rethink and said we could get over one defeat. He said the club was going well and we'd be able to turn round the team. He talked me out of quitting. If he'd not done that, my career would have been history.

'I was working as an estimator at Bett. I'd have stayed there – and I shudder at the thought. If every club nowadays had a chairman like Sam, football would be in a better place. But I was lucky with many of the chairmen that I had, the likes of Dick Donald at Aberdeen and David Murray at Rangers.'

Knox even took Forfar to play Guelph Oaks, a team coached by Sam Smith's son, Graham, in Ontario, Canada. Almost 2,000 fans filed into Alumni Stadium on the University of Guelph campus to watch the 'soccer' match. Graham Smith recalled: 'Forfar had a successful three-game tour, including beating Guelph Oaks 3-0.

'Archie turned Forfar around. All they were playing for before he arrived was whether they'd be bottom or second-bottom of the old Second Division. He turned them around to be a team that challenged.'

They challenged for league and cup honours, winning the 1978/79 Forfarshire Cup final against Dundee at Station Park.

Knox recalled: 'We were winning 2-1 in the Cup final with about ten or 12 minutes still to play. Forfar's club secretary, Jimmy Robertson, came on the tannoy and announced, "The cup will be presented to Forfar immediately after the final whistle."

'I couldn't believe it – talk about putting pressure on ourselves! Luckily, we held on and we did indeed get the cup.'

That cup win came just a season after Forfar's greatest night, a League Cup semi-final classic against Rangers at Hampden. Rangers, who would go on to win their second Treble in three seasons under Jock Wallace, led through Derek Johnstone's opener. But goals from Kenny Brown and Brian Rankin turned the tie on its head and threatened to propel the Loons to their first-ever major final.

Rangers substitute Derek Parlane bagged a late equaliser to send the semi-final to extra time as the injury-ravaged part-timers began to tire. Alex MacDonald scored before Parlane's second goal took the tie away from Forfar and ended their dreams of a return to Hampden for the final. Johnstone, who would win two Player of the Year awards that year and go to Argentina for the World Cup finals with Ally MacLeod's Scotland squad, netted a fifth goal near the end of extra time to put an undeserved gloss on the final scoreline of 5-2.

Johnstone recalled: 'Forfar gave us a big scare. They were very unlucky not to reach the final. We didn't equalise until near the end of normal time. We battered them in extra time when our superior fitness came through.

'I remember Rankin taking the ball off Tommy McLean and running the full length of the pitch to score a fantastic goal.

'We were really up against it, even though we'd been playing well as a team for the majority of that season.

'Forfar have never played a better game in their history and it would have gone down as their greatest win. We'd been making jokes about Forfar bridies before the semi-final and I think we probably thought we'd turn up and win easily. Every Forfar player will probably still look back on the semi-final and think they should have won.

'Archie and I both come from the Dundee area but I didn't know him until I played against him when he was at St Mirren. Of course, I've got to know him so much better in the last few years after he joined Walter Smith at Rangers.'

Forfar would finish sixth in the Second Division that season, a fact which only serves to heighten the sense of achievement at their cup exploits.

The *Forfar Times* front-page headline of 2 March 1978, proclaimed: 'You did us proud'. Photographs of the goals by Brown and Rankin dominated page one, relegating to page three a story of the Kirrie 2nd Brownie Pack heading for Dundee to watch the newly-released *Star Wars* movie. The empire had struck back in the shape of those four late Rangers goals, but Knox can now look back with a sense of pride at simply pushing them so hard. 'We had hardly played a game for about seven weeks because there was a cold snap and all the pitches were frozen. I think the referee was Douglas Downie from Edinburgh. We had a goal disallowed and a stonewall penalty turned down. It was 1-1 at the time. We took the lead after the break and it was looking good for us until Derek Parlane scored right at the end.

'Their full-time training and the fact we hadn't played for so long caught up with us when the game went into extra time. We were a part-time team and we were running on empty. But we gave it a right good go and no one would have thought we could even have taken Rangers to extra-time.'

Alex Rae was a midfield mainstay for Forfar under Knox, having famously scored Partick Thistle's opening goal in their 4-1 League Cup final victory over Celtic in 1971.

By now working as a printer and playing part-time for the Loons, Rae – who'd take over as boss after the brief tenure of Knox's successor, Steve Murray – still believes they could have beaten Rangers. 'In the second half, Rangers had become very predictable in their attacks and I honestly felt we were going to make it,' he recalled. 'Only when they sent on Derek Parlane near the end and his aerial prowess began to cause us problems, did the game change.

'Archie was an old-school player. He was solid and he played it very simple. He and I would not get a game nowadays because we were players who liked to put the foot in in the days when tackles were allowed.

'I didn't know an awful lot about Archie until I went on a coaching course to Largs. I'd been freed by Cowdenbeath and went down to the coaching course for the first time. I must have done something right because Archie asked me if I fancied coming to train at Forfar. I was there for six years as a player, coach and manager, so it worked out great.

'The thing that impressed me about Archie from the very start was the way he took part in the full training. When I went flat out and did everything, I could hardly speak. But he was a player-manager who led from the front, did everything he asked the players to do and could still communicate his points. He ticked all the boxes for me as he was a straight-talking guy. He was very enthusiastic and very single-minded. He didn't leave any room for doubt about how he wanted to do things. If you weren't doing it the way he wanted it done, he would tell you. But we also had an arrangement where if I'd done anything he didn't like, he would tell me in private. I was at the tail end of my career and I didn't need to be told off in front of young lads. Archie understood that and I appreciated his style.'

So, too, did the Loons fans who had been starved of success for so many years but were now jousting with the likes of Rangers and Dundee in thrilling cup ties.

Among those supporters was Lord Lyell, a one-time Conservative Whip in the House of Lords and Honorary Patron of the Loons.

His path would cross with Knox's over four decades as he was also a shareholder in Everton.

Archie said: 'Lord Lyell had an estate at Kirriemuir and was a great supporter of Forfar for many years. He also supported Everton and he'd send postcards to me from his travels all over the world. He would come to many Everton games when I was at Goodison and we became firm friends. He actually took me into the Foreign Office one day to sort out a visa for me when I was visiting Alexei Mikhailichenko in Ukraine. Sadly, he passed away at the start of 2017. He had been a great friend and a terrific supporter of the two clubs which meant so much to him.'

David McGregor had also been a Forfar fan from the 1950s and would go on to serve the club as chairman and director. 'Archie is very much remembered as one of Forfar's all-time greats,' said McGregor. 'We have a lounge named after him at Station Park. He came back recently for a speaking engagement and the event sold out inside a day. He is so popular in these parts. Archie has never forgotten his roots and there have been plenty of Forfar folk, myself included, who have enjoyed days out at Old Trafford and Goodison over the years.

'When he first came to Forfar as a player in the mid-60s, he became part of one of our most successful sides since the War. By the time he came back a few years later, we were on our uppers again. But he gave us some great times. He lifted the whole place but I still kid him on to this day that we needed to bring in Doug Houston before we actually won something – the Second Division title in 1983/84!

'The League Cup semi-final against Rangers had originally been scheduled for November 1977 but it was frosted off in the days before Hampden had undersoil heating. It was eventually played on a Monday night in February 1978, but that caused problems for us in terms of injuries. We were already short at the back then we lost Alex Brash to an injury against Stenhousemuir on the Saturday. It was a full-scale defensive crisis but Archie stepped in at centre-half alongside Kenny Brown for the game. Kenny scored the equaliser and Brian Rankin put us ahead with a fine run and shot past Stewart Kennedy, who would be playing for us two years later.'

Knox's place in the pantheon of great Forfar bosses was assured by that run to the semi-final and the Forfarshire Cup victory over Dundee.

Houston would later take the Loons out of the bottom tier before, in more recent times, promotions and cup shocks have been achieved by Dick Campbell.

Knox and Campbell have been close friends since they were thrown together at Dundee United almost half a century ago. And they still argue over whose name should take pride of place at Station Park. Campbell said: 'I signed for Dundee United in 1970. I could have gone to Leeds or Liverpool – but they didn't want me! I moved into a house off Ballinard Road in Dundee. There must have been about a dozen of us in there. I was still only 15. It became very clear very quickly that Archie ran the place. He must have been 21 but he didn't let anyone slacken off.

'He is a great man, one of my closest friends, and he is also a great football man. He deserves great credit for all his achievements in the game.

'I wind him up by telling him that I won a proper trophy when I was Forfar manager, which was more than he achieved. I don't count that Forfarshire Cup! I had eight years at Forfar and when I arrived there were three Portakabins at Station Park – named after club legends Stewart Kennedy, Ian McPhee and Archie Knox.

'When we took Forfar up from League Two in 2010, I was still at the ground and I got a telephone call from Spain. Archie's voice came over the line, saying, "Don't get too confident – you might have won promotion but you still don't have a Portakabin named after you!"'

Unsurprisingly, Knox again had the final word when Campbell's side finally achieved a mark of revenge for Forfar over Rangers in a cup competition.

Knox said: 'When Forfar beat Rangers in the League Cup in 2013, I phoned Dick again. I said, "Never mind a Portakabin, it'll be The Sir Dick Campbell Stand at Station Park now".'

CHAPTER FIFTEEN

FISTFIGHT WITH A COWBOY AT THE DENS CORRAL

SO, TEDDY SCOTT was right. Someone did come calling for Archie Knox. Dundee offered him a route back to frontline management. And this time in the Premier League. Going toe to toe with the Old Firm, squaring up to Jim McLean. Clashing directly with Alex Ferguson and the Aberdeen team he'd just left behind. Walking in the footsteps of Bob Shankly more than two decades after he'd worshipped the Dark Blues' title winners. This was too good an opportunity to pass up. The chance to boss his boyhood heroes and perhaps bring back a touch of the glory he'd witnessed as a wide-eyed kid on the terraces at Dens Park.

It was never going to be an easy task. Knox knew he'd have a battle on his hands when he returned to the club in 1983. He just didn't expect to have a bare-knuckle scrap with a captain called 'Cowboy'. Jim Duffy, who played at the back for Dundee under Knox and would later become manager, recalled the square-go between the boss and John 'Cowboy' McCormack. 'There was an infamous fight between Archie and Cowboy. I don't mean a bit of pushing, shoving and arguing – I mean a proper fight. This was manager versus captain. They were punching each other, wrestling with each other, pinning each other down. A bona fide fight.

'We were playing Celtic that night and I think it had all started when Cowboy was told he'd be on the bench. To Archie's great credit, when we got to Celtic Park he named the team and then named the subs with John among them.

'He said, "If it takes a fight to clear the air, so be it." He never looked at John differently, treated him differently or ostracised him – it was as if nothing had ever happened. It's testament to the guy Archie is – he just wanted what was best for the team.'

McCormack recalls the rumble but also remembers the background to one of Dens Park's greatest scraps. 'Archie signed me from St Mirren but I knew him before then from coaching courses. He was robust, shall we say. He liked winners, people he could rely on to give their all. Don't get me wrong, he brought in good players too and he built a team at Dundee.

'I'd been having problems with a knee. I'd had operations on it but I was struggling. My wife wanted back down the road to the Glasgow area because we felt I might just have a couple of years left playing with the state of my knee. Archie reluctantly agreed to speak to the board about my future and they accepted my wishes to go.

'I was back in the team to face Celtic in the Scottish Cup at Dens. I played well and, when I came off, Archie told me how well I'd done. The replay was on the Wednesday night. We came in for a loosener before the game and Archie named the team. I wasn't in it. I couldn't believe it, especially after all the praise I'd received after the first game. I followed him out of the door into the corridor and asked what was going on. He told me I wanted to leave so it was either going to be a case of me taking the piss out of him or him taking the piss out of me. I just lost it and the next thing I knew we were rolling around on the floor outside the dressing room. The boys must have heard the noise and wee Albert Kidd opened the door to see what was going on. He didn't try to interrupt, he just said, "Give him one for me" and went back inside!'

Knox said: 'He had a proper swing and a proper connection as well. He caught me with the first punch and it was a dull one. I was still jabbing as I was going down. The irony was that there were injuries in the squad and we ended up having to put him on the bench.

'News travels fast in football. Walter Smith was down the road at Tannadice and had heard about it within an hour. But, amazingly, it never got to the newspapers.'

Maybe it wasn't so surprising that news of the dust-up travelled along the street to United's home ground. After all, Jocky Scott – Knox's No.2 and a Dundee legend who'd later have three spells as boss in his own right – was quickly informed of the rumpus and it was the talk of the place.

Scott said: 'After training, I'd run the first-team players back to Dens and then return for the younger lads and the kit. The day of the Celtic game, Archie had ended training a bit early so I was charging about trying to get everyone back. By the time I'd arrived back at Dens with the younger lads, I was confronted at the door by Audrey the cleaner. She was distraught. She said, "Jocky, you need to help – the manager has been rolling about on the floor with one of the players!"

'I'd missed it all. But when I went into the manager's office, Archie was behind his desk with a bruise under his eye. I took one look at him and just burst out laughing. Then he burst out laughing and said, "I don't think he liked being left out of the team".'

Most witnesses to Knox's three-year spell as boss at Dens tell the same story. They all credit him with adding character in the dressing room and quality on the pitch. In the former camp were the likes of Cowboy and John Brown, in the latter were players with the skills of Robert Connor and Stuart Rafferty. This was at a time when Aberdeen and Dundee United were in the midst of unprecedented success at home and abroad. Celtic were still fighting on every front while Rangers were regrouping and poised to kick-start the Graeme Souness revolution. Competition for places at the top end of the Premier League was as fierce as it has ever been – even to this day. But Dundee fought their corner under a boss who would try everything to squeeze an extra ounce from his players.

Brown, who would later be a cornerstone of Rangers' Nine in a Row success with Knox, recalled: 'When I signed for Dundee, I'd had six knee operations by the age of 22 and I'd had all of my cartilage taken out. Signing for Dundee and having the platform to play in the Premier League with the likes of Connor, Rafferty, Duffy and McCormack was terrific.

'Archie's training was great. I'd been a welder and come from part-time football at Hamilton, so this was terrific. We went to Seattle, Calgary and Portland on an end-of-season trip not too long after I had signed for Dundee. Jocky Scott had played in Seattle and it was something to do with that link-up. Archie let the boys enjoy themselves and we had a right few drinks. But when it came to game time, he was enormously competitive and warned us it wasn't a holiday.

'It was a real eye-opener for me, the first time I'd had a real sight of the competitive streak which Archie possesses.

'We went to Germany one pre-season, too. Jocky had stayed at home with the reserves, so Archie and Eric Ferguson were with us. Archie had to go home after a bereavement, so a pal of his – the German agent who had arranged the trip – stepped in to help out.

'Of course, the boys just took advantage and had a couple of big nights out when Archie was back home in Scotland. Everyone was sworn to secrecy and, when Archie came back, he told us he'd heard how well we'd trained and how well we'd behaved. He said he'd reward us with a night out. On one hand, we were thrilled to have got away with it but, on the other, another night out was the last thing we needed. Once we'd had a couple of beers, we were feeling no pain and I think most of us finally fell into our beds at 2 a.m. The next thing we knew – at 6 a.m. – Archie was banging on all of our bedroom doors and ordering us to be downstairs ready to train in five minutes. He'd known all along what we'd been up to and this was our punishment. He ran us into the ground and I've never spewed so much in my life.'

Brown, like Duffy and Scott, would later manage the club – and brought back Knox as a scout during that spell. But he remembers the end of Knox's period in charge, at the conclusion of the 1985/86 season, as a sad day for Dundee. 'Archie had the nucleus of a decent squad which was punching above its weight and looking to grab one of the European spots.

'One of my best memories from my playing career was actually scoring a hat-trick against Rangers in November 1985 at Dens Park. Ally McCoist got Rangers' goals in a 3-2 Dundee win. Jock Wallace was the Rangers manager at the time and I remember thinking that by getting a few goals he might want to sign me. That never materialised but it was a still a proud moment scoring three goals against a side that had the likes of Bobby Russell, Davie Cooper, Ted McMinn and Coisty in it. I was playing in midfield back then and in the game we had Tosh McKinlay sent off when the score was 0-0. For about 70 minutes, we were down to ten men so that made the result even more special. For a change I got the match ball at the final whistle and Coisty didn't!

'But Archie would probably admit that the bank manager was controlling the club and he had to sell any decent player who came along. I think he probably realised he had taken Dundee as far as he could in the circumstances and felt a return to Aberdeen was the right thing for him.'

It was great while it lasted, with two sixth-place finishes in the league, one cup semi-final – against Fergie's Aberdeen – and three more quarter-finals in his three seasons at the helm.

Strachan's late clincher at Tynecastle in the 1984 Scottish Cup semi would send the Dons towards their third consecutive Cup win, with Knox having been involved in the first two.

Knox recalled: 'We'd brought the likes of Robert Connor, John Brown and Stuart Rafferty to Dundee and the team was good enough to kick on. But I always felt we'd reach a certain level and the club would allow those good players to be sold on. As it turned out, we signed Connor for Aberdeen after I went back there. Brown went to Rangers and that team did split up.

'I'd watched Brown play for Hamilton against Dundee United a few weeks before we took him to Dens. He was a hardy boy and could play centre-half, left-back or in the middle of the park. I liked the look of him. But he failed the medical when he first came to Dundee. The medical people were worried about the cartilage – or the lack of it – in his knees. He'd had cartilage ops at 18 or 19 and Eric Ferguson told me he'd only last for two or three more years and he'd be done. I told Eric, "We probably won't be here in two or three years' time so let's just sign and worry about that later."

'He was playing regularly for Hamilton but he had failed a medical at Hearts. He seemed to have a history of it. When he signed for Rangers, they were worried about his heart. But it turned out that his heart rate wouldn't come down simply because he was so excited to be signing for his boyhood idols.'

Excitement was growing around Dens in the mid-80s with the competitive streak of Knox and Scott driving them on. Scott still laughs when he recalls some of the scrapes they managed to get into. And the way Knox, like Fergie at Aberdeen, hated to lose. 'I'd take the kids for training in the afternoons and this day

Archie wanted a game of five-a-side behind the goals at Dens. I picked my side and he picked his side. I asked how long he wanted to play and he said half an hour. At the end of the half-hour, my team was winning and I shouted for time up. But he wanted another half-hour of extra time. My team was still winning, so he announced the next goal would be the winner. Of course, my team scored it. He was going daft at the boys in his team. He pointed to the floodlight pylons and told them to climb up them and stay there until they were told to come back down!

'But he was great for the club. For me, it was brilliant to have someone of Archie's experience and knowledge. He also signed some very good players for small fees. He brought in half a dozen players who improved the team, and he showed a professionalism which hadn't been there before.'

Captain Cowboy was among that number and warmly remembers his time under Knox at Dens – fistfight notwithstanding. 'I remember playing a friendly at Montrose and Archie ranting at half-time. He'd just signed Stewart Forsyth from Arbroath and was having a right blast at him. He shouted, "You've got the attitude of a guinea pig."

'I said, "Hold on a minute, where did that one come from?"

'He was raging and said, "And as for you . . ." All of a sudden, I was on the receiving end. But it had taken the heat off poor Stewart, who was shivering in his boots. There were times when it was hard not to laugh in the middle of Archie's rants.'

Forsyth wasn't the only newcomer to feel the wrath of Knox if they didn't instantly reach his high standards. Duffy recalled: 'Archie was very demanding and his training was tough. I'd only been at Dundee for a couple of weeks when we went to Germany for a pre-season trip. Archie named me as captain for a friendly against Eintracht Frankfurt and I thought I played quite well. After the game, he came in and went round the players one by one giving them both barrels. He said to me, "Captain? You couldn't captain the Boy Scouts – that was money down the drain."

'That was an eye-opener for me that Archie didn't suffer fools gladly.

'Early that season our keeper, Tam Carson, made a mistake which cost us. I think he'd cost the club £50,000 from Dumbarton. In the middle of his after-match rant, Archie told Tam, "I'd have been better driving down Clepington Road [the big street up from Dens] throwing fifty grand out of the car window rather than wasting it on you." He was waving his arms round gesturing as if he was actually chucking the notes in the air. We were desperately trying not to laugh!'

Duffy, who has enjoyed a fine career as a boss in his own right, was a great admirer of the job Knox did at Dens. 'Archie's big strength was team-building – and I don't mean days out to go-karting or ten-pin bowling. I mean actually building a team. He knew how to structure the team and brought in some big characters like Cowboy, John Brown and me. He brought in talented lads like Robert Connor and Stuart Rafferty. He brought through youngsters like Colin Hendry, Tosh McKinlay and Rab Shannon. He liked big characters and you couldn't be a shrinking violet and play for Archie. You had to be able to handle the expectations. The younger boys at the club had chores to do – and they had to do them properly. They cleaned the boots, they cleaned the dressing rooms, they cleaned the bath and they cleaned the showers. Even the grout between the tiles had to be clean. Archie had high standards and, personally, I never had a problem with that.

'He cracked up with Cowboy at half-time in one game and told him he was coming off. Cowboy took off his jersey and threw it down in anger. When he'd finished his teamtalk and told us to go back out, we realised that he'd not sent anyone on in his place. We were going out with ten men – then he looked at Cowboy and said, "What are you doing still sitting there?"

'Cowboy replied, "You told me to come off."

'But Archie said, "Get that jersey back on and get back out there."

'He knew he'd get the perfect response from Cowboy and that he'd go out and run through brick walls for him. Archie had picked on the toughest guy in the team knowing he'd get a response, not only from him but from the rest of us as well.

'Archie would have confrontations with John Brown or me, too. He never went over the top but he knew which buttons to press to get the reaction he desired. He knew we'd not throw the toys out of the pram, we'd just show more determination to improve things. He knew which players he could go to and flick their switch and he also knew which players to leave alone.'

Albert Kidd, scorer of the goals which famously denied Hearts the league title on the final day of the 1985/86 season, had his own share of run-ins with Knox. 'I really liked Archie. After Don Mackay left Dens, there was a feeling that the job would go to either Walter Smith – who was still assistant manager at Dundee United – or Archie.

'Archie got the job and inherited no fewer than 44 full-time players. It is incredible to look back and remember it.

'I knew Archie because he'd coached St Columba's Boys' Club in Dundee where I'd played with Bobby Glennie. Archie was a shouter. I remember coming home from Australia years later and Archie inviting me to go to Ibrox to see him and Davie Dodds, another pal from Dundee who was on the backroom team at Rangers. I asked Archie if the veins still stuck out in his neck when he screamed at the players, the way they did in the good old days. He told me he'd mellowed. He said to get the best out of world-class talents like Paul Gascoigne and Brian Laudrup, you had to make sure they felt good about themselves. I told him he should have tried that approach with me and the boys at Dundee and he might have got more out of us!

'To be fair, he brought in some really talented players like Rafferty and Connor. He kept Dundee sixth in the Premier League, which was a great achievement considering they were only behind Celtic, Rangers and those strong Aberdeen and Dundee United teams.

'I remember Archie pulled me one Friday and said he wanted to use me at outside-left against Celtic the next day. He talked me through matching the runs of Danny McGrain, and he urged me to force him back and get crosses into the Celtic box with my left foot. The next day, we went for the pre-match meal in Dundee and Archie named the team. I wasn't in it. I tried to draw his attention to this as I assumed it was a mistake. He named the subs – and I wasn't among them either.

'I just flipped. He was starting his teamtalk but I just got up and walked out. My parents lived fairly close to Dens and I went up to their house to tell my dad the story. On the Monday, Archie listed me to play with the youth team at East Fife. I was the club's record signing at the time – a record I'd held for five or six years. I was also fined a week's wages for my outburst. But I wasn't going to accept that and I went to Tony Higgins at the players' union. Tony told me that he could probably get me the money back but the cost would be a seat in the stand for the rest of the season.

'The next thing I knew I was being listed to play in the reserves away to Morton down at Cappielow. Jocky took the reserves and I remember the bus stopping in Glasgow so Archie could get off and watch a player in the Old Firm reserve match. When we reached Greenock, Jocky told me I was on the bench. The bench. For the reserves! I went to see Archie on the Friday and said, "Look, it appears to me there's only going to be one winner here."

'He said, "You're damn tootin." I accepted the fine and was stuck back into the first team the following day. I scored two goals but the moral of the story was that players were never going to win an argument with Archie. And he still owes me that week's wages.

'I've lived in Australia for a few years now and work in the media. I've even had Archie as a guest on my radio show in Adelaide and the chat was terrific.'

Midfield maestro Connor was plucked from Ayr United in the old First Division and transformed into a player who'd later star for Aberdeen and Scotland. He, too, recalls crazy days at Dens but believes Knox should be credited enormously for aiding his development. 'Archie was a huge influence on my career but if I could sum him up in one word it would be "intimidating". To be fair, there were quite a few managers around at the time who had a similar style – the likes of Alex Ferguson and Jim McLean. I'd come to Dundee from Ayr where my manager had been Willie McLean, Jim's brother and a man best described as "crabbit". He'd blow his top all the time, but I think the experience of working under him helped me when Archie took me to Dens.

'Archie had that big, square jaw and always seemed to be in your face. He was like that because he was passionate – but he was also fair.

'I often thought back to those days when I saw Fergie in his 70s on the touchline at Manchester United games. I'd wonder how a man of that age could get so worked up about decisions in a football game. But it was his passion, just as it was Archie's passion.

'Archie was the bad cop at Dens. He had Jocky Scott and Drew Jarvie there as the good cops. All three were brilliant coaches. I'd been part-time at Ayr and I couldn't believe the high standard of coaching from the three of them at Dundee.

'But Archie's passion almost spilled over one Christmas

when the reserves were playing a rearranged game at home to Dumbarton. The game had been moved to December 23 and, as the first team didn't have a game until New Year, he decided he wanted us all to play. The Glasgow-based lads, including myself, had been promised they'd be allowed home for Christmas and most of the wives and girlfriends had already gone down the road. We had a nightmare, the game ended 0-0 and Archie was going bananas. He ordered us in for training on Christmas Eve. The problem was that most of the lads had arranged to share cars down to Glasgow after the game and some of us didn't even have house keys as the wives had taken them.

'Cowboy was the captain and we sent him in to see Archie to ask him to relent. He said he was totally disgusted by the performance and made us sweat in the dressing room for ages before finally agreeing to Cowboy's request.

'I also remember a League Cup tie against Hamilton Accies on a quagmire of a pitch at the old Douglas Park in 1985. We were losing 2-1 in the dying seconds of extra time and the winner had the prize of Rangers in the next round. We got a penalty right at the death. I was the penalty taker at the time but I missed it and we missed the chance to go to a shoot-out. The final whistle went straight away and the next thing I knew Archie was over barging me with his shoulder. There were a few choice words but the ones I remember were the ones about me costing the club £50,000 from a tie against Rangers. Needless to say it was the last penalty I ever took for Dundee – my choice. But Archie was just a big character whose passion shone through.

'When I followed him to Aberdeen in 1986, I couldn't believe it when I was told Archie was the *good* cop. I remember John Hewitt pulling me to the side and telling me Fergie was the nutter and Archie was the calm one. I was terrified.

'I had fantastic times with Archie, especially at Dundee. He signed some real quality players for the club. He wanted more money to make signings to take Dundee that extra step but the directors wouldn't give him it and he ended up going back with Fergie at Aberdeen.'

The last chapter of Knox's Dundee story, though, was perhaps the most famous as they denied Hearts the championship and came within a whisker of European qualification themselves.

Knox recalled: 'There was an amazing list of possibilities on the final day of the 1985/86 season – and not just for the championship. Rangers were playing Motherwell and if we had bettered their result then Dundee would have qualified for Europe at Rangers' expense.

'I threw on Albert late in the game and, of course, he scored the two goals which denied Hearts the title. I think he won six Celtic Player of the Year awards that summer and he's dined out on the goals ever since.

'He's done really well for himself in Australia and actually interviewed me for a radio show he's involved with over there.

'He tells people that when he came back into the dressing room at Dens Park after the game, I said to him, "Albert son, what have you done?"

'I don't remember saying it but I think Albert has repeated the story so often over the last 30 years that even he believes it now!

'I do remember handing big Colin Hendry his first start at centre-half in the game. He was only 20 and he didn't give Sandy Clark a kick.'

Kidd remains adamant that his version of events is the correct one, insisting: 'Archie came in and said, "F*** sake, Albert – what have you done?" I wasn't sure whether he was praising me or the opposite. He was sitting down – which was unusual in itself in the dressing room – right opposite me.

'I asked him, "Are you not happy?" But it was such an unbelievable way for things to pan out that everyone was just stunned.'

CHAPTER SIXTEEN

EUSEBIO, BROWN AND A WHEELCHAIR BY THE SEASIDE

IF FIRST impressions truly do last, it's a real surprise that Archie Knox and Craig Brown ever worked together.

The pair, of course, operated hand in hand with the Scotland national team and, later in their careers, at Motherwell and Aberdeen. The veteran coaches were christened 'Jack and Victor' in deference to the ageing characters in the hit TV comedy *Still Game*. But they were young scufflers when their paths first crossed – with Brown seething at the on-field tactics of Knox.

Brown said: 'I was manager of Clyde. Sean Sweeney was playing up front for us and clashed with Archie, who was player-manager of Forfar at the time. The pair of them hit the deck. Archie got up quicker and I was sure I saw him put his studs onto Sweeney's ear and twist them.

'I went daft and ran onto the pitch. I had my Clyde blazer on but I ran after Knox and wanted to get at him. I was a bit of a hothead when I was younger and although Knox could probably have turned and planted me, I found myself chasing him in the centre circle.

'Billy McNeill was in the stand watching the game and said it was the funniest thing he'd ever seen in football. Billy had been Clyde manager before me – he actually got me the job – and always had a fondness for the club. He'd gone to Aberdeen but had come down to Forfar to watch his old team. I think he enjoyed my run more than he enjoyed the game!'

After unfortunate beginnings, a friendship grew between Knox and Brown as their paths crossed time and again at the SFA's coaching courses at Largs. The likes of Jose Mourinho, Andre Villas-Boas and Pedro Caixinha would come from abroad to learn under what became known – and not always in a complimentary way – as 'The Largs Mafia'. But Knox and Brown remain fiercely loyal to the programme on the Ayrshire coast, even if the former wasn't always on the winning side in the extra-curricular activities.

Brown recalled: 'When I was manager of Scotland, I had seen a disabled football team when I was out in Russia to watch their national team before we played them in a qualifier. I was so taken by the wheelchair football that I demanded the SFA give each club in the country a grant to improve their facilities. I got involved with Richard Brickley, who is based in Glenrothes and is the doyen of disabled sport in Scotland. I asked him if he'd bring one of the wheelchair teams to Largs so the managers could see how good they were. They were all there – Knox, Alex Ferguson, Walter Smith, David Moyes, the late, great Tommy Burns, Graeme Souness, Gordon Strachan, Roy Aitken, the three crabbit McLeans and Jimmy Calderwood in the days when he was still white!

'Richard said the kids were starstruck at seeing so many big names and asked if any of them would fancy playing against them. We managed to find six wheelchairs for a six-a-side game and I picked our team. I had Bryan Gunn in goal and I think Smith, Ferguson and Burns, among others, wanted to play. I ended up with one spare chair so I chose Knox. Looking back, it might not have been my best selection decision. After five minutes, my team was 3-0 down. One wee lad from Castlemilk had scored all three goals for them. Every time he scored, he wheeled round to Knox and shouted, "How do you like that you big bastard?"

'Archie was getting angrier and angrier and muttered something along the lines of, "I'll do you, son."

'I don't think the boy thought he was serious but after this had happened another couple of times, Archie cemented him from the side. Both wheelchairs toppled over and the two of them were sent sprawling across the floor in the gym we were using. To be fair, Archie immediately got up and apologised and helped the lad back into his wheelchair before picking up his own chair.

'The game restarted but very quickly Archie was shouting over to me that he'd have to come off as he was struggling. He was moaning that his arms were knackered and he was toiling to keep up with the rest of the opposition. The wee man grinned and shouted over to me, "No wonder he's knackered – I pulled on his brakes when he knocked me out of my chair".'

Few folk managed to put the brakes on Knox during his coaching career, not even the great Portuguese superstar Eusebio. Brown said: 'Andy Roxburgh brought Eusebio to Largs to teach us the importance of free-kicks. We had a great time with him. We ended up playing against some of the students. I think we had a team involving myself, Archie, Alex Ferguson, Paul Sturrock, Frank Coulston and others. I think it was 2-2 when we got a penalty near the end. Would you believe Knox pushed Eusebio out the way to take it? And he missed it! But Eusebio loved him and loved the fun we all had together.'

It goes without saying that Knox's version of events differs slightly from that of Brown – and he has witness statements to back him up!

Knox said: 'We had some great times in Largs. We had the great Eusebio down at one stage to put on a session for the coaches. He hardly spoke a word of English but was showing us a set-piece routine which involved targeting a defender in the wall who looked the most scared. Eusebio tried to tell us that if we targeted the most frightened player then he'd be the most likely to dodge out the way of your free-kick. Brown and I weren't convinced but I was selected to try it out. I just blasted the ball and, sure enough, a lad moved out of the way and it flew into the top corner. Eusebio was suitably impressed that I'd taken his lesson on board. Brown still tries to tell a different version of events so I don't get the credit!'

Frank Coulston, a doyen of the SFA courses and a close pal of Knox and Brown to this day, prefers Archie's story. Coulston, a League Cup winner with Partick Thistle in 1971, said: 'Archie and Walter Smith first came down to the course at Largs when they were young players at Dundee United. They were naturals from the start and showed great promise, even though they were still young men in their 20s. They didn't hit the headlines as players, although they did underestimate their own quality, but they were outstanding coaches.

'There was always great camaraderie at Largs, going back to when Wilson Humphries – who was Archie's manager at St Mirren for a time – was there. Archie and Walter later came back as staff coaches, even though they'd moved on to bigger roles at Aberdeen and Dundee United. In even later days, they were at Manchester United and Rangers – two of the most successful clubs in the country at that time – but always came back. They were great to socialise with, they still are, and had great humour. But they were serious when they got onto the pitch.

'I remember Archie going to the airport to collect a young Jose Mourinho when he came to study for his coaching badges. He was there with Eusebio, too, and the Portuguese link has brought Andre Villas-Boas and Pedro Caixinha to Largs. And despite what Broon says, he *did* score that day when he pushed Eusebio out of the way. One of our pals, Jim McSherry, still has the photo of Archie and the rest of us with Eusebio. It's a great memory.'

Knox added: 'We had some great laughs at Largs and made friendships which have lasted a lifetime. We had big names from overseas but we also had some of the best managers in Scottish football. John Lambie, who had great success with Falkirk, Hamilton and Partick, used to come down to Largs. He'd have us in stitches – and not always intentionally. One day he was recalling playing for St Johnstone in Europe back in the day. He said, "I'm sure we were playing in Italy – aye, that's right, in Madrid".'

Brown and Knox were reunited when the former drafted in the latter as No.2 with the national team. Brown said: 'When I was playing at Dundee in the early Sixties, Archie was a supporter. When we won the league in 1962, he was at every home match. He was at Ibrox when we beat Rangers 5-1 and Alan Gilzean scored four. I was 21 and I didn't play often in the title-winning team. But I did play in a 0-0 draw against Celtic which was crucial to the championship.

'It was Bobby Lennox's first-ever game for Celtic and I bled his nose with my elbow. Archie was on the terraces as a 14-year-old supporter. Celtic had a great team with Pat Crerand and some of the lads who would go on to become Lisbon Lions. I was Man of the Match, but I think Archie would be even happier.

'It was more than 35 years later that we worked together with Scotland. I wanted someone I could trust when I lost Alex Miller to Liverpool – and I'd trust Archie with my life.

'It was strange for me when Archie joined me at first because he wanted to take all of the training sessions. Alex Ferguson and Walter Smith had left most of the training to him, but I'd tended to do most of it on my own. Archie said to me, "That's not your job," and I was quite pleased because I was having trouble with a knee and was limping about the place. His preparation and his training were meticulous and the boys loved it. He still has folders of every training session he's ever done.

'He's the most genuine, trustworthy man and, despite all those hardman stories, he's really just a big pussycat.

'When I was at Preston, I had a couple of spare rooms in my flat and Archie moved in while he was working for Bolton. He is the most sensitive, caring man – not the hard man everyone perceives him to be. You couldn't have that kind of popularity without having those qualities.

'When I decided to leave the Scotland job in 2001, Archie tried to talk me out of it. He reckoned the SFA wouldn't sack me and I should carry on. But I'd been eight years in the job, we hadn't qualified for the World Cup in Japan and South Korea – and I just felt people were fed up with me.'

Shortly after Brown's decision to quit Hampden, the Everton management team of Smith and Knox were shown the door at Goodison Park. It kick-started a remarkable decade in which he would work for no fewer than seven different clubs while also enjoying a brief return to Hampden as Scotland youth team supremo. Long-time pal Jimmy Bone wasn't surprised that he landed so many jobs, given the high regard in which he's held within the game. Bone, a former Scotland striker, said: 'Archie's enthusiasm always shone through and so did his charisma. I'd watch some of his sessions from the side of the pitch at Largs. He could have players going in all different directions and he'd be standing in the middle in total control of it all.

'He would take time out with young coaches, too, to explain things to them. He could lavish praise on them, but could also deliver a kick up the arse.'

Unfortunately, Knox wouldn't be immune to receiving a kick up the arse in the next few years with his Everton dismissal proving the first of many such setbacks in England.

He would assist former Aberdeen strikers Mark McGhee and Eric Black after they were handed control of Millwall and Coventry City respectively.

And Knox remains astonished at the manner of their sacking from both clubs, at a time when results were more than respectable.

He said: 'I'd been involved in some great derbies – Dundee United v Dundee, Aberdeen versus both Dundee sides, the Old Firm game and United versus City in Manchester. The Merseyside derby was good, too, but the wildest of them all was Millwall against West Ham – especially at Upton Park. We went there with Mark McGhee. West Ham had the statue of their three World Cup winners from 1966 – Geoff Hurst, Martin Peters and Bobby Moore – outside the ground. But they had to barricade it before the derby to prevent it from being attacked. It was that kind of game.

'There was always trouble at the game. Even travelling from the hotel to the stadium required a police escort for the Millwall team bus.

'Mark had been at the New Den for around three years and asked me to go down to help after his assistant, Ray Harford, took ill. Ray had been at Kenny Dalglish's side when Blackburn Rovers won the Premier League title in 1995 but he tragically passed away.

'I had been at Millwall for about three months and the team was doing well at the top end of the Championship. We had a decent team – Tony Warner, who'd been at Celtic and Aberdeen, and Kevin Muscat, who'd been at Rangers. Dennis Wise and Tim Cahill were in the midfield and Neil Harris, who'd go on to manage the club, was up front.

'Craig Brown and Billy Davies brought Preston North End down to the New Den in October 2003 and managed to win 1-0.

Craig and Billy came in for a drink after the game and we were sitting in Mark's office when the chairman, Theo Paphitis, stuck his head round the door. People now know him from *Dragons' Den* on TV. At that time, he had big ambitions for Millwall and wanted to speak to Mark. Mark said he was still having a drink with Craig and would pop upstairs in a bit – but the chairman was insistent. Craig and Billy headed off and about 90 minutes had passed when Mark came back into the room and asked if there were any beers left. I said, "Yes," and he said, "Right, let's take them back to the flat and drown our sorrows." In those days, we shared a place in Bromley.

'I said, "It's hardly a case of drowning sorrows – we've only lost 1-0."

'Mark said, "I know, but we've still been sacked!".

'We went back and sank the rest of the beers. In the morning, about seven o'clock, Mark brought me a cup of tea into my bedroom. I said, "Can we just go over what happened at the club last night?"

'Mark said, "It's simple – we've been sacked."

'I replied, "Well, I know the chairman sacked you – but did he mention he was sacking your assistant as well?!?"

'Mark said, "It's all your fault anyway." I'd only been there for three months.'

McGhee, who has worked most recently as assistant to Scotland manager Gordon Strachan, wasn't quite as shocked at his Den departure. 'I think Theo was quite restless at that time as he was thinking about leaving Millwall. He wanted to exert his influence more and more and our relationship was becoming an increasingly anxious one. I never felt it was a real problem because Theo was the best chairman I ever had – and I've had a few good ones.

'I had sensed for a while time was running out for me at Millwall. I knew Theo wanted to make changes. We'd been through a lot together. We'd been promoted, lost a play-off and witnessed the riot against Birmingham when the police wanted to shut the place. Theo and I had to fight to keep the place open. But there were many more problems aside from that. ITV Digital went down and caused financial issues for many of the clubs outside the top flight.

'Of course, we lost Ray Harford as well which was terrible. That's when I brought Archie in. I felt it would be better to appoint someone with experience to bridge the gap until we saw how it all shook down. I knew Archie was very good at his job and I knew he would hit the ground running when he came here. It all came to a head that night after we lost to Preston and I went upstairs to have a long chat with the chairman. I told him if there were things he wanted to go and do at the club then maybe it was time to let me go. I'd been at the club for three and a half years, we'd been promoted and had then been beaten in the play-offs to go up again. I was satisfied my time was up, we shook hands and went our separate ways. And I went back downstairs to tell Archie and gather up a few beers.

'I said, "Right, we're out of here." I think he thought I meant we were going home, but I had to tell him we were out of there for good.

'I remember Walter Smith phoning him as soon as the news of our departure broke and telling him he was a "jinx".'

There was more pain to come at Highfield Road as the same fate befell Black at the hands of an ambitious chairman. Knox recalled: 'Eric was placed in charge at Coventry when Gary McAllister stepped down to care for his wife, Denise, who tragically passed away. We went down to Gillingham for a game in the old Division One and won 5-2. We'd been 3-0 up and cruising, they got it back to 3-2 and then Gary McSheffrey and Richard Shaw scored late on to clinch the points. The next morning, Eric took a call to go and see the chairman. I thought they were going to hand him a new contract because he'd been doing well. But the chairman, Mike McGinnity, told him that we could have lost the game and he wasn't best pleased. Eric agreed that it could have gone the wrong way but said the players had done well to hold on and then score those goals at the end. Sadly, it wasn't enough and the chairman sacked him.

'The club was still at Highfield Road at the time – a big club, a good club. It's a shame to have watched them tumble down the divisions to the fourth tier of the English game.

'I remember going to Highfield Road with Everton when Gordon Strachan was Coventry manager. A boy jumped a barrier to get at Wee Gordon and we had to get him up the tunnel to safety. It was crazy.

'It was a real shame for both Mark and Eric, the way it ended for them at the two clubs. I'd like to see more Scottish managers, not less, get the chance to work in England. If you look at the Premier League in England and even the Championship clubs, it's nearly all foreign managers in charge at the moment. Some of the best managers ever have been Scots, going back to Shanks, Alex Ferguson, Walter Smith, and Jim McLean. A lot of them have made their mark down in England, so I don't see why more of our guys can't do the job now.'

Black, who has gone on to work for several top-flight clubs in England and most recently helped Southampton to the League Cup final, insists Knox was the obvious appointment as his assistant. Those days babysitting the Knox girls seemed a long way off when they were plotting success for the Sky Blues. Black said: 'I took Archie to Coventry as my assistant and he was different class. He was the ideal man for a young coach like me. It was great to have all that incredible knowledge sitting across the desk from you. I remember him talking me through a game at Walsall after they'd gone down to ten men. We went from 1-1 at half-time to a 5-2 win. Having that type of knowledge on your shoulder during games was fantastic.

'He could also put the fear of death in all of our players, even the big 6ft 4in Bosnian centre-half Mo Konjic. Some things hadn't changed!

'We averaged two points in every game during our time there and won six away games in a row, which was the best in the club's history. They still binned us, which was a disgrace.

'When I went into Coventry, I wanted to take charge of everything. I was checking what sugar went in the tea, what filling was in the sandwiches. I was trying to control everything. Two days in, Archie said, "Just one thing, Eric. What am I doing here, because you appear to be doing everything?"

'He was right – I was even going out early and putting out the cones. I ended up taking a step back, which was the right thing to do, and let Archie do the things he's good at.'

No one needed to tell Walter Smith about the things Knox was good at, hence his appointment as national youth teams coach by the SFA in July 2006. On the day of the appointment, the late SFA chief executive David Taylor said: 'Archie commands great respect from the players and other coaches. He has had a successful career to date and his ideas, enthusiasm, and organisational knowledge will be of great benefit to the work of the SFA.'

Smith, then in charge of the national team, added: 'Archie is an excellent appointment, as his experience and knowledge will be of considerable benefit to the young talent which is coming through the ranks today. The SFA is placing increasing emphasis on developing our age group international squads, and having Archie here will allow us to build on the considerable progress that has already been made.'

Looking back today, Smith added: 'It was an obvious move for me to take Archie into the Scotland set-up. But, like me, I think he found the circumstances of not having day-to-day contact with the team difficult to handle. Archie is not the type to be sitting behind a desk. He likes to be out on the pitch taking training and working.'

Knox was at Smith's side when Scotland savoured the rare high of winning an international tournament on foreign soil – the Kirin Cup in Japan in 2006. He also enjoyed success with a youth team at a competition in La Manga in Spain during his spell with the SFA. But a whispering campaign laid a portion of blame at the door of the SFA for 'losing' Glasgow-born James McCarthy to the Republic of Ireland. The criticism still irks Knox, who has sought to set the record straight over the Hamilton Accies kid who developed into an FA Cup winner with Wigan Athletic and £10 million star with Everton. Knox said: 'To suggest I was asked to watch McCarthy and deemed him not good enough is nonsense. The laddie and Billy Reid, who was his manager at Hamilton at the time, did articles in the paper saying Scotland hadn't shown interest in him and he was going to Ireland. That's his right.

'Ross Mathie, who was in charge of the Scotland Under-16s and 17s at the time, decided the boys in his team were as good as McCarthy. That's fair enough. But after they did the articles I went to see Billy and told him it was wrong to say we hadn't shown an interest. I urged Billy to tell the boy not to put all his eggs in one basket. We were happy for him to go and look at the Republic's set-up but we never closed the door for him or felt he wasn't good enough.

'He burst onto the scene for Hamilton but Ross decided to stick with the squad he had. No one at the SFA closed the door and maybe if James had been more patient he'd have got his chance with Scotland. People make outrageous claims about players as teenagers. It has always been that way and continues to be so. I have heard it with the likes of Billy Gilmour, the lad who has moved from Rangers to Chelsea. I just think it puts unnecessary pressure on the lads. But you can never tell if they'll make it. As I've said many times before, in my entire career there were only two I'd have put money on – Ryan Giggs and Wayne Rooney. I worked with David Beckham and Paul Scholes at 14 and 15 but would never have said for sure that they'd be top players. To be good enough, you have to stay quiet and prove yourself.'

CHAPTER SEVENTEEN

SNODDY AND BIG CHEERS

MANY YOUNG managers seek to copy the style of coaches they've enjoyed working under during their playing careers. In Archie Knox's case, they haven't just tried to emulate him – they've tended to employ him. Mark McGhee took him to Millwall in his hour of need and Eric Black lured him to Coventry City. Paul Ince would later hand him a job as his No.2 at Blackburn Rovers. Perhaps Knox's most colourful season working under one of his former players, though, was at Livingston with Richard Gough. Together they'd helped Rangers seal Nine in a Row and edge within 90 minutes of the first-ever Champions League final. But this was a wholly different challenge as they fought – all the way down to the final seconds of the campaign – to keep Livingston in the top flight.

Gough recalled: 'I played against Archie when I was a 17-year-old at Dundee United and he was still playing for Forfar Athletic. Jim McLean had us playing four games a week and we'd take on the Angus clubs in friendlies all the time. I think I smashed him at a corner kick. I couldn't miss that big jaw and that big bridie heid!

'Of course, we worked so well together at Rangers and Everton – and I wanted him by my side when I got a job as a manager. I was appointed Livingston manager on the same day Walter Smith was appointed Scotland manager in 2004. I wanted Archie as my assistant but feared he'd go with Walter. I was desperately hanging on for him.

'He called the day before I was confirmed in the job and told me he'd come with me. It was an enormous boost.'

A boost for Gough, a fillip for the ambitious club – and a real positive for a squad packed with emerging talent. Scotland winger Robert Snodgrass, now a £10 million English Premier League superstar at West Ham United, was among Livingston's exciting crop of kids at the time. Snodgrass recalled: 'When big names like Archie and Richard come in, there is respect straight away. Archie had a fear factor and he would take no nonsense. But, if you gave him everything, you would get it back. I was just a young boy coming through and I didn't want to cross him. He always put pressure on you to improve. He was a great coach. I'd been used to young coaches making their way in the game – the likes of Allan Preston, Paul Lambert and Richard. When Archie came onto the training ground, he had a presence and his coaching was great. He had a presence about him off the field, too.'

Knox's presence would be missed by rookie gaffer Gough after a rare touchline disagreement early in their partnership in West Lothian. Gough remembered: 'Having Archie was huge for me. I was going into something I'd never experienced before and he was the best. He's the best No.2 ever. Just look at the managers he worked with – he was trusted by two of the best of all time in Sir Alex Ferguson and Walter Smith.

'I remember my first day. I wanted to make a positive impression and get in early. I was in there at 7 a.m. – and Archie was already in the office sorting out training routines.

'Coming down the stretch that season, he was invaluable to me. But we didn't always see eye to eye. There was a game when I wanted to throw on Derek Lilley as an extra striker before half-time and really go for it. Archie wasn't convinced as he felt we'd be caught out at the back. I remember saying, "Let's go for it, if we're going to die let's die with our boots on."

'I also said, "I'm only playing Devil's Advocate," but Archie replied, "Devil's Advocate? You've only been a manager for two minutes – right, I'm going home."

'I said if that's how he felt, he'd be as well f***ing off home. At that, he turned and stormed down the tunnel. I thought he'd gone to the dressing room but when we got there at half-time, he wasn't there. All the players were looking for him because he always had a lot of input at half-time. I spoke to the boys but I was quite despondent because I was sure he'd left and I was worried about how I'd get on without him. We went back out for the second half but there was still no Archie. The game restarted then, all of a sudden, he appeared over my right shoulder.

'I said, "I'll speak to you after the game but I apologise for my behaviour." He said it was okay as emotions always ran high.'

Emotions certainly ran high in a chaotic and often ill-tempered fight for survival at the foot of the Scottish Premier League. Livingston were deeply immersed in a relegation fight when Gough and Knox were drafted in to succeed Allan Preston in December 2004. Two of Knox's former clubs, Dundee and Dundee United, were also embroiled in a four-way relegation scrap. So, too, were Dunfermline Athletic, who had almost taken on the pairing of Gough and Knox just a few months earlier.

Gough said: 'I'd almost become Dunfermline boss the previous summer and I was going to take Archie with me to East End Park. My interview had gone very well and when I told them that Archie would be my No.2 they thought it was brilliant.

'When we arrived at Livingston, they were a few points off the pace and Archie felt we were three players short. Alec Cleland was already there as a coach, which was great, but we did have our run-ins with Pearse Flynn and Vivien Kyles, who were in charge at the time. I remember Archie pulling out an old training plan that AC Milan had used in the 90s. It only allowed the boys one touch between the two penalty boxes. He decided it was maybe a bit early for our Livingston team!

'I started training with the boys but Archie didn't think it was a great idea for the 45-year-old manager to be keeping up with the rest of the squad so he pulled me out and made me watch. Little bits of advice like that were so vital to me. He was great to have at my side when we were fighting to stay up.'

With Knox requesting three additions to bolster Livingston's survival chances, the club invested in former Southampton and Morocco winger Hassan Kachloul. Signed outside the transfer window and officially employed as a 'commercial executive', Kachloul provided crucial on-field experience in the run-in. Never more so than on 21 May 2005 – the afternoon which would define the tenure of Gough and Knox at Livingston. Dundee, a side supported and managed by Knox in previous decades, arrived at Almondvale needing a win to stay up. To add even more spice to the occasion, they were bossed by Jim Duffy – a key player under Knox at Dens in the 1980s.

The visitors struck early through Callum MacDonald, but Kachloul provided the cross for Craig Easton to equalise before the interval. A nerve-shredding second half witnessed chances at both ends with Dundee's Tam McManus striking a post in the final seconds.

Snodgrass, a late substitute for Kachloul, said: 'I remember the day we drew with Dundee to stay up. I'd gone on as a sub and had a chance to score and ease the nerves. I was so nervous and so tense that I couldn't even run through and I didn't even manage to get a shot away. My legs just seized up and I couldn't shoot.

'It was pressure but I think it was a different type of pressure to that which Archie and Richard had been used to. They'd been used to the pressure of trying to win leagues. Now they had the pressure of trying to stay in a league. But they had a calmness which came over to the players.'

Knox said: 'We kept Livingston up on the last day of the season. It was one of those games which could have gone either way. Easton scored the goal for us but McManus could have won it for Dundee near the end when he hit the post. We sent on a young Robert Snodgrass near the end and he should have scored a goal to ease the nerves.

'I was raging as we should have put on Graham Dorrans instead of him. I was sure Dorrans would have taken the chance.

'That was May 2005 and it's amazing to think that those two young lads have gone on to carve out such fine careers down south. When Snodgrass missed that chance, you wouldn't have thought he'd be bought and sold for all those millions in the English Premier League! But he's enjoyed a superb career and, of course, Dorrans is now back in Scotland with Rangers.'

Dorrans, who returned to Scotland with Rangers in the summer of 2017 after spells at West Bromwich Albion and Norwich City, credits Knox with aiding his development during his year at Livingston. The Scotland international midfielder said: 'Archie was old-school. We had been used to having more modern coaches at Livingston but his arrival was brilliant for me. I loved it when he and Goughie were there as they had done so much in the game that they earned instant respect.

'I think the boys were taken aback that a club of Livingston's size had been able to attract them.

'We knew there were boundaries and we knew that Archie would put you in line if he needed to do so. But I grew up watching Rangers and seeing Archie at Walter Smith's side in all those big games, so this was great for me. This was somebody I had watched when I was growing up and was now coaching me. We all sat up and took notice when someone of Archie's stature came in. These were two big figures from the Rangers' Nine in a Row era and here they were taking us at Livingston. It was amazing.

'They weren't at the club for too long and, to be honest, it wasn't long enough for my liking. But they gave me my debut against Kilmarnock when I was just 16 or 17 and I'll always owe them for that. I spoke to Goughie recently and he told me he'd have given me my debut even earlier but Archie said I was too young!

'It was great to work with them and the only coach I've worked with in my career who I could compare to Archie would be Roy Hodgson at West Brom. He was old-school, too, but probably not as "out there" as Archie.'

Remarkably, Gough and Knox had intimated in the days prior to the Dundee draw that it would be their final game in charge of Livingston. Their relationship with chairman Flynn had deteriorated since a defeat to former club Dundee United three months earlier. But they would leave with the club's top-flight place secured and their heads held high as Paul Lambert took charge.

Knox recalled: 'Pearse told us we didn't show enough emotion on the bench and we should shout at the players more. I'd had one or two run-ins with him and he told Goughie that he'd support him if he wanted to facilitate a change to his staff. Of course, Goughie came straight to me and told me everything. And I immediately called the chairman to ask what was going on. Goughie and I met with him and I told him that everything I did for the club was for the manager and not for him.'

Livingston's players, including Snodgrass and Dorrans, bemoaned their exit in the wake of a run-in which had seen the club edge up to tenth place in the final table. Snodgrass said:

'I would have liked to have worked with them for a lot longer. But I'm not sure they got on well with the chairman at the time. They made some great signings at Livingston. They brought in the likes of Hassan Kachloul, who had real quality.

'When I was at Hull City later in my career, you could see Steve Bruce had some of the same traits as Archie after their time together at Manchester United. Steve also wanted hard work from his players and showed that same determination to win.

'People speak about old-school managers and modern-day managers. I'd say Steve adapted from being old-school to modern-day.

'I always remember Archie telling me about what life was like working with Sir Alex in the early days at Aberdeen. He said there was a day when he said to Alex, "I don't know why you've brought me here – you want to do everything yourself. Why don't you go upstairs and let me do something here?" Fergie said that was the best thing he ever did. Archie was an on-field guy who loved getting his point across to players.

'He always had great banter. He came down to Hull to see Steve Bruce when I was playing there. We have a mutual friend, Ewan Chester, and we were all chatting together.

'I chat with Archie when I see him now and he always gives you good advice.'

The final chapter of the Livingston tale was a full-scale SPL probe into the signing of Kachloul. It ruled that the club had paid the player the equivalent of a professional wage despite registering him as an amateur. There was no suggestion that the management team were involved in this rule breach – but the club was fined £15,000.

Dundee's plea for a points deduction – one which would have kept them up and relegated Livingston – fell on deaf ears at Hampden.

Gough would return to his family in the United States, while

Knox's next jobs would be south of the border. Sammy Lee, having briefly succeeded Sam Allardyce at Bolton Wanderers, employed him as assistant.

And Ince, the one-time firebrand who had clashed with Knox at The Cliff in their Manchester United days, handed him a similar role at Blackburn Rovers.

Both positions were relatively short-term as the two managers lost their jobs in double-quick time. But the spell at Bolton in particular opened Knox's eyes to a new wave of techniques to prepare players for games. Not all of them to his liking. 'At some of the clubs I was with in England, you would take a load of guys to away games. At Bolton they had about 20 staff going to away games – sport scientists, analysts, masseurs, warm-up guys, even boys who dish out the water. That's what happens now. I can't see that making any difference to how people perform on the field but that's how it is these days. You say to yourself, "Do we really need all this?"

'I remember saying to one guy during pre-season, "You need to be doing a wee bit more than that, do you not?" I could have done that level of training myself and I was in my 50s at the time. But he said we had to hold back as the players were in the "red zone".

'He told me that when the players' heart rate was up you didn't want to be pushing them above that. I went back to the reply I gave Brian McClair about finding another colour of zone because red wasn't going to be high enough for my liking!

'The amount of training we did with Jim McLean and Alex Ferguson and the rest, it was incredible.

'I remember being at Bolton when I was helping Sammy. There was a squad of folk helping but I didn't know what they were for. I phoned Sir Alex at Manchester United and asked if he had all these boys working for him. He said, "I think so but I don't have anything to do with them."

'He didn't rely on them on how to pick a team. It was all about what he saw with his eyes. I think what you see tells you how these boys are actually performing. You can't tell a lack of confidence in a boy by stats or anything like that. Maybe you can tell they haven't run or sprinted as far – but you need to know the boy. You need to know the individual players and what they are capable of, what they are giving you or whether they are holding something back. That bit is easy enough if you have the manager's eye or your experience will tell you that. You can't rely just on stats and stuff like that if it's going to dictate how you pick a team. If you think back to the Aberdeen days, we were playing 60 games a season and people like Willie Miller played all the games. That's because we knew him and knew he could do it. I think we maybe overdo all the analysis part of it nowadays. It's the same with players when you are doing set-pieces and stuff like that. I can remember at some of the clubs where the analysis people would have screens in the dressing room and keep on rolling out footage of opposition free-kicks and defensive walls. They'd be shouting, "There's the wall, there's a free-kick out there coming diagonally into the box, where you are lining up, are you playing zonal or man-marking?"

'By the time the players were walking out onto the pitch you knew to some of them it wouldn't make the blindest bit of a difference.

'Was it Jock Stein who said of set-pieces, "There's only one ball and if it comes into your area head it or kick it away – that's basically it."

'At Rangers, Goughie would be a spare man at set-pieces. He wouldn't be against anybody but wherever that ball was you'd expect him to be on the end of it heading it the right way. He didn't need a big support staff to explain it all to him. He just knew he needed to keep the ball out of our net.'

Knox enjoyed that brief stint at Bolton, though, as Lee – a

member of that great Liverpool team under Bob Paisley – shared his boundless enthusiasm for the game. He recalled: 'I left my job at the SFA to go down and work with Sammy. He gave me the opportunity to return to day-to-day contact with players. I had enjoyed the work at the SFA but missed that day-to-day involvement on the training ground. Even though it didn't last too long for us at Bolton, I felt it was just what I needed at that time.

'I knew Sammy from my days working with Everton. I would see him at games or see him around Liverpool. I could never understand a word he said with that thick Scouse accent. Mind you, I'm not sure that he understood me either – or listened to any of it.

'Sammy was so enthusiastic for the game. You would see him out running at half past six in the morning.'

Knox has relied on his eyes and his experience since those early days learning under the likes of McLean and Ferguson. He has passed on those tips to a succession of up-and-coming coaches at Largs over the years. Even the SFA's own director of coaching, Jim Fleeting, admits he's learned from him. 'I'd always been involved in the development department at the SFA but had never worked with a team until Archie came to Hampden,' said Fleeting. 'He took me out to work with the Under-21s and we were staying at the Westerwood Hotel in Cumbernauld to prepare for a game. He convened a team meeting with myself and Maurice Malpas and I have to admit I was quite nervous. I even brought down a pencil and notepad, although I hid them from Archie. He told me at the start that I'd be in charge of "the BBC". I was terrified because I'd never been very good at giving interviews. I asked what I was expected to do when they came in with their cameras but Archie said, "Not that BBC – I mean the balls, bibs and cones".'

But Knox didn't always deliver the one-liners and Fleeting remembers a night when he was lost for words – as he was trapped in a phone box. 'We had a night out when we were on a coaching course down at Largs. We just nipped out for a couple of pints. Archie offered to go out and phone a taxi to take us back up to our accommodation. It was in the days before mobile phones. Brian Whittaker and Roddie MacDonald, two very good defenders in their day with Celtic and Hearts who were on the course, followed him out. Archie asked if they wanted him to phone a taxi for them but they insisted they were happy just to walk back. They waited until Archie was in the old red phone box and then casually lifted a concrete seat which was next to it and placed it across the door. After Archie called the taxi, he turned to get out and found he was trapped – with Brian and Roddie sitting on the seat.

'The taxi duly pulled up, Brian and Roddie got into it and headed off – leaving Archie stranded in the phone box. By the time the rest of us came out to find out where he was, he was banging as hard as he could on the windows of the phone box to attract anyone's attention.

'All the way back up to the accommodation, he was threatening to do all sorts to the pair of them in the morning.'

CHAPTER EIGHTEEN

RANTS WITHOUT PANTS

AT DUNDEE, it was Knox versus Cowboy. At Motherwell, it was Brown v Boyle. In terms of bareknuckle brawls, the two flashpoints scarcely stand comparison. But the latter skirmish in the Fir Park tunnel highlighted how valued the contribution of Craig Brown and Archie Knox had been in their brief spell at Motherwell. The veteran pair had been brought in by Well chairman John Boyle in December 2009 to replace the axed Jim Gannon. They led the Steelmen not only to safety but to a fifth-place finish in the SPL which would guarantee a passport into the Europa League qualifiers. Trips to Iceland, Norway and Denmark followed before they were lured away by Aberdeen, almost exactly one year after arriving in Lanarkshire.

Motherwell accused the Dons of a 'gross discourtesy' in swooping for the pair – who were working without contracts – just days before the teams were due to meet at Pittodrie. And a bitter sense of injustice was clearly still being felt by Boyle when his erstwhile management team returned to Fir Park with their new side four months later.

Knox recalled: 'John had appointed Stuart McCall as manager after we went to Aberdeen but, when we came back down, he wasn't at the game. We didn't realise at the time but he'd been dropped off at the front door just before the final whistle and had come straight down the tunnel to get to Craig.

'He started having a go at Craig and I couldn't believe what I was seeing. I grabbed him and asked, not too politely, what he thought he was doing. We got him back up the tunnel but, in the end, we were the ones charged by the SFA. It was nonsense – Craig did nothing wrong at all.

'I'd fallen out with John before. We'd had words during a conference call and I told him he knew nothing about football. The next time he saw me at the ground, he jabbed a finger at me and warned me never to speak to him like that again. I warned him never to jab a finger at me again. It was one of those relationships but, if I saw him at a game now, I'd shake his hand.

'We had a great time at Motherwell. We were there for that 6-6 draw against Hibs and we have nothing but fond memories of the place.'

Brown recalls the lingering build-up to the incredible flashpoint with Boyle, but believes the feud should not overshadow the job he and Knox did at Fir Park. 'Motherwell owed us bonus money and weren't going to pay it so we got the managers' union involved to fight our corner. I think a telephone call had gone into Motherwell the day before we went back with Aberdeen and emotions were running high. When we went to Motherwell at the start, they had lost seven games in a row. But we managed to get hold of the place. I think our best run was 11 games unbeaten and, of course, we managed to lead the club back into Europe.'

Long-serving Motherwell defender Steven Hammell played in the Brown versus Boyle game – a 2-1 win for McCall's side – and still laughs at the post-match fracas. 'The bust-up with Craig Brown and John Boyle made the TV highlights package and all the boys were talking about it. But I don't think John would have made the same comments to Archie that he made to Craig that day!'

Team-mate Keith Lasley added: 'I think John was lucky that Archie didn't clock it straight away and it was only Craig who chased him. Archie was in the dugout when it started and, although he saw a commotion, he didn't see it all. I think John knew the script and he maybe picked his target wisely.'

Hammell has spent the vast majority of his career with the Steelmen, shattering all manner of appearance records at home and abroad. He has savoured the highs of cup finals and Euro clashes – and the lows of nerve-jangling relegation play-off battles. But one clash at Celtic Park and a post-match dressing down (or undressing down) from Knox stands as one of his abiding memories of his lengthy spell with the club. 'We were playing at Parkhead and were winning 1-0 at half-time. This was at a time when Celtic were running over teams. Archie was firing us up at half-time but by 50 minutes we were 3-1 down. By the end, we'd lost 5-1.

'When we came back in, Archie didn't miss anybody. But he didn't give me much criticism and I thought I must have done okay. I was starting to get changed and I just had a towel round me, but he caught my eye and started on me. I looked up and he had his shirt and tie on, his socks on up to his knees and his shiny shoes on – but no pants or trousers. He put his foot up on a bench. I thought it was a wind-up but it couldn't have been because he was hammering me. I tried to maintain eye contact with him but all I could see were these things dangling in front of me. He was shouting at me to the extent that spit was flying out his mouth and all I could think about was maintaining that eye contact. I knew I'd be dead if I even laughed. Even after he finished with me, he was marching round the dressing room half-naked. It was a surreal moment. I didn't know whether to laugh or cry. He was so serious – and that was his style.'

Well's chief operating officer, Alan Burrows, insists the Parkhead incident wasn't the only time Knox was caught with his pants, er, off. 'I don't know if he still does it, but Archie used to get dressed in a most unusual way. It was socks and shoes first, then shirt and tie. Finally, it was pants and trousers over the top of his shoes.

'One day, he'd put on everything apart from his pants and trousers when Craig was addressing the team. Craig asked Archie if he had anything to add and Archie said yes. He just stood up – still with no pants or trousers – and started speaking. He was going off his trolley about something and, all the while, everything was hanging out. All the boys were trying so hard not to laugh.'

Knox admits: 'I always got dressed that way. Shoes and socks first then shirt and tie then I'll comb my hair and finally it's the drawers and trousers.'

Burrows also recalls being on the wrong end of a Knox-inspired wind-up after he revealed the Motherwell team line-up to the media before a game. 'I remember us going to Kilmarnock for a league game after we'd faced Odense in a European play-off match. Craig had made some changes to the team and one of the BBC reporters, Al Lamont, asked me how we'd line up. We had a young lad called Jonathan Page starting and I told Al that, while I couldn't say for sure, I thought he'd maybe play at right-back. Al then asked Craig about Jonathan playing at right-back. Craig asked him how he knew and he said, "Alan told me."

'Craig told Archie who went mental and told me it was a sackable offence to reveal team details to the press. He was screaming in my face and warned me that I'd be sacked on Monday morning if we lost the game. Fortunately, we won 1-0. Esteban Casagolda set up the winner – about the only thing he ever did for Motherwell – and Nick Blackman scored.

'I could have kissed Nick when the goal went in. But I was still petrified all weekend after getting the hair dryer treatment from Archie.

'I went in on the Monday morning and they pulled me in and told me they'd only been kidding!

'We had some great times and there were some great fall-outs between Craig and Archie and John Boyle and Leeann Dempster, our former chief executive.'

Euro clashes with the likes of Odense, not to mention the record-breaking 6-6 draw with Hibs, didn't seem likely when Knox was first approached for a role at Fir Park. He recalled: 'Jim Gannon had left the club and I remember getting a call out of the blue from Craig one Sunday night. Bill Dickie, the Motherwell director whom we'd worked with at the SFA, had asked Craig if he could step in. John Boyle was in Australia at the time and they actually only wanted us for three games until they decided who they wanted to bring in as permanent manager. Craig asked me if I'd help him. I was doing nothing else at the time so we went in on the Monday morning.

'We didn't have a contract – we never had one at Motherwell – but we got a few results and we stayed on.'

Former club captain Lasley, who was appointed assistant manager to Stephen Robinson in the summer of 2017, recalls the instant impact Knox and Brown made at Fir Park. 'The biggest thing for us after Jim Gannon left was that Craig and Archie came in. It was like chalk and cheese.

'It was instant respect for the two of them with everything they'd done in the game. I can imagine Archie had mellowed from his days at Manchester United and Rangers but he still had a steel about him. When he walked into the dressing room, people sat up. Some of the younger boys probably didn't appreciate everything these men had done in the game. Some of our boys know nothing pre-2000! But they soon got the message. It was respect straight away and that was reflected in our results.'

Hammell added: 'We were playing in the indoor astroturf at Hamilton. It was the day Jim was sacked. We were playing a little game among ourselves and we spotted Craig and Archie watching us. At that point, the standard of training picked up instantly.

'They had a great balance. Craig was softly spoken and would have a full teamtalk without talking about anything on the pitch. If the hammer or the hair dryer needed to come out, that was Archie's area. The balance that they had was excellent.

'The upturn in results from the day they came in to the day they left was excellent.'

The media loved portraying the veteran management team as Jack and Victor, but Brown and Knox were deadly serious in their pursuit of success for Motherwell – and the players loved their methods.

Lasley said: 'Archie took 90 per cent of the training. His enthusiasm, given everywhere he'd been in his career, was terrific. He had an incredible hunger to improve guys like us. That was the biggest thing I took from it. It was inspirational to see someone with the passion to do everything properly every day. There was never a day when he gave less than 100 per cent at Motherwell. It's the standards he was used to from the start of his career.

'I still meet Archie now and what a gentleman he is. He came to Motherwell after being at two massive clubs.

'But guys like me who wanted to go into coaching and management could only marvel at his enthusiasm. You can stand and have a conversation with him about the game now and he's still as passionate as he was when he started out in the game. Even when Archie was having a go at you, it was always clear that he was doing it for the right reasons. It didn't happen often.

Maybe that was a reflection on results, which more often than not were pretty good.

'They could make you feel ten feet tall. They had a way of using words to make you feel good. They worked well together.

'When I look back, they probably saved me from leaving Motherwell. I was out of there under the previous manager. I have to thank Craig and Archie for keeping me at the club. It also coincided with my best spell for Motherwell and a large part of that was down to Archie and the way we trained and the confidence he instilled in me again. Under the previous manager, me and some others felt as low as a snake's belly. I was a couple of weeks from leaving the club so I've a lot to thank Archie for. The two of them coming into the club was a big moment in my career and Archie was a massive part of that.'

Hammell added: 'Archie was so humble despite everything he'd achieved in the game before he arrived at Motherwell.

'Having a go at you wasn't the only tool he had. He had the right balance and he did it better than most. He would compliment the younger boys and take time out to try to improve everybody. We were seen as the experienced ones and he still wanted to improve us.

'I remember after a game at Kilmarnock, Archie and Craig came in and said it was one of the best results they'd had in their careers. We were going through a tough stage but we went down to Killie and won 3-0. You felt like they genuinely meant it and it wasn't just a wee trick they were trying to pull to raise our confidence.'

The 6-6 draw at home to Hibs in the final home game of the 2009/10 season was the highest-scoring game in SPL history. Well came from 6-2 down in a scintillating final quarter, with Lukas Jutkiewicz smashing home a spectacular equaliser in the dying moments.

Less well remembered but equally noteworthy was a 3-3 draw with champions Rangers at Ibrox just four days later. Motherwell this time scored twice in added time – through Steve Jennings and Jutkiewicz's penalty – to earn a point on the last day of the season.

The start of the next campaign featured Europa League clashes with Breidablik, Aalesund and Odense. Domestically, they won seven games from nine just before Aberdeen chairman Stewart Milne made his move.

In a strongly-worded club statement, Motherwell raged: 'We wish to make clear that as a board we believe that the conduct of the board of Aberdeen in this matter has been wholly inappropriate and in clear breach of SPL rules, as well as basic courtesy.

'At no point did they inform us or seek our permission to speak to critical employees of our club and to seek to entice them to leave our employment.

'We realise the desperation they are feeling and the pressure they are under from their fans for their own performance as a board, but to go about their business in this way is a matter of gross discourtesy.'

Little did the Fir Park hierarchy realise that, as they penned their statement, Knox was helping to prep their next manager.

Stuart McCall, who'd worked with him at Rangers during their Nine in a Row heyday, revealed: 'Archie was a larger than life character. He has been brilliant with me in recent years, too, and is always in touch to help me out. I was driving up the road to be interviewed for the Motherwell job after Archie and Craig had left for Aberdeen.

'Archie had a sniff that I might be getting it and he called me and spent 20 minutes on the phone giving me the full rundown on the players, the staff and the club. He also came away with us on a few Scotland trips when I was working with Gordon Strachan and Mark McGhee in later years.

'His stories and anecdotes are brilliant. You could stay in his company all night and listen to all the tales.'

CHAPTER NINETEEN

SEEING RED AGAIN – QUITE LITERALLY

RYAN JACK caused something of a stir when he left Aberdeen to sign for bitter rivals Rangers in the summer of 2017. But some say trading Pittodrie for Ibrox paled into insignificance when set against his feud with Archie Knox. Craig Brown takes up the story, one which he regards as the most remarkable of his own stellar managerial career.

He recalled: 'Archie was giving Ryan pelters in a game against Hibs at Easter Road. Ryan was right in front of the dugout and lost possession to Lewis Stevenson. I couldn't believe what I was hearing but Ryan turned to Archie and said, "F**king shut up" or some such insult. I'd never heard anything like it in all my years in the game.

'I told our physio Davie Wylie, "Right, get him off the park now." But Davie said, "Gaffer, you've used all your subs already."

'We still had three minutes of stoppage time to play and the game was 0-0. I wanted to take him off but couldn't risk losing a goal with ten men.

'Archie kept saying, "Wait until I get him in there." I thought there was going to be a bloodbath. When the final whistle went, I intercepted Jack and told him he'd have to apologise to Archie. I'd dealt with international players for 16 years and never even remotely heard dissent like it. I kept him outside the dressing room in the hope that Archie had calmed down. When we finally went inside, the place was absolutely silent. Archie was sitting on the treatment table and you could have heard a pin drop.

'I was sure Ryan would apologise but he just sat down.

'I instantly started a post-match teamtalk in the hope of buying him some time. It must have lasted 20 minutes – and there was nothing to say as it had been an awful goalless draw.

'Archie stood behind me revving up to get to Ryan.

'I then said, "Right, the bus is leaving in five minutes so make this the quickest shower you've ever had."

'The players all disappeared into the showers and Archie moaned, "The wee bastard – I wanted to get into him."

'I said, "I know, that's why I kept talking."

'If I hadn't kept talking for so long, it would have been an assault case!'

Jack, who'd go on to become Aberdeen captain under Derek McInnes, can afford to laugh at the flashpoint now. 'We weren't doing so well in the game and Archie was having a go at a few of us. Emotions were running high. He had a go at me and I said, "Go take a f*** to yourself." It was just something I said when I was caught up in the emotion of the game. I remember him going mad at Craig to sub me and Craig saying he'd already used all three subs.

'We had a throw-in near the bench and I could hear him shouting, "Right Jack, you're coming off."

'I knew they'd used all the subs but I could hear him saying to Craig, "I don't care – just take him off now."

'When the final whistle went and we'd drawn the game, Craig got me at the side of the pitch and told me to stay out of the way because Archie would flip his lid with me. He tried to calm it all down. It's funny now to look back on it. Craig was trying his hardest to be the peacemaker but Archie was still raging.

'When things calmed down after the Hibs game, Archie said emotions had run high but he warned me not to do it again. No one knew but I missed the next game, a cup replay against Queen of the South, because of that incident. Craig told me I wasn't playing and told me I'd better get my head right. It's funny now but it wasn't so funny at the time, having Archie Knox on my case!'

Knox had returned to Pittodrie more than 24 years after leaving with Sir Alex Ferguson to embrace the challenge of Manchester United. Results had dwindled and so had the crowds, with just 5,600 attending a home game with Dunfermline shortly after Brown and Knox succeeded Mark McGhee. Knox said: 'Aberdeen was a totally different club with totally different people when I went back there with Craig. I don't think there was a single person left from the day I'd left for the second time at the end of 1986. It was awkward for me because my friend, Mark McGhee, had been sacked. You don't like jumping into a pal's shoes. The job could be awkward at times, too, with budget pressures and the fact we lost some talented young players.

'We tried to get Adam Rooney, long before he signed for Derek McInnes, but the club didn't have the budget at the time. We lost a few of the young players as well.'

Jack was one of the home-grown youngsters Brown and Knox did manage to retain during their three seasons at the club. Echoing the reaction of Keith Lasley and Steven Hammell at Motherwell, he reveals the Dons' squad were in awe of the newly-appointed management team. 'As a young player who'd grown up watching Scottish football, Craig and Archie had been real figureheads in the game. Craig had taken Scotland to a World Cup. Archie had enjoyed so much success with Sir Alex

Ferguson and then at Rangers. It was a big deal when they came to Aberdeen.

'Archie had us doing some of the old stuff that he'd done back in the day during his first spell with the club. He'd have us down on the beach, training on the sand.'

Brown, who still serves Aberdeen as a non-executive director, stands by their dugout record in their spell in the Granite City. Like Knox, he still wonders if they could have achieved even more given a more favourable financial wind. 'When we went to Aberdeen, they were bottom of the league. They'd lost 9-0 at Celtic Park and we watched from the stand as they lost 5-0 to Hearts at Tynecastle. Derek McInnes has had great runs of eight or nine successive home wins but, on two separate occasions, we were 13 unbeaten in all. It wasn't an easy time because the financial circumstances meant we were forced to lose some key players. Sone Aluko, Chris Maguire, Richard Foster, Jack Grimmer, Fraser Fyvie and, of course, Ryan Fraser all went. The club wouldn't pay Kari Arnason – who is actually now back for a second spell with Aberdeen – to stay and he ended up starring for Iceland in the win over England at Euro 2016. Add in the fact that we lost Paul Hartley and Yoann Folly to injury and you can see some of the problems we faced.

'The likes of Ryan Jack and Andrew Considine were already there and we managed to bring in Mark Reynolds, Niall McGinn and Jonny Hayes.

'Having Archie at my side was huge for me as it guaranteed us extra respect from the fans after his earlier spells at Aberdeen.

'Aberdeen put us up in the Atholl Hotel and we'd leave at 8.15 every morning and take turns with the driving. There was a lollipop man positioned on the pavement outside the hotel and sometimes we'd have to stop to let the schoolkids cross the road. One morning, when Archie was driving, the fella stuck out his lollipop and stopped us – even though there wasn't a kid in sight.

Archie was going daft and shouting at him to get out the way. He kept his lollipop in front of the car bonnet and motioned for Archie to roll down his window. Reluctantly, Archie finally rolled it down and was ready to give the fella a mouthful until he said to us, "Mr Knox and Mr Brown, I'd just like to wish you all the best in your new jobs".'

Knox and Brown were soon away from the hotel and into permanent accommodation in the Granite City. Archie added: 'I have enjoyed Craig's company and value his friendship.

'During those years, I also enjoyed the friendship of Maggie McAlister. I met Maggie at Bob Hopcroft's son Michael's wedding and we spent a lot of time together. Maggie taught English as a foreign language and also threw herself into charity work with the Crafty Things design collective in Aberdeen. I valued her friendship and I still do today.'

Back on the pitch, centre-back Reynolds had worked under Knox and Brown during their time at Motherwell and gladly signed for them on loan after a spell with Sheffield Wednesday. Reynolds said: 'The only reason I went to Aberdeen was down to Archie and Craig. They were the deciding factor.

'It wasn't going well for me at Sheffield Wednesday, they'd just gone to Pittodrie and they offered me the chance to go back up the road.

'The first thing Archie said to me was the Aberdeen shirt suited me.

'I said I'd have to get used to the red, but he said, "You'll need to get used to the two stars on the shirt – you're at a f***ing massive club now, son."

'Craig said it wouldn't be long before Archie told me that he was responsible for those two stars – one for the European Cup Winners' Cup win and one for the European Super Cup win – being on the shirt in the first place!'

Reynolds agrees with Jack's assessment that the mere presence of Brown and Knox had a positive impact on the whole club. They raised the Dons to ninth place – a dozen points clear of relegated Hamilton Accies – after only six months in the job.

Another ninth-place finish, followed by eighth place, were achieved as they laid the foundations for McInnes' revolution.

Reynolds said: 'When Archie spoke, everyone listened. They are the best management team that I've ever worked with. It just clicked. They seemed to appreciate the qualities that I had as a player and, of course, I appreciated what they did for me as coaches.

'I really enjoyed my time with them, both at Motherwell and Aberdeen, and they were successful times. We played European football at Motherwell and then they went up and steadied the ship at a difficult time for Aberdeen. Everyone up in Aberdeen acknowledges the fact that they laid the foundations for much of the success the team is enjoying under the gaffer now. They brought in four or five players, they made the team solid and they got a really good side together.

'There was no ego with Archie. He had bad words to say to you, but never a bad word to say about you. He could go through you in the dressing room after a game on a Saturday night. He could nail you to the wall. But it was all forgotten about on the Monday morning when we were back in the dressing room. Nothing was ever allowed to fester.

'He would get showered with the players after a game and Craig would tend to start talking to the players. Don't get me wrong, Craig could rant and rave with the best of them and he'd start if we'd played badly. Archie would come out the shower and get changed. Socks and shoes, shirt and tie . . . I remember a game when he decided, at that point, that he needed to wade in and give us some stick. He would stand there going mental and, just as Steven Hammell has said, you'd be thinking to yourself, "What is he doing?"

'He would hammer you and you didn't want to look up because you knew he was naked from the waist down – apart from the socks and shoes, which were on perfectly. I had this vision of him just putting on his suit jacket and walking out of the dressing room like that. He didn't care. If he had a piece to say, he'd say it – no matter what the situation was.'

Of all the home-grown kids who headed out of Pittodrie to balance the books, the exit of Ryan Fraser pained the management most. Now a Scotland cap and starring in the English Premier League with Bournemouth, Knox had spotted his potential straight away. Reynolds recalled: 'When I went up to Aberdeen, Ryan Fraser must have been only 15 and he'd hardly been seen around the first team. But Archie would tell us all, "This lad can play". He knew straight away. He had worked with so many top players over the years and knew Ryan could do it.

'Ryan had to make Archie's tea and toast, and we would hear Archie shouting down the corridor at him inside Pittodrie.

'Archie knew he had the ability but this was his little test to see if he could take a bit as well.

'Now he's in the English Premier League, playing against the best in the world, but Archie knew all those years ago that he could do it.'

Knox recalled: 'Ryan was a quiet, quiet boy but you could tell straight away that he was a player. He was quick and he was brave, and we got him involved in training with the first team. He played quite a bit for us, too. He's done very well in his career since going down to Bournemouth.

'He used to get Kieran Gibbons to help him make the tea and toast, though, because he couldn't seem to do it on his own.'

Despite being into his 60s when returning to Pittodrie, Knox made a point of building a rapport with the young players. Working with club captain Russell Anderson, he brought in a system of fines for any dressing room breaches. There were no longer any baseball bats or games of Tips. Then again, he no longer had Steve Cowan waving a dissenting finger at his minibus.

Times had changed. He'd never seen Alex McLeish or Gordon Strachan wander into the home dressing room at Pittodrie on a mobile phone.

But Knox recalled: 'I'd go into the youth dressing room. If I caught one of the young lads on their mobile phone, I'd send them to Russell and they'd be fined for using it in the dressing room.

'I caught five of them one day. I sent them along to Russell, who would decide the size of the fine. It was normally just a couple of quid.

'They would also get fined if they got caught not wearing flip-flops in the shower.

'The same day I caught five of them on their phones, I was aware that two others were in the shower – and I suspected without flip-flops. I sent someone in to check but I told him not to let on that I was hiding behind the door. I could hear him say to someone – who turned out to be Kieran – that Knox was on the warpath and he'd already fined five of the boys. He said Kieran better beware that I didn't catch him without flip-flops. There was a pause, then I heard Kieran reply, "Tell him I couldn't give a f***."

'The lad told him that he'd be fined for it, but Kieran said, 'Tell him I won't be f***ing paying."

'At that point, I stepped into the shower and said, "You'll be f***ing paying all right."

'We held a kangaroo court in the dressing room the next day and I sat on a plinth in the middle of the room with a towel on my head like a judge's wig.

'We had one of the lads as Kieran's defence lawyer, we had another as the prosecution lawyer and we had various witnesses.

When I started asking questions of the defence lawyer, he quickly jumped ship and that was the final straw. Guilty as sin.

'The folk from Red TV – the club's in-house television station – got wind of the trial and asked if they could film it for the club website. Can you imagine? I'd have got the jail, never mind Kieran!'

Dons legend Willie Miller has maintained strong links with the club over the years and insists Brown and Knox deserve immense credit for the work they did in trying times. 'Archie's undoubted strength has always been on the coaching field. You could see it back then when we played and you could see it when he returned to the club with Craig. He was never one for boardroom meetings or the diplomacy you'd have required to manage Aberdeen at the time Alex left for Manchester United.

'I was on the board at Aberdeen when Archie returned with Craig. Mark McGhee had left and they stabilised the ship. Those were turbulent times. Mark, as a former player, had endured a difficult time and I think Archie and Craig were just what the club needed.

'Craig never referred to Archie as his assistant or his No.2. He was always his "colleague" and they won't take umbrage when I say they were the older heads the club needed at that time. They did a good job. They brought in Niall McGinn and others and they stabilised things at a difficult time.'

Their successor, McInnes, finally ended a wait of almost 20 years for a major trophy when he brought back the League Cup after a penalty shoot-out victory over Inverness Caledonian Thistle at Celtic Park in 2014. Since then, he's maintained Aberdeen in the top six of the Premiership and been runner-up to Celtic in the 2016/17 Scottish Cup final, League Cup final and league title race.

Brown said: 'I became a director at Aberdeen and I was involved in the recruitment process when Derek was appointed.

To be honest, I didn't know Derek very well so I asked Archie, who'd had him as a player at Rangers many years earlier. Archie gave him an outstanding recommendation which I was able to relay to the board and played a big part in Derek getting the job.'

McInnes, having savoured his spell under Knox at Rangers 15 years earlier, talked to him about succeeding Brown at the Pittodrie helm. 'I spoke to Archie before taking the Aberdeen job on. He always knew I'd been keen on coaching and management and had always been very supportive. I always felt Archie had my back when I was player. He saw the limitations in me but liked me as a player and a person. It was a mutual respect. I often saw him at games – I still do – and his opinion on a player is one that I will always respect.

'I remember going to one of the PFA exit trials for freed players at Broadwood when I was manager of St Johnstone. I was late and I was running in the front door five minutes after kick-off when I met Archie on the way out. He said, "Del, get back in the motor – you're wasting your time here. It's called an exit trial because these boys are exiting out the game!"

'He was always to the point. He could be brutal in his assessment of a player, but he was always very honest. He had a great phrase he used to use and I still mention it to him to this day. He used to say, "You can't turn sh*** into honey".'

Other than a few scouting missions for Dundee when John Brown was at the helm, Knox has spent the seasons since his Aberdeen exit as an avid spectator of the beautiful game. He may no longer stand on the game's frontline, but his standing within Scottish football remains undiminished.

In writing this book, it's been incredible to discover how the name 'Archie Knox' can open so many doors. From Sir Alex Ferguson and Walter Smith to countless players who have performed under him, they have all wanted to share their memories of a career less ordinary.

Knox's own memories are now mainly shared with pals and peers over a coffee at Jim McSherry's pub in Ayr. McSherry, once of Ayr United and Kilmarnock, now runs the Wee Windaes and hosts some of the greatest names of a magnificent era for the national game.

He said: 'Archie and all his pals come to the Wee Windaes on a Wednesday and have a great time telling all the old stories. Sometimes we'll have him, Craig Brown, Frank Coulston, Willie McLean, Joe Filippi, Neil Hood, Johnny Hubbard, Robert Reilly and Robert Connor.

'I've known Archie for years and remember him as Dundee manager when I was playing against them for Ayr United. I had a running battle with Rab Docherty, who'd just broken into the Dundee team and was giving me a hard time. After the game, Archie asked me what had gone on and I told him Rab was kicking me and calling me a "has-been". Archie summoned Rab into his office and, although he wasn't bothered about the kicks, he warned him not to call me a "has-been".

'I was quite chuffed until Archie went on to say, "McSherry isn't good enough to be a has-been – he's a never-was." Typical Archie.

'He has been good to me down the years and I remember him bringing a Rangers team down to Kilwinning to play a game when I was manager there.

'In more recent times, he has done Question & Answer nights in the Wee Windaes – and you could hear a pin drop in the place when he's speaking.

'He's one of the most likeable men in football and is very kind to people. We always have a great laugh together.'

Hard Knox, right enough. But he has left so many with smiles on their faces.

CHAPTER TWENTY

ARCHIE KNOX'S DREAM TEAM

'I WAS asked to pick a "Dream Team" to end this book and I thought it would be easy to select my top 11.

'When I was struggling to whittle it down, I tried to list a "Scottish XI" from my days north of the border and an "English XI" from my time down south. To be honest, that didn't make the task any easier – so I've decided to go for a bumper squad of brilliant players and great friends. Apologies to those who didn't quite squeeze into my big squad of 50. You were ALL in the selection process so don't give me a hard time. But here is the list of players who perhaps played the biggest parts in my career and also in my life outside football. Without doubt, they could all play a bit – well, most of them could!'

GOALKEEPERS

ANDY GORAM & JIM LEIGHTON: I make no apologies for being unable to split them. Both superb keepers and they competed for Scotland's No.1 jersey for more than a decade. We had Jim at Aberdeen and Andy at Rangers.

GARY BAILEY: You always felt you had a safe pair of hands in goal when Gary was playing. He was already at Manchester United when we arrived and he was a commanding figure who would come and take crosses.

DEFENDERS

RICHARD GOUGH: Now my old pal Stuart Kennedy will say Goughie was a centre half so he should be my right-back! A great player who helped us win a Merseyside derby at Anfield when he was almost 40 years of age.

STUART KENNEDY: A terrific right-back for Aberdeen – even if Alex Ferguson wasn't always convinced by his crossing! Injury denied him a start in Gothenburg but a fine player who went to the 1978 World Cup with Scotland.

ALEX McLEISH: A terrific partner for Willie Miller and a great defender for club and country. Mind you, Alex Ferguson used to tell him off for taking too many elbows from Davie Dodds in the games against Dundee United.

WILLIE MILLER: Great penalty box defender – there are not many like him nowadays. He wasn't the biggest but not too many could get to the ball before him in the box. Great awareness and always where he needed to be.

MAURICE MALPAS: Another great defender, I worked with him during his Scotland days. Incredibly, he was a part-timer in his early years at Dundee United but a one-club man who deserved all the plaudits that came his way.

JOHN BROWN: I signed Bomber for Dundee and we were later reunited at Rangers. When he was 22, I was warned he'd only be able to play for a couple more years because of his knees. They didn't take into account that big heart.

PAUL HEGARTY & DAVID NAREY: Dundee United's answer to McLeish and Miller. A wonderful pairing for Jim McLean at Tannadice. They both played for their country, with Narey managing that famous 'toe-poke' against Brazil.

STEVE BRUCE: You'd stake your life on him. A terrific defender who wasn't the quickest but would anticipate everything. He'd put his head on everything – and I even managed to shout at him to stop trying those big diagonals!

GARY PALLISTER: We brought him to Manchester United from Middlesbrough and he was a terrific centre-back. A cultured player who would prove an excellent partner for Bruce and would earn caps for England.

SCOTT NISBET: That goal against Bruges in the Champions League was enough to get Nizzy into the team on its own. A great lad who brought an awful lot to the Rangers squad in his heyday.

ARTHUR ALBISTON: A fine left-back for Manchester United and Scotland – and he even played for Dundee before hanging up his boots. Put in many years of service at Old Trafford and was an excellent defender.

BOB HOPCROFT AND BRYN WILLIAMS: Even I couldn't argue they were on a par with, say, Narey and Malpas at United. But they were good players and, much more importantly, lifelong friends to me and my family.

DAVE WATSON: A great defender in the penalty box and you could always depend on him. He was in the twilight of his playing career when we went to Everton but I don't recall him ever missing a game or even a training session. A great lad.

DENIS IRWIN: One of the best full-backs I've ever worked with. A top-notch defender with great pace, excellent use of the ball and could play on either side. He had every ingredient you need in a great full-back.

CRAIG BROWN: I was a Dundee supporter on the terraces at Dens Park when Broon played a part in the Dark Blues' last title triumph in 1962. I was still at school – just to prove he's a good bit older than me!

GARY NAYSMITH: Such a reliable player who was good in the air, a good user of the ball and a really good defender. I'd worked with him in the Scotland squad and convinced Walter Smith to sign him for Everton.

PAUL McGRATH: An outstanding footballer with great pace who was comfortable dribbling the ball out of defence. You never worried when he was one-on-one with a striker because no one could run past him.

JOE FILIPPI AND NEILLY HOOD: If we ever have to pick a five-a-side team in the Wee Windaes on a Wednesday morning, they'll be in that side. Two good players who have become great pals to me over the years.

MIDFIELDERS

GORDON STRACHAN: He was a cross between a winger and a midfield player. We had him at Aberdeen and

Manchester United, and he'd just work his socks off for the team. He could produce quality out wide or by coming inside.

PAUL GASCOIGNE: Gazza was unbelievable for the couple of years we had him at Rangers. Crazy at times off the pitch but he never gave us a single headache in training. One of the most talented players of them all.

IAN DURRANT: I didn't see him in his early years at Rangers and he was still coming back from injury when I arrived. But he had phenomenal talent and I'll always remember his goal against Marseille in the Velodrome.

BRYAN ROBSON: One of the best players I've ever worked with. A captain, a leader and a boss on the field for the players. Captain of England, a great goalscoring record and one of the best players of his era.

PAUL INCE: The Guv'nor, as he liked to be called, was a really powerful midfielder. He had great recovery pace and his ability to get back to people was phenomenal. Nobody got away from him, and he was hard to leave out of your team.

WALTER SMITH: Walter always says we weren't that good as players. Frank Coulston maintains we were better than Walter suggests. But, of course, I'd have to stick my old Dundee United team-mate into the squad.

BILLY KIRKWOOD: Such a hard worker at United, he was one of those lads who made the most of his ability to have a terrific career. Kirky also became a fine coach at Rangers and has served the club with distinction.

STUART McCALL: He might not have liked my driving on his first day as a Rangers player but he was a great signing. Scored at the 1990 World Cup for Scotland, too, and has had a great career as a player and manager.

ALEXEI MIKHAILICHENKO: He didn't like warming up and he didn't like playing when the sun was shining. But the lad could play and he had a wonderful career, including that great spell at Ibrox.

DAVID BECKHAM: We used to go and watch him when he was still playing for his school team in London. We got to know his parents and his sister and got him to sign for United. He didn't turn out to be a bad player!

PETER WEIR: A great signing in our first spell at Aberdeen and he started the move for the winning goal in the European Cup Winners' Cup final against Real Madrid in Gothenburg. Great down the left flank.

JIM McSHERRY: Captain and manager of the Wee Windaes Select. A top player for Ayr United and Kilmarnock in his day and even played in Cyprus. I was only kidding when I said he was a 'never-was' all those years ago!

ATTACKERS

BRIAN McCLAIR: If Choccy played the way he trained, he'd never have got near the team. He was one of those lads who would just turn up and play – and you could always rely on him. A great lad and funny, too.

NORMAN WHITESIDE: I don't think I ever saw him give the ball away, even in training. He had no real pace but he could run a game from the middle of the park simply through his use of the ball. A wonderful talent.

RYAN GIGGS: I first saw him at 13 and knew then that he'd be a superstar. A fantastic player who had everything in his game. He was known as a winger but could also play in the middle. A true Manchester United legend.

BRIAN LAUDRUP: The Great Dane could produce something different from anyone else. He was a big man but was a terrific dribbler and had great pace. He was a team player, too, and scored the goal to clinch Nine in a Row.

BRIAN KIDD: A European Cup winner as a teenager alongside Bobby Charlton, Denis Law and George Best. Kiddo was capped by England and went on to star for clubs of the size of Arsenal, Everton and Manchester City.

ALLY McCOIST: His 355 goals tell you what he brought to Rangers. He was always in the middle of things trying to sniff out a goalscoring chance. A great character who came alive in the penalty box.

MARK HATELEY: A great partner for Ally and the man whose goals won the 1990/91 title against Aberdeen. It was only my second game after arriving at Rangers and it was a vital win for Walter Smith after Graeme Souness left.

PAUL SCHOLES: One of United's Class of '92 who signed their first deals while I was at Old Trafford. You would play him off the front and he would run the game. An incredible talent.

WAYNE ROONEY: I first saw him as a 13-year-old and we tried to play him in the English Premier League at 15. He became Manchester United and England's greatest-ever goalscorer and fulfilled all of that potential.

MARK McGHEE: He played under us at Aberdeen and was later manager when I was his No.2 at Millwall. A great player and a great lad. He even managed to cross a ball with his left foot once…

ERIC BLACK: Babysitter, goalscorer, manager. He arrived at Aberdeen as a kid in the summer of 1980 and turned into a fine forward. Scored in Gothenburg and has held so many top coaching positions.

MARK HUGHES: After he recovered from that broken rib I inflicted on him, Sparky returned to doing what he did best – scoring goals. A powerful striker who had starred for Barcelona and would become a top boss.

FRANK STAPLETON: He had scored bags of goals for Arsenal and the Republic of Ireland before arriving at United. He was a fine player for us when we first arrived at the club and one of the best strikers of his era.

ALEX FERGUSON: This book started with his foreword and I couldn't end it without putting him in my squad. One of the best bosses of all time, but that sometimes obscures the fact that he was a very good frontman in his earlier years.

ARCHIE KNOX HONOURS

European Cup Winners' Cup: 1
1982/83

UEFA Super Cup: 1
1983/84

Scottish Cup: 5
1981/82, 1982/83, 1991/92, 1992/93, 1995/96

FA Cup: 1
1989/90

Scottish Premier Division: 6
1991/92, 1992/93, 1993/94, 1994/95, 1995/96, 1996/97

Scottish League Cup: 3
1992/93, 1994/95, 1996/97

Forfarshire Cup: 2
1978/79, 1985/86